CONTEMPORARY FRENCH PHILOSOPHY

CONTEMPORARY FRENCH PHILOSOPHY

MODERNITY AND THE PERSISTENCE OF THE SUBJECT

CAROLINE WILLIAMS

THE ATHLONE PRESS

LONDON AND NEW YORK

THE ATHLONE PRESS
A Continuum imprint
The Tower Building, 11 York Road,
London SE1 7NX
370 Lexington Avenue, New York, NY 10017-6503

First published 2001

British Library Cataloguing in Publication Data
A catalogue record for this book is available
from the British Library

ISBN 0 485 00432 1 (Hardback)
0 485 00632 4 (Paperback)

Library of Congress Cataloging-in-Publication Data

Williams, Caroline, 1966-
   Contemporary French philosophy : modernity and the persistence of the
subject / Caroline Williams.
      p. cm.
Includes bibliographical references.
ISBN 0-485-00432-1 (case : alk. paper) – ISBN 0-485-00632-4 (pbk. : alk. paper)
   1. Philosophy, French. 2. Subject (Philosophy)–History. 3. Philosophy,
Modern. 4. Philosophy, French–20th century. 5. Subject (Philosophy)–History–
20th century. 6. Philosophy, Modern–20th century. I. Title.
B1809.S85 W55 2001
194–dc21   00-067642

Typeset by Aarontype Limited, Bristol
Printed and bound in Great Britain by
MPG Books Ltd, Bodmin, Cornwall

CONTENTS

ACKNOWLEDGEMENTS

Every work is inscribed by the works of many others, and hides many debts, some of which are difficult to record. However, the names of Diana Coole, Gregory Elliott, Peter Lukács, Warren Montag, Susan Stephenson, Margaret Whitford, Abbas Vali and David Wood, are important ones for offering critical insights, thoughtful discussion, advice and, at crucial moments, support. I would also like to record my thanks to the department of Politics, Queen Mary College, for giving me study leave in Spring 1998, and for offering a stimulating, collegial environment in which to conduct research. As fellow travellers of this work, Pete Lukács and our daughter Rosa helped me in so many personal ways, lightening the weight of writing with love and play.

London
August 2000

Will you, as a self, accept taking this self as problematic,
as fictive, and nonetheless more necessary than if you were able
to close up around yourself like a circle sure of its centre?

Maurice Blanchot, *The Infinite Conversation*

It is impossible to *know* anything about men except on the
absolute precondition that the philosophical (theoretical)
myth of man is reduced to ashes.

Louis Althusser, *For Marx*

This book is dedicated
to the memory of
my father

INTRODUCTION

One common feature which marks out the preoccupations of European philosophy during the last 30 years, particularly its French component, is its focus upon the question of the subject. Indeed, over the years, the concept of the subject has been interrogated, dislocated, deconstructed and recomposed, in a multitude of different modes of philosophical thought. At the same time, however, many important arguments have gone astray, and discussions around the fundamental theme of subjectivity have been reduced and simplified, forgotten or overlooked, and, on occasion, simply bypassed. Instead of understanding the question of the subject as something which eludes and fascinates philosophers, even those who claim to abolish it, much contemporary debate conceives the subject as an entity which is dead and buried, or as something which is due for resurrection. The aim of this book is to investigate the question of the subject and to mine some of the rich reserves present within what often appear as 'established positions' on the question of the subject. The book's central claim is that *the question of the subject persists* in all contemporary philosophical perspectives, be they perspectives that seek to abandon it altogether, or perspectives that supposedly reposition it within discourse.

If we extend our focus beyond the concerns of the last three decades, it is clear that attention upon the mode, appearance and status of human subjectivity has defined modern philosophy since Descartes. Many philosophers also contend that the problem of grounding subjectivity, of providing a foundation for thought, even if that foundation may enclose and determine subjectivity as an element of the cosmos, has been present since the founding of the Greek *polis*. Certainly the Greeks did not conceive of a being that could be reduced to the status of a subject with specific attributes and functions; philosophy was to undergo several revolutions in thought before anything approximating a self-contained subject could be imagined. Rather, for the Greeks, being was understood as *hypokeimenon*, namely, that which lies before, that which looms up. It was not yet a distinct self and certainly not yet an ego in the modern sense of the term, rather *hypokeimenon* refers instead to the powerful presence of the world which confronts being. However, the presence of this early formulation does indicate that the focus of the study which follows and the theoretical problems which pervade it are not exclusive to the late-twentieth-century concerns of philosophical discourse but have engaged the project of philosophy for centuries.

Furthermore, a study of some central positions in modern philosophy (the aim of Chapter 1) amply confirm that the unity of consciousness and the singular intentionality of the subject have rarely been sustained. Rather fragmentation, fragility and contingency would appear to characterize the modern subject of philosophy. For example, Descartes doubted the unshakability of the *cogito's* self-evidence: on what could it base its judgements if such an exigency was undermined? Spinoza drew attention to the imaginary character of the subject's knowledge and devised a philosophical system which posited the subject as an effect of substance rather than an autonomous creator of knowledge. Kant recognized the concrete, empirical limits of the sensible subject and sought to generate a transcendental system which could respond to this contingency. In short, moments of contingency and fragility are co-present within all rational systems and methods which claim to *bring the subject to order*. To locate these moments of contingency, it is necessary to follow the movements of an *undercurrent* within philosophical thought, to trace its many self-reflexive questions that seek ultimately to enjoin thought and concept in a more unified, tranquil current of philosophical consciousness. In his reflections upon the various presentations of the historical and philosophical shapes of consciousness, Hegel writes that 'no content occurs which functions as an underlying subject, nor receives its meaning as a predicate.'[1] Rather, with Hegel, something comes to stand in for the subject at particular conjunctures, incites its function and stability within philosophical discourse, and legislates against its dissolution and its defeat. The effort to contain the subject, to bring meaning to the world of objects is an achievement of philosophical thought. Moreover, this effort demands a degree of mastery on the part of philosophy that is conducted only at great cost to thought itself.

It has been a commonplace, if parochial, activity within contemporary thought to proclaim the death of the subject. However, these postmodern voices announce the subject's dissolution and defeat with

undue regard to the residues of subjectivity which still echo in their pro-
nouncements. In view of the observations above, the widely discussed
death of the subject so often associated with contemporary French
philosophy is more accurately portrayed as a somewhat reductive and
misguided reading of a philosophical problem that is *ineluctable*. Contemporary critical thought, post-structuralism in particular, is anything
but an exit from philosophy and a break with the discourse of subjectivity. Rather it embraces a range of problems which have been central to philosophy for centuries. Far from being dead and buried then,
the problematic of the subject persists and orientates many of the
questions of contemporary critical thought. The central aim of this
book is an investigation of the question of the subject's persistence.

How should the discourse of the subject be approached? The theoretical and historical conjuncture which marks out the focus of this
work upon the conceptions of the subject adopted by Althusser,
Lacan, Derrida and Foucault can be encountered in many different and
competing ways. Clearly, these four thinkers share an involuntary
connection in that they are each located within the same temporal,
historical and intellectual space, a space unified somewhat by its questions and preoccupations. There are also more deliberate connections,
recognitions, dialogues and debates which unite these thinkers. This
study chooses a path which at first may appear to be largely philosophical. It is not concerned with the historico-political background of
the writers, although this background arguably shapes, and reverber-
ates upon, the construction of philosophical thought. An intellectual
genealogy, useful as this may be, would detract from the central
questions of this work, namely: what are the *challenges* posed by the
peculiar, ambivalent status of the subject in modern philosophy and
what are the implications of these challenges for a critical philosophical
and political thought? It is philosophy which opens up a site of freedom,
a space of reflection for thinking about the question of the subject.
However, this thought will always begin to flourish from the point of
view of the present, that is, within the context of the concerns and
questions which must occupy us today. Nonetheless, on a more general
level, despite the ahistoricism and anti-subjectivism of structuralism,
the historical and philosophical cannot easily be separated, particularly
in discussions about the subject.

The theoretical construction of subjectivity has significant historical
roots and is bound up with the collapse of the ancient world and the

development of the modern, scientific, bureaucratic, rationalist society. The concept of the individual *subject* as *subjectum* is a distinctly modern formulation which is tied to the commencement of an age where the self becomes the Archimedean point from which the world achieves meaning. It is the *subject* that is posited as the focal point, the origin of truth claims, and knowledge becomes specifically *human* knowledge. It is also the subject who becomes the central reference point for political theory as questions of contract and right, submission and consent, sovereignty and freedom take on an explicitly human dimension, that is, the concept of the subject is politicized, it becomes subsumed by the political. These two moments, epistemological and political, could not have taken place without the structural transformations which, broadly speaking, mark the late seventeenth century.[2] The level of philosophical thought (however we understand it) cannot be abstracted from the world of things because metaphysical reflection *presupposes* ontico-political conditions. It is important then, to place emphasis upon the political, economic, cultural and scientific changes occurring at this time which were to have such a profound effect upon the philosophical structure of human existence and experience.[3] As will become clear in the chapters that follow, the approach to the concept of the subject herein recognizes no distinct boundaries between the political and the philosophical; instead it understands the two as intricately woven together at the theoretical level of concept formation.

Another approach to the study of the subject might be to ask: *what* or *who* is the subject? Yet according to what method or framework may this singularly important question be guided and delimited so as to give it unity? There is *no single framework* for approaching these philosophical problems. Instead there is a rivalry inherent in the very notion of the subject: *hypokeimenon, cogito, ego, ipse*, to name but a few.[4] The subject is a concept which, at origin, is a plural configuration yet to be formulated; it is always a bare sketch which still requires the colours of philosophical position. To this end, the subject's conceptual form is always shaped by a philosophical model or style. Indeed, the history of philosophy situates the question of self and subjectivity in distinct and different formulations. As Paul Ricoeur notes, '*The* philosophy of the subject has never existed; rather, there have been a series of reflective styles, arising out of the work of redefinition which the challenge [to the subject] itself has imposed.'[5]

The problem becomes, at this introductory stage, one of how to present, and how to interpret, the range of different styles and theoretical possibilities of the concept of subjectivity contained within this book. The form and structure that a philosophical discourse takes will itself *structure* and very often *confine* the possible formulations of subjectivity. This is what I would call, following Althusser's formulation, the problematic (*problématique*) of the subject. This shapes, in a literal sense, the mode of questioning and dictates the presence and absence of certain concepts and possibilities; the problematic forms the possible horizon for thinking about the subject. Hence we cannot form easily a telos, a system or even a dialectic of the subject's constitution because this would ignore the specificity, variety and rivalry inherent within the concept of the subject. To seek a system to contain the heterogeneity of these philosophical positions would be to impose *a priori* a mode of conceptualizing these differences as they appear across time and space. Similarly, to understand them sequentially, dialectically, as sublating and refining that which has gone before according to a higher purpose, may impose a certain *telos* upon the subject's variable constitution. Whilst both of these systems, the transcendental and the dialectical, produce a concept of subjectivity which is of interest to the present study, the systematizing that governs their individual methods in turn conditions the ways in which the *styles* of subjectivity are themselves represented. We must be vigilant, in order to recognize the ways in which 'systems' and 'theories' may themselves often be imposed retrospectively upon a particular problem or question to close off its multiple possibilities. Indeed, the very duality between subject and object cannot be assumed to be ontologically natural or given. It carries certain judgements and priorities, it embodies ways of understanding knowledge and the relationship between existence and world.

Taking these considerations on board, a more important starting point for the present study is an awareness that the *mode of questioning* regarding the form and the attributes of the subject will itself shape the concept of the subject. To ask: *what* or *who* is the subject? or even, who comes *after* the subject?[6] may already presuppose a certain ontological style of thinking about subjectivity. As Nietzsche and Derrida have shown, it is a question which brings an imposition of meaning from some other hidden or assumed viewpoint.[7] The question will always bear the weight of the thought that moves it; it may seek to gather together, or sublate, that which it anticipates to be (or, perhaps, *desires* to be) the *answer* to the question. Contemporary French thought brings a certain anxiety or uneasiness to the question of the subject, because the question is itself *a calling into question of what precisely is already an open question*. This reflexive question gives rise to an inescapable paradox which we will discuss more fully below, and in the Conclusion to this study. It is this paradox which opens up creative thinking about the space of subjectivity.

Bearing in mind the necessary, indeed inescapable, exigency of the question, the kinds of initial questions which are asked here and open up what could be described loosely as an approach, are the following: why has the principle of subjectivity been so central to philosophical discourse? What is it about the *kind* of questions posed from within particular philosophical positions that leads them to embrace, challenge and sometimes even to destroy the activity of this principle of subjectivity understood (variously) as principles of containment, sufficiency, substantiality, constancy, security, presence, certainty and rationality? According to what developments and transitions has philosophy arrived at a conception of the subject with such a primary status and function within philosophical and political discourse? Has this status been undermined by contemporary critical thought, or has it repositioned the subject, creating new figures and new forms of thought?

Each of these questions is important to a philosophical and political interrogation of the concept of the subject. *The status of the subject is inseparable from the status of the question* precisely because our mode of questioning, our framing of a project may also gesture towards certain exclusions. The way in which we establish certain problems and questions, the language of conceptualization that we proffer are all in themselves *interpretations* of the subject; they may structure the questions as purely formal claims regarding the function of the subject in the field of truth and its relation to knowledge, they may view the subject primarily as a historical subject thereby subordinating the field of truth to that of historicity. What does it mean for the subject to be constructed or constituted by certain presuppositions rather than others? What, moreover, are the philosophical and political effects of the constructions of the concept of the subject? If it is the case that a particular construction of the subject has come to fill a structural function in political discourse, thereby delimiting the nature of its concerns and practices, usurping its space of creativity and possibility, what are this subject's attributes and what are its effects? These are the questions which concern us in this book.

How, then, to begin? As we shall see in Chapter 1, Descartes' starting point was to question the reliability and certainty which could be attached to knowledge derived by the self. Whilst the problems that troubled his own epistemology do not – and indeed could not – embrace the concerns of this introduction, the spectres of doubt and insecurity, the questioning of ground, origin, *telos*, the limits of experience, and hence human knowledge, preoccupied Descartes and those after him in much the same way as they form the horizon for thinking for the writers considered in this work. Derrida has noted that, so long as questions regarding the constitution of the subject are tied to the ontological question which deals with the *subjectum*, they must remain post-Cartesian.[8] Althusser, Lacan and Foucault are all considered to be post-Cartesians, according to this observation. Of course, the status of this view must remain, at this early stage of our investigations, open to debate. Even when this movement of questioning appears to be overshadowed negatively as a *crisis* of thought or a *doubting* of subjectivity (as it is for Descartes) the *openness* of a mode of questioning, the calling to accounts of the subject, may still produce new figures of thought, and create new forms of subjectivity, *before* any egological containment of the subject takes place.

This return to beginnings, to first principles and to 'the things in themselves' shorn of all substantial relations was a journey taken by Husserl's phenomenology. It is often claimed that the three philosophical masters to influence the writers considered in this work were Marx, Nietzsche and Freud, who replaced the centrality of Hegel, Husserl and Heidegger in contemporary French philosophy. However, it is likely that such a picture of the philosophical transition in post-war France goes furthest in accounting for the decline of existential humanism which was influenced primarily by what Descombes refers to as 'the three H's'. Hegel, Heidegger, and particularly Husserl's, influence continued within contemporary thought and the latter's attempt to reduce subjectivity to its barest essence, to question the mode through which consciousness may constitute its world, is a project which may even be seen to seep, through categorical inversion, into the discourse of structuralism (see Chapter 2). All philosophical positions which place subjectivity under erasure owe their beginnings, in part, to Descartes, Kant and Husserl who, by subjecting consciousness to doubt, a transcendental framework and the phenomenological reduction respectively, sought to secure, ground and isolate the central characteristics of, and limits to, subjectivity. Nevertheless, if contemporary conceptions of the subject are concerned with the problem of beginnings, or the question of *the before*, this focus is without chronological or teleological reference. The beginning or origin does not simply precede the construction of the subject, or the political for that matter, rather it co-exists with, and accompanies both as their necessary counterpart.

In this particular work, Althusser, Lacan, Derrida and Foucault may each be understood to question the status of subjectivity in philosophical discourse. Whether we investigate 'structuralism' or 'post-structuralism,' each of these thinkers may be understood to have transformed, repositioned and reconstituted the question of the subject.[9] Whilst the chapters below indicate theoretical parallels in their positions and a certain common locus of concern, as Derrida similarly observes, the problematic of the subject cannot be reduced to a homogeneity.[10] Each chapter of this book identifies a particular theoretical milieu for its reflections upon the question of the subject; each is organized according to diverse frameworks encompassing language, psychoanalysis, discourse, power and ideology. Very often the perspectives developed in the chapters overlap; sometimes they even reduce or disrupt the construction to the subject. For example, in Chapter 2 we will examine the presence of Spinoza's philosophy in Althusser's Marxist epistemology, and the place which both philosophers assign to the subject; in Chapter 5, we will examine the trajectory which takes us from Althusser's conception of ideology to Foucault's perspective on power, and compare their respective discussions of the subject as an effect of ideology and power.

However, whilst each thinker appears to reposition the subject in relation to a distinct locus of problems, it is clear that they all share one important philosophical problem, namely *the paradox of the subject* which draws each of the thinkers into its mire – even as they seek to undermine, transcend or evade it by repositioning and reconstituting the subject in other forms. The paradox is that the subject is both in the world (as an empirical subject) and also an object of the world (a transcendental subject or object).[11] The paradox of the subject expresses the ineluctable aspect of thought attempting to think its own (absent) ground. In his *Philosophical Fragments*, Kierkegaard describes the paradox as the passion of thought 'wanting to discover something that thought cannot think', something without demonstration or presupposition. As both burden and passion, the paradox bequeaths a risk to contemporary thinkers of the question of the subject: neither to resurrect the subject *tout court*, namely, *in one piece*, nor to ignore its insistence, its ineluctable significance.[12] Can contemporary thought remain close to this weight of the paradox in order to reconfigure the subject productively and creatively? We can begin to offer some hints of response here.

The paradox finds a place in contemporary thought because the concept of the subject is at once viewed as a requirement of analysis *and* something which must be radically displaced. Thus, references to the subject always seem to assume the existence of some form of subjectivity, even though it is precisely this which is open to question. This paradox introduces a circle of referentiality because it *appears* that in its desire to account for the emergence of the subject, contemporary thought risks resurrecting precisely that which it seeks to question. The thinkers considered in this study are aware of this paradox of subjectivity to a greater and lesser extent. Althusser will try to contain the subject within the realm of ideology and avoid its reflexive exigency, even though it continues to haunt his formulations, marking his later writings in significant ways. Derrida, on the other hand, will root out this paradox continuously, tracking and unravelling the assumption of a punctual subject, self-present and always 'on time'. What is clear however, is that the paradox of the subject cannot be simply put to one side because it will always throw up problems for those trying to analyse its significance. Rather, we must recognize this conceptual slippage inherent in the order of subjectivity as an announcement of the *subject's persistence*, a persistence which can take many different forms, styles and modalities in the philosophical perspectives under consideration in this book.

This paradox must also be attached to the unavoidable *historicity of the subject*. Whilst the subject *may* be reinscribed in another theoretical register or perspective, it may often still remain tied to previous conceptions of subjectivity and to a historical and philosophical genealogy from which it is difficult to escape.[13] This point really provides the context for Derrida's observation noted above regarding the Cartesian underpinnings of some conceptions of subjectivity. It may also apply to other philosophical positions that draw upon distinct genealogies of the subject, be they Spinozist, Hegelian, or Nietzschean. It is not the intention of this book to offer a history of the concept of the subject. However, it is crucially important to observe – and attempt to locate – the philosophical displacements that have been undertaken within contemporary thought. Only then can we respond to the question of a *break* with the philosophy of the subject and expose its fictional basis. The question of philosophical inheritance is a complex one, not least because contemporary thought poses its own unique questions to the past; in effect, it rediscovers past philosophers and makes them our contemporaries. Chapter 1 will trace this historical relation and the question of philosophical inheritance for its effects upon the various discourses of the subject.

The arguments and explorations of the status of subjectivity in the following chapters will also draw attention to the insuperability of the political horizon of philosophical questions. *The re-opening of the question of the subject cannot be viewed in isolation from the re-examination of the possible structure of the political.* We have noted above that philosophical and political levels are interwoven. Philosophical thought is the conceptual lining of the political, and philosophical questions are always ontico-political ones. We can go further: philosophical and political thought share a common history and philosophical foundations are always political in their effects. Hence, if the consideration of the ontological shape of the subject gives rise to political questions, then ontological questions are themselves politicized just as the political, too, must become an ontological category with all the accompanying risks that such categorization brings. Each thinker considered here is cognizant of this fundamental relation. Indeed, from Lukács to Foucault, epistemological problems are folded into political ones.

Moreover, philosophical questions regarding the subject also entail ethico-political decisions. The decision (both conceptual and political) shapes the form, content and possibility of the political. To tie the question of the subject to the structure of the political in this way is not to map a theory of the subject *upon* the political neither is it intended to reduce the subject to an effect of a constitutive political structure. Both of these theoretical manoeuvres risk determining the shape and content of the subject and inverting the problematic of subject to that of the political.[14] The claim in this study is that the emergence of a particular problematic of the subject – and the extent of its constitution – itself shapes and delimits the conditions of possibility of the political. When the fragile, contingent nature of the subject's constitution is emphasized, the groundwork of political thought is itself re-opened. We shall view the ways in which the philosophical and the political are inextricably bound and simultaneously give rise to each

other, by pursuing the various presentations of the subject in each of
the following chapters. Our first task, however, is to situate the subject
upon the terrain of modern philosophy and to consider, in turn, the
question of the philosophical inheritance of contemporary accounts of
the subject.

1

INHERITING PROBLEMS
AND PARADOXES

SUBJECTIVITY AND MODERN
PHILOSOPHY

> All concepts are connected to problems without which they would
> have no meaning and which can themselves only be isolated or
> understood as their solution emerges. [Concepts] link up with each
> other, support one another ... articulate their respective problems,
> and belong to the same philosophy, *even if they have different
> histories*. [Deleuze and Guattari, *What is Philosophy?*[1]]

The concept of the subject poses a philosophical problem which has
many different historical presentations. From Descartes to Husserl and
beyond, the question of the subject has taken up elements of past
philosophies but has nonetheless posed the question anew. This makes
the history that comes to predominate in philosophy's many tales about
the subject, a particularly exclusive one. It is one which ties securely the
event of knowledge to a substantial subject equipped with the attribute
of thought and always returns the subject to itself, enclosing truth
within the ambit of self-consciousness. Within modern philosophy, it
has often been the case that the subject has been conceived of as a
subjectum, as the objectifying ground for knowledge and as the foundation for all possible being. Vincent Descombes describes lucidly this
subject of modernity as 'the name given to a be-ing whose *identity* is
sufficiently stable for it to bear, in every sense of the word (sustain, serve
as a foundation for, withstand), change or modification.'[2] Here, the
subject appears to serve primarily an epistemological function, delin-
eating the field of intelligibility where the representation of the object is

the result of the thought, perception and knowledge *of* subjective consciousness. Such a subject appropriates what is outside itself and brings everything within the purview of its own substantial centre.

However, as we have pointed out in the Introduction, the subject cannot be reduced to an homogeneity. Neither can the subject be constructed solely within an epistemological problematic, that is, in relation to what it is possible to *know*. What is the 'subject of reason,' or the *subjectum*, when isolated from its ontological ground, that which breathes existence and possibility into it? The region of ontology is as important as that of epistemology, and if in this region too, a particular kind of being, as determination, as self-origin, and as pure self-presence, has been viewed as dominating the order of the subject, then so too must this hegemonic position be questioned. There are as many histories as there are conceptions of the subject; *the* history of *the* subject does not exist. Is it, therefore, only retrospectively that a particular, determinant structure of the subject can be identified?[3] Any such retrospective history would appear to disregard the openness of the subject in the posing of the question of its existence: the doubt, contingency and finitude which accompany the moment that seeks to inaugurate certainty and self-evidence. What is distinctive about contemporary reflections on the subject is that they begin with an empty horizon for thought; they do not seek to determine the subject's structure, or to fill out a metaphysical subject of plenitude and certainty.

We have also argued in the Introduction that the problem of the subject is best conceived of as a *question*, a question not answered once and for all, but a question which can only achieve a temporary theoretical stabilization. The subject is a project, an event of philosophical thought and it cannot be reduced to a single delineation. If contemporary perspectives on the subject bear the imprint of the philosophical tradition, this is a stamp inscribed with diverse marks, a multiplicity of philosophical names and a whole gamut of problems (for example, grounding thought, achieving certainty, ensuring truth, setting up the boundaries for what it is possible to think and know, but also with thinking its temporal becoming, the presence of otherness, the infinite possibilities of thought).[4] The question of the subject cannot escape this history of problems. An investigation of some of its philosophical styles and conceptual shapes can aid our understanding of the contemporary theoretical field by presenting some of these problems. If the history of the concept of the subject is a multiple one, then the positions on the subject considered in this study (mainly structuralist and post-structuralist) cannot easily be reduced to a single precursor.[5] The following chapters will draw upon diverse philosophies of the subject. The aim in this chapter is to identify and elaborate three important conceptions of the subject developed by Descartes, Spinoza and Hegelian phenomenology. Each throws up a range of problems encountered in the constitution of the subject and each offers a valuable exercise in the project of thinking the form of subjectivity. In the following discussion, we will see that philosophy ultimately sheds its purely epistemological dressing and reveals its concrete preoccupations with the *question* of the subject.

I. DESCARTES AND THE BIRTH OF THE MODERN *COGITO*

No philosophy of the subject can take its bearings without reference to Descartes. Whilst most twentieth-century philosophers would agree that the subject is a site of contestation, it is clear that the birth of modernity and the rationalist orientation of knowledge charted by, among others, Michel Foucault in *Les Mots et Les Choses*, cannot easily be separated from the Cartesian thinking subject and, later, the Kantian transcendental subject of knowledge. The Cartesian dualism between mind and body and the separation of a space for pure thought, *res cogitans*, from the sensual, reactive and non-discriminatory site of the body, *res extensa*, had a profound effect upon the subsequent history of modern philosophical and political thought. Whilst Descartes' conception of the subject may be contested on an epistemological level as illustrating merely one of the many philosophical styles of subjectivity, it is clear that the construction of a modern, rational subjectivity was inaugurated by this dominant Cartesian problematic.[6]

Descartes responds to the Renaissance concern for the fragmentation of the self in relation to worldly truth by creating a new foundation for knowledge and constructing a stable, thinking subject able to verify the new scientific method which marked the modern age. However, it was not according to certainty that the *cogito* was grounded. Cartesian metaphysics arose from a deep scepticism about the possibility of claiming certainty *for* reality from the point of view of the human subject. This 'epistemological insecurity'[7] leads the subject to doubt its own interpretation of reality, and even more significantly, to doubt that any criteria for truth can be ascertained. Hannah Arendt describes this state in the following way:

the outstanding characteristic of Cartesian doubt is its universality, that nothing, no thought and no experience, can escape it.
[It] did not simply doubt that human understanding may not be
open to every truth or that human vision may not be able to see
everything, but that intelligibility to human understanding does
not at all constitute a demonstration of truth, just as visibility did
not at all constitute proof of reality.[8]

If our intellect is finite and our capacity for knowledge is limited to
common-sensical, natural ideas and beliefs which are, at best, confused
and mystified attempts to assert the truth, how can knowledge be
universal and judged to be so by the subject? As Descartes writes in the
first meditation:

> I have for a long time had in my mind the belief that there is a God
> who is all-powerful and by whom I was created and made how
> I am. And who can give me the assurance that this God has not
> arranged that there should be no earth, no heaven, no extended
> body, no figure, no magnitude, or place, and that nevertheless
> I should have the perception of all these things, and the persuasion
> that they do not exist other than as I see them?[9]

This radical doubt, the inability to distinguish between fantasy,
imagination and reality, the existence of the object from the inaccurate
sensory perceptions of it, precipitates an anxiety in the subject in
relation to objectification. For Descartes, this anxiety can only be elim-
inated and mastered by the creation of an authentic *cogito* able to
distinguish in a rational way between these different existential states.
Arguably, it is this Cartesian framing of the problem of the subject that
continues to orientate, if not to *haunt*, many contemporary constructions of the subject. For Descartes, epistemological security and the
containment of truth can only be achieved by reducing (and eliding?)
this fundamental problem between the experience and being of the
subject and the structure of representation. The problem must be cast in
terms of a *more geometrico* which can be amenable to cognitive understanding *whatever* may be the state of the subject. Descartes' example
here is the difference between sleeping and wakefulness. Whilst in the
state of sleep our dreams can often persuade us of the verity of mere
illusion, it is nonetheless clear that 'whether I am awake or sleeping,
two and three added together always make five, and a square never has

more than four sides.'[10] For Descartes, we can always be assured of our
cognitive capacities, and it is this resolution (partial at this stage) which
forms the basis of *ego cogito ergo sum*: I think therefore I am. Furthermore, the mind's capacity for thought, for distinguishing between true
and distinct ideas and those which remain untrustworthy, can always
be underwritten by geometric laws which act as a measure for clarity
and distinctiveness. If thought – and the role of perception is also
important here – continues to be clouded by delusions, this can only be
the result of affections, immediate experience, in short, the imprint
of the body upon cognition, all elements which should be subjected to
deliberate and assiduous control.

Cartesian philosophy constructs a subject who is author of thoughts
both clear and deluded, a volitional, thinking subject who begins to
take responsibility for the structure and form of knowledge and truth
where previously these had been designated to the will of God. This
move, however, from the authority of God to the responsibility of the
subject, is made only by designating God as the guarantor, the certifier
and the cause of clear and distinct ideas. Thus, as in the case for
Hobbes, who follows this epistemological path in his own account of
the state of nature, the subject's faculties are God-given. As Genevieve
Lloyd points out, the human mind is itself made God-like; it is conjoined with God and in its purest reflections has the same capacities as
the divine will. Hence, 'we avoid error by schooling the will to assent
only in the presence of ideas that are clear and distinct.'[11] Once this
step into faith, security and substantiality is made, our knowledge of
the universe follows in close pursuit. In this way, the sceptical doubt
that plagues the newly modern age, has its source in *human* and not
worldly imperfection. The Cartesian subject must bear the weight of
the world in more than one sense. Not only is it now conceived as the
author of knowledge but it is also fully responsible for the *wrong* use
made of these God-given powers of clear and distinct thought.

What is the ontological content of the Cartesian subject? Descartes
does not present us with an ontology of the subject because thought is
still conceived as being one with substance. Descartes does not begin
with an analysis of the experience of existence of the self, or consider
that the presence of others may be required to verify the *cogito's*
powers of speech.[12] This solipsistic subject is a 'fictitious creature, bodi-
less, senseless and forsaken'.[13] Furthermore, this Cartesian subject must
be fixed in time. It requires no recourse to natural philosophy which
merely drags age-old beliefs and mystifications into the timeless world

of geometric form. The origin of subjectivity is not deciphered historically or dialectically as it will be later for Hegel. For Descartes, the essence of subjectivity is given by the cognitive capacities of the self alone, which require no spatio-temporal relation to the world and others, but are discovered through inward-turning and internal reflection on the powers of the intellect. It is thus a pure, wholly atemporal, self-enclosed, reflective consciousness that will recognise instantaneously the perfectibility of the intellect and create, in this process, rational and self-certain knowledge.

Whilst Descartes may appear here to overcome the spectre of doubt and scepticism concerning the possibility that the subject may not be able to maintain its position as the source of all claims to truth and objectivity, future philosophies of the subject could not lose its shadow. Epistemological doubt became *a fissure within all discourses of subjectivity*. It has a bearing (sometimes indirect) upon all the philosophical problems discussed within the chapters of this book, even though the philosophical configuration of the subject that we will consider far outstrips the philosophical specificity of Cartesianism. It would surely be a mistake to view the repression of doubt and anxiety as producing a new foundationalist theory of the subject. In psychoanalytic discourse, for example, it is precisely this repression which disrupts foundational theories of the subject. For the psychoanalyst Jacques Lacan, whose writings are the focus of Chapter 3, objectification, the representation of the object by the subject, can be obtained only at a cost: doubt is harboured within and is forever ready to disrupt attempts to secure the truth. Furthermore the linguistic subject of the verb *I think, therefore I am*, can never experience itself in language but will remain forever split in its identity. The Cartesian subject is thus taken as the point of departure in psychoanalysis.

Western philosophical discourse, in particular Kantian philosophy, continued to negotiate this antinomy between an abstract, transcendental subjectivity, devoid of particularity, and a concrete, empirical subjectivity, bound up with relations to time and space and a specific existential relation to the social world which influenced its structure of experience. If Hume's scepticism stalled the rational progress of this antinomy towards various resolutions by viewing the subject's identity to be in continuous flux and lacking any solid ground,[14] Kant radicalized the Cartesian problematic of the thinking subject, by grounding subjectivity upon the distinction between the subject and object. Human intelligence, that is reason, became set against a series of categories structured by universal laws. The knowing subject was conceived as an absolute, transcendental being, 'a transcendental unity of apperception'; this subject became the condition for the possibility of knowledge. As Kant writes in *The Critique of Pure Reason*, 'The conditions of the *possibility of experience* in general are at the same time the conditions of the *possibility of the objects of experience*.'[15] Like Descartes, however, Kant recognized the limits of human experience as a source of absolute knowledge. Transcendental subjectivity is an ideal conception that cannot coincide with empirical, practical consciousness. Significantly, error, illusion and confusion remain, as they do in Descartes, potential disruptions to the security of self-certain forms of knowledge.

The conception of subjectivity discussed above has been viewed by many to constitute the dominant paradigm in Western political and philosophical thought. It points towards a privileging of subjectivity over objectivity, ensuring the latter is dependent upon a truth disclosed by the subject. For Heidegger, one of its dominant critics, the Cartesian *cogito* inevitably transforms philosophy into anthropology, and secures thinking as an assertive act of representing the world to the subject. In 'The Age of the World Picture', Heidegger writes: 'the superiority of the *sub-iectum* (as a ground lying at the foundation) that is preeminent because it is in an essential respect unconditional arises out of the claim of man to a *fundamentum absolutum inconcussum veritatis* (self-supported, unshakable foundation of truth, in the sense of certainty).'[16] This Cartesian conception of the subject as the unshakable ground of certainty forms is taken, according to Heidegger, as the paradigm of modern forms of thinking even as it reifies that thought. Such a view makes Spinoza's anti-anthropomorphism a somewhat misplaced perspective in the genre of modern philosophy. Spinoza's philosophy stands as an anomaly between Cartesian and Hegelian conceptions of the subject but it does have very interesting repercussions for the philosophy of the subject within contemporary thought. It is to Spinoza's anti-subjectivist account that we now turn.

II. SPINOZA'S PHILOSOPHY OF SUBSTANCE: THE DECOMPOSITION AND RECOMPOSITION OF THE SUBJECT

Spinoza's influence upon the structure and form of contemporary thought has been considerable. His philosophical discourse offers an account of subjectivity that displaces the primacy of the *cogito* which remained central to Descartes' construction of the rational subject. Spinoza places the subject within a complex schema of interconnected relations where its volition, its desires and its self-understanding of the world are viewed not as *self*-caused but rather as *effects* of a systemic, rational order, that which he calls substance. We should say at the outset that this conception of substance is not easily equated with the absolute, as a kind of godly substance. Neither can it be interpreted as a form of pantheism. Spinoza uses the term substance in a metaphoric and a real (or concrete) sense. It is metaphoric in that substance is nothing if it is not conceived in terms of the infinity of its possible attributes. The possibilities for being and knowledge emanating from substance have yet to be fully explored by human understanding and this openness to possible modes of being (and hence to endlessly divisible attributes of substance) must be borne in mind.[17] Substance is real in that it is natural, material, it pertains to life; it is not simply an ethereal and abstract substance.[18]

Spinoza's *Ethics* is concerned in part to expose the epistemological limitations of Cartesian dualism which considers the intellect (mind) as that which can become independent from the world of objects, events and bodily affects. Such a dualism between mind and body splits the subject into two contradictory realms, the first is isolated from the world, independent of the passions (or at least, through inward-turning, able to sever itself from their effects) and seeks resemblance in God; the second is what we may call the being of the subject, but it has, in Descartes, no real temporal expression because it lacks a relation to the world and a sense of embodiment. According to Spinoza, the form of knowledge that emerges from such dualistic thinking is one that gives full power to the imagination, ushering in an artificial construction of knowledge which is unable to recognize the *mode* through which an idea and its corresponding object is constituted. As we shall see, for Spinoza, an understanding of the form of subjectivity and the structure of knowledge can only be achieved through a recognition of the interconnectedness of body and mind, the passions and the intellect, and the way in which concrete existence affects the claim to absolute knowledge.

Spinoza shares with Hegel the attempt to embody the relation between subject and knowledge. However, whereas Hegel understands this relation to be based ultimately on a dialectical reconciliation of subject and object, Spinoza's conception of substance has no room for the initial separation established by Hegel between subject and object (this important difference is discussed more fully in Section III below). Indeed, one of the primary criticisms of Spinozism by Hegel and others is that Spinoza's monist conception of substance denies to subjectivity historical becoming and agency.[19] Hegel ultimately conflates the positions of Spinoza and Descartes, viewing both philosophers as pursuing an abstract conception of thought derived in accordance with a mathematical model. The French theorist, Pierre Macherey, whose work on Spinoza comes out of the Althusserian school, describes Spinoza's conception of substance and its attributes as a concrete system with unlimited possibilities for being and knowledge. It is readings such as Macherey's which signal the profound influence his philosophy would have for contemporary theories of the subject, structuralist and post-structuralist alike. Indeed, Spinoza's critique of empiricism, his account of the imaginary basis of knowledge and subjectivity, and his reflections upon the way in which the passions may delimit, discipline and contain the *potentia* of mind and body (both individual and collective), anticipate in important ways Althusserian and Lacanian constructions of the subject discussed in Chapters 2 and 3 of this book. This section will indicate aspects of Spinoza's thought which have had an influence upon the contemporary philosophical conjuncture.

We have noted that Spinoza's aim is to construct an account of knowledge which is not predicated upon an ontological dualism between subject and object. His endeavours are also theistic and directed towards an attack upon a theology which dupes man to accept a doctrine of religious *telos*, where God directs all worldly activity according to a fixed pre-given end. Such a teleological and *a priori* conception of reality as imbued with the logic of final causes is, for Spinoza, a false account of our relation with nature, a figment of the imagination which fixes our understanding of God in ignorance. Awe takes the place of a rational understanding of our place in nature; by accepting the constructions and rationales of the imagination as evidence for the absolute presence of God, philosophers have taken particularistic and essentially contestable images of God's effects to be symbols of his cause in the world. As Spinoza writes, 'he [the philosopher] mistakes for reality the way his imagination is affected.'[20] Misperceptions and misinterpretations of the world are folded into human knowledge; they are built upon an originary chasm between the rational understanding of the will and our passionate exchange with nature. If this deep antinomy is built into our forms of knowledge, Spinoza seeks to show us the error upon which it is founded.

Spinoza constructs a single, structured totality which purports to contain the elemental conditions of knowledge and the means to attain absolute truth. Neither are predicated upon a self-contained act of the mind as rational will. The role for a reflective self-consciousness is severely limited by the structure of forces and affects that compose substance. Consciousness does not extend outside of this *milieu*; the subject is not the creative agency of ideas nor the autonomous experience which, opposed to the object, creates the conditions of possibility for knowledge. 'The essence of man', Spinoza writes, 'is constituted by definite modifications of the attributes of God [Substance].'[21] Similarly, 'in the mind there is no absolute, or free, will. The mind is determined to this or that volition by a cause, which is likewise determined by another cause, and this again by another, and so ad infinitum.'[22]

As Gilles Deleuze notes, bodies and minds 'are not substances or subjects, but modes'.[23] In contrast to Descartes, Spinoza understands mind and body (whilst they are separate domains) as two amongst an infinity of attributes of a common substance. Thought and extension must be viewed as modifications of the existence of this primary substance. In her book *Part of Nature*, Genevieve Lloyd summarizes the relation thus:

> for Spinoza, ... the self is not at all the primary object of knowledge. Self-knowledge becomes a reflective dimension on our knowledge of the world – a world whose existence is never in doubt. Knowledge begins as immediate awareness of substance under the attribute of extension.[24]

In this way, thought, intellect, will and perceptions, like ideas, objects and forms of knowledge, all arise through their immanent and necessary relation to substance, (primary matter, existence). It follows that the subject (or *cogito*) must be situated within this rational totality and understood as a mode of being or a modification of substance. For Hegel, it is this pantheistic move that ensures Spinoza's totality is governed by an objective logic which denies self-consciousness its participation in determining the rationality and actuality of the object.[25] Nevertheless, Hegel's interpretation also confounds two issues which remain interesting for the broader theoretical questions at stake in later chapters of this book. The first concerns the status of the concept of idea in Spinoza, and the second concerns the process of signification, the production of the *sign* of truth; in other words, the role of language and imagination in the constitution of bodies, minds and knowledge.

Ideas and images, bodies and minds

> The order and connection of ideas is the same as the order and connection of things.[26]

For Spinoza, the mind is an individual subject only because it is also a particular idea of the body. Ideas are seen to have physical, material form. However, the body is also a site of multiplicity, affected in many ways by its experiences, and able to retain and contain impressions of past experiences in memory. This implies that the order of ideas in the mind and the body may not be derived as adequate, clear and distinct representations of ideality and existence. Instead knowledge may be rather confused, partial and particularistic in form. With this important distinction between clarity and distortion, Spinoza does not reintroduce the dualism established by Descartes. Ideas cannot be represented by the mind or *cogito* under the attribute of extension; indeed the metaphor of representation is deemed inappropriate here because it points to a *separation* between mind and body which Spinoza rejects. For Spinoza, mind is the idea of the body *in thought*, it is *thinking body* and cannot be disconnected from it.

Given this crucial interconnectedness between mind and body, and the significance of the body as the physical and material site of ideas (the mind in fact cannot *know* the body, it may only come to *think* it through the affections of the body as an idea in thought), how may Spinoza develop a pure knowledge that may conform to substance viewed as the totality of life? How may he both reject Descartes' construction of the subject of certitude *and* rescue the concept of idea from fragmentation and confusion caused by the body as a site of multiplicity? Can Spinoza construct a structure of subject adequate to this task? Spinoza's theory of knowledge offers an important solution to this dilemma.

Spinoza differentiates between three kinds of knowledge, a schema which also serves as a very important historical observation of different conceptions of the subject in modern philosophy. If it is the case that particular conceptions of the subject will create different epistemological effects within the possible structure of knowledge then Spinoza's three forms of knowledge serve as an elucidation of such effects. For Spinoza, each form of knowledge corresponds to a different mode of being and a different relation to substance; each offers a specific account of the relation of the subject to the construction of knowledge and truth; finally, each embraces a specific conception of the idea in a certain relation to knowledge.[27]

The first kind of knowledge is derived from casual experience where 'individual objects [are] presented to us through the senses in a fragmentary (mutilate) and confused manner without any intellectual order.'[28] This form of knowledge always embraces inadequate ideas because it draws its significance solely from the experience of the passions, emotions and bodily affects. As Deleuze notes, this form of knowledge is 'constituted by the linking together of inadequate ideas and of the passion-affects that result from them.'[29] Here, knowledge may be seen to correspond to a stark empiricism which takes the plane of subjective experience as the material for the construction of knowledge, material which is swayed and bent perpetually by the abstract notions of philosophy. It can thus provide nothing but a fiction in the realm of knowledge, based as it is upon images taken directly from a multiplicity of bodily experiences. This first kind of knowledge is also derived from symbols: 'from having heard or read certain words we call things to mind and we form certain ideas of them similar to those through which we *imagine* things.'[30] Spinoza makes an important distinction between an idea as adequate to itself, requiring no object of representation (see the discussion below), and an idea that is tied to the image it conjures up in the imagination, or the word or sign it produces in the mind. The *imaginatio* can confuse this uneasy relationship between ideas and images, hence creating erroneous knowledge. It can deceive the subject of the latter's mode of being, namely as a modification of substance; it can even delude the subject into constructing a framework of knowledge based upon the representation of ideas where it views itself as the author of ideas and as the moral adjudicator between good and evil. For Spinoza, our moral distinctions, together with the imperatives which follow from law, have their source in the imagination: order, goodness and beauty may appear as transcendental categories but they are deducible from nothing other than the relativism of the imagination. Thus, 'if the motion communicated to our nervous system by objects presented through our eyes is conducive to our feeling of well-being, the objects which are its cause are said to be beautiful, while the objects which provoke a contrary motion are called ugly.'[31]

In his study of imaginary forms of knowledge, Spinoza points to a problem which had occupied Greek philosophy, particularly the Sophists, and was to become significant in the writings of Hobbes, Rousseau, Nietzsche and, later, post-structuralism. Language, in both

its written and its spoken form, might not close the gap between representation and truth, rather it may be subject to deception, distortion and
illusion. Through symbols and signs, mind creates inadequate ideas
and, whilst these may come close to the ideological fictions which
legitimate certain kinds of bodily action, they come nowhere near a
form of knowledge that can express the essence of life, its form and
ideas. To put this in other words, for Spinoza, language is reactive, it is
tied to imagination and conditioned by the responses of the human body
to the motion of objects upon it, and the inadequate ideas that become
tied to these bodily affects. As Christopher Norris points out, language
distorts 'because its nature aligns it with the sources of inadequate,
confused or "imaginary" ideas.'[32] Like Nietzsche, Spinoza thus points
to the materiality of the idea and its concrete connections over and
above its linguistic form. Language and subjectivity are intricately tied
together. Descartes' announcement: *ego cogito ergo sum* involves a
grammar of *evidence* ('Yes, it is I') which sustains and supports this
conception of the subject. Spinoza thus recognizes the power of language, through its grammatical structure, to call the subject into being.

The second kind of knowledge that Spinoza discusses, arises 'from the
fact that we have common notions and adequate ideas of the properties
of things'.[33] This form of knowledge is important as it acts as a bridge
between the first and the third pure kind of knowledge. Common
notions are evidence that thought is able to present generalities that are
not founded on the immediate experience of the body. Common notions
illustrate the interconnections, the necessary integrations and classifica-
tions that derive from the mind's ability to reason and *understand* the
unity of affects of different bodies. Significantly, Spinoza is also pointing to the existence of an area of thought about which we may, at
present, have very little knowledge, (for Deleuze, this is an unconscious
of thought), in so far as our imagination is able to predominate and
determine our reception of adequate ideas.

In Parts III and IV of the *Ethics*, Spinoza produces a complex schema
of the passions in order to represent and differentiate bodily affects.[34]
His aim is to understand and account for the ways in which the
imagination may generate illusory, inadequate ideas, and give rise to
imaginary identifications. Specifically, in Part IV, he discusses the
ways in which a multitude of bodies can be held in bondage by an
authority, be it theological or political. Spinoza traces the vacillation of
the passions between love and hate, joy and sadness, hope and fear,
and their constant source of conflict and instability between men.[35]

In *Spinoza and Politics*, Etienne Balibar points out that, for Spinoza, a multitude must be formed by a process of 'mutual recognition'. Thus, the passions may move the body according to an idea which the mind has formulated when swayed by another object (i.e. image or will of another). Such imitations or identifications constitute the subject as part of a multitude and create, in turn, an obedient, slavish social bond. It is this deep exploration of *affectuum imitatio* (the imitation of the affects) which anticipates in important ways the psychoanalytic construction and disciplining of the body by the material practices of ideology in the work of Louis Althusser.[36]

Whilst the 'physics of bodies' developed in the middle part of the *Ethics* may appear to emphasize the vulnerability and perpetual oscillation of the passions as they are composed and recomposed according to different political forms, this reading must not be detached from Spinoza's more encompassing schema discussed above, one which differentiates between three kinds of knowledge. As we come to understand the encounters that modify the body and produce affects, we are able to form somewhat predictable generalities about them, and begin to transcend the mind. Reason, for Spinoza, as it will later be for Hegel, is also a kind of embodied reason, but it is dialectical only in a very formal sense. For Spinoza, it is only by thinking the body reflexively and understanding the passions that common notions can be derived. It is at this point that the immanent *potentia*, the freedom and power of thought, may become manifest.

This degree of understanding is illustrative of the autonomous capacity of thought, that which Spinoza calls intellect. Intellect is a mode of the attribute of thought; it is timeless, infinite and belongs to substance. Indeed, as attributes of substance, both finite body and mind (and indeed all the other modes of substance about which we know almost nothing) contain the possibility of intellect. Intellect is a form of critical or pure thought for which essence and existence are the same thing. It is here that the third kind of intuitive knowledge becomes possible. The construction of knowledge does not require the existence of objects according to which we formulate ideas. The idea comes *before* the object for Spinoza.[37] It is the effect of none other than the attribute of thought. The idea is therefore immanent to itself and requires no *ideatum*. In what we may now view as a fundamental critique of empiricist conceptions of knowledge, Spinoza makes an important distinction between the idea of an object produced by a subject's sensory perception, which, as we have noted, produces knowledge of the first kind, and the idea of an object *in thought* which is prior to the perturbations of the finite body and mind and contains a multiplicity of different impressions and object-traces.[38] Coupled with Spinoza's rejection of anthropomorphism and hence any conception of a subject of consciousness, Spinoza's third form of knowledge does not link subject and object together in a relation of inequality but rather poses consciousness as reflected substance where the order and connection of ideas is the same as the order and connections of things.

Knowledge of the third kind is based on immanence and not transcendence of the concrete-particular. As Yovel notes perceptively, Spinoza remains outside the tradition of transcendence.[39] This conception of knowledge is immanent in two important respects already discussed above. Let us rehearse these once again. First, Spinoza's conception of knowledge is not founded upon a dualism between mind and body which requires a retreat from the passions in order to be achieved; rather both are attributes of Substance and thus contain (modally) the conditions for reflexive (immanent) knowledge. However, because of what we may call the socialized nature of the Spinozan body,[40] these conditions often elude thought, which remains confused and fragmentary, and hence generate inadequate ideas. Second, we have seen that immanent knowledge is built upon a growing adequation and generalization of ideas of the body and the mind. There is a parallelism between body and mind which demands both the interconnectedness of knowledge, and that any graduation from reason to intellect in one mode *must be paralleled* by an increased awareness by the body as an affected object. There is, we might say, an identity of Being between Substance and its modes which allows for no original, ontological difference or ruptural negativity of a Hegelian kind. This ensures that developments in knowledge will be immanent in both finite thought and infinite intellect. However, we must be careful not to see in Spinoza an *a priori* conception of substance. Clearly, there is a system of rational causality which contains Substance and its modes but this is not built up in opposition to the world of objects and ideas; neither does it presuppose some *final* cause which is the origin of all modes of substance. If there is an infinity of possible modes of substance then how can we reduce their origin to a singular one? Spinoza, let us remember, has already warned us of the power of imagination.

Spinoza presents us neither with a philosophy of the *cogito* nor with a conception of absolute subjectivity. In Spinoza, we find the first theory of structure; moreover, it is one that avoids every risk of categorical inversion from structure to subject. Spinoza distributes the modes of being, which could be said to compose a philosophy of the subject, over many different planes of existence; the recomposition of the subject into a discrete, self-contained identity can only be the result of an inadequate, imaginary form of knowledge. With this account of substance and its attributes, does Spinoza distance himself from the paradoxes inherent in the conception of the subject, or does he, too, require a certain conception of the subject, even if only as a model to depart from? Clearly, Spinoza's concept of a structured totality devoid of subjectivity has an important relation to anti-humanist positions within contemporary critical thought. Spinoza's *structured totality*, which would have such a profound influence upon the epistemology of Louis Althusser, reframes the questions of subject and object. Both subject and object are constructed by imaginary forms of knowledge that remain ignorant of their real plane of existence. These forms of knowledge cannot penetrate the *core* of objects; they can only interpret them through the play of an erroneous imagination. For Althusser, all imaginary forms of knowledge are ideological and cannot achieve the status of a true knowledge; for Lacan too, this imaginary is inseparable from the ego of the subject, to whom the *cogito* must always refer. The questioning of the order of the subject by Spinoza is a radical philosophical attempt to recompose its function. However, phenomenological conceptions of subjectivity view Spinoza's subject-less structure as leaving little room for self and human agency. For Hegel, as Lloyd remarks, 'Spinoza casts self and world into the abyss of the one identity.'[41] Hegel's system claims no such reduction. Let us assess the philosophical strength of this criticism.

III. HEGELIAN PHENOMENOLOGY: CONSTRUCTING THE SUBJECT OF HISTORY

The return to Hegel initiated within French philosophy in the 1930s, and the burgeoning interest in Heidegger which accompanied it, posed a serious challenge to Cartesian and Spinozist forms of rationalism. It was also a return to the theorization of the historicity of consciousness which had been all too easily delimited or ignored within the rationalist tradition. This new regard for Hegel opened up ontological and epistemological questions within the space of history. Questions concerning the relation of the individual to society, action to history and knowledge to humanism which had been earlier posed by left Hegelians in 1830s Germany now set the scene for a reopening of the Marx–Hegel relation.[42] Contemporary reflections on the question of the subject often bear the marks of this Hegelian problematic – even as they try to distance themselves from it. The translation and interpretation of *The Phenomenology of Spirit* by Jean Hyppolite, the lectures given by Alexandre Kojève, texts by Jean Wahl, Maurice Merleau-Ponty and Jean-Paul Sartre, reorientated French philosophy and provided the question of the subject with new conceptual resources.[43] Indeed, this problematic had already been anticipated in Lukács' seminal work, *History and Class Consciousness* which preceded the translation of Marx's *Paris Manuscripts* by more than a decade (see Chapter 2).

Phenomenology, in this distinctly Hegelian formulation, is tied to the historical experience of consciousness.[44] Hegel's speculative philosophy views the journey of thought and experience as a quest for meaning and truth, for a knowledge that is ultimately absolute and can coincide with self-consciousness. For Hegel, subjectivity may be analysed in a number of ways: in terms of its universality, its specificity or particularity, and its singularity. *Phenomenology of Spirit* draws these three dimensions together in a dialectical method.[45] The dialectic is a relation which is able, through the process of sublation, to overcome and incorporate opposites, contradictions and differences into a synthetic unity. The logic of the dialectic enables it to synthesize the contrary movements within both knowledge and history, illustrating how each exists relationally and is meaningless outside of any dialectical construal.

Hegel's phenomenology can be viewed as a dialectical analysis of the history of the philosophical subject and the gradual emergence of self-consciousness as *Geist*. *Phenomenology* contains, therefore, the seeds of Hegel's method which brings a historicized subject to the scene, one with weighty limitations but one which also contains, by ontological necessity, the possibility of absolute knowing and the certainty of truth. Significantly – and this is certainly important for twentieth-century interpretations – truth, rationality and the absolute are viewed as *achievements*. As Hegel writes in the retrospective preface to *Phenomenology*, 'Of the Absolute it must be said that it is essentially a *result*, that only in the *end* is it what it truly is; and that precisely in this consists its nature, viz. to be actual, subject, the spontaneous becoming of itself'.[46] It is through the process of historical and subjective becoming, in the articulations of difference and contradiction, the traversing and dialectical mediation of new cultural paths and the shaking off and learning from old cultural formations, that the actuality of truth and reason are to be realized. In short, without movement and without the temporality of the self, thought and being cannot posit or exceed themselves. Certainly, the language of origin and *telos*, closure and finality, appear as wholly inadequate descriptions of the form of Hegel's dialectic. As Jean Hyppolite remarks, 'What is important in Hegel, is not that we view it [the dialectic] as a rational system but that we focus on the movement within thought.'[47] Hegel's system is not static but dynamic and transformative. As we have noted above, the categories of time and space are given a new significance. They offer up the possibility of an ontology of the self which was untheorized by Descartes and understood in a limited way in terms of *a priori* categories by Kant. Hegel's attention to movement, motion and becoming, give rise to a view of the subject as the *principle of movement* itself. How is this dynamic subject conceptualized?

For Hegel, the subject can not be assumed as a fixed point, suspended in time and space. The task of philosophy is rather to '[free] determinate thoughts from their fixity'.[48] Indeed, the knowing subject that posits itself as the ground upon which the act of predication proceeds, establishes a realm external to the self; it becomes an object to itself and creates in the process an antithesis between being and knowing. Cartesian dualism, and what Hegel calls the 'monochromatic formalism' of Kant's philosophy, are examples of forms of subjectivity which extricate otherness and contradiction, hence ignoring the fundamental relation between essence and existence that only dialectical thought is able to synthesize.

However, if Hegel may be seen to rid the subject of its modern alienation, the ontological structure of the subject as set out in the *Phenomenology* does not seem conducive to any such transcendence. Hegel marks his concepts of Substance and Subject with an originary difference or fissure – that which he calls negation. It is negativity, the power or force whose self-movement turns the subject into being, which gives existence to its essence. It is, Hegel writes, 'a bifurcation . . . [t]he doubling which sets up opposition'.[49] Both Substance and Subject (they are ultimately of the same mode for Hegel), contain their own negation.[50] This ontology is tied to history and this allows for a structural distinction between the self and the subject (which we may call consciousness and *self*-consciousness), a distinction which sets the subject on an arduous and self-alienating journey in search of satisfaction of a desire for self-recognition and self-consciousness, and a desire for the wisdom of Absolute Knowledge. Consciousness, it seems, must live in forced exile, losing its identity over and over again in order to achieve a full sense of itself in the absolute. It is this conception of the desiring subject that will be developed not only by Kojève and Hyppolite (discussed below) but also by Jacques Lacan in his psycho-analytic construction of the subject (see Chapter 3). Furthermore, by questioning the status of the absolute and the transcendence of nega-tivity, these three thinkers generate more sensitive readings of the subject's adventures in history.

The basis of Hegel's criticism of what, for him, constituted Spinoza's metaphysical monism should be all too apparent now. By reducing the complex structure of the subject to a mere modification of Substance, Spinoza's objective logic offers no opportunity for subjective becoming. Whilst Spinoza's parallelism constructs a rational knowledge with the unique and, for some, revolutionary aim of distinguishing it from the world of fictions produced by the subject's *imaginatio*, for Hegel, this can only institute a dualism in Spinoza's philosophy which separ-ates the concrete subject from the attainment of a Universal knowledge. We have seen in the previous section precisely why Spinoza wants to break with all anthropomorphic forms of knowledge. Hegel's dialec-tical conception of expressive totality together with his concept of negativity respond to the important problem of the subject's agency, will and action; they embrace the world of finite, particular selves. They are seen by Hegel as important *correctives* to Spinoza's abstract Substance, allowing for the concrete expression of difference and particularity, reciprocity and recognition, and the active becoming of consciousness in history. These elements of Hegelian philosophy, as we shall see in due course, were to be reworked by twentieth-century thinkers such as Kojève and Hyppolite.

Before turning to focus upon the French reception of Hegel and the impact and rethinking of the problematic of the subject his writings necessitated, the transformations wrought to the Hegelian conception of the subject by Marx must be brought into this discussion. There is no easy way of characterizing the Marx–Hegel relation; indeed the relation often remains a lacuna in the work of Lukács and Althusser despite their rigorous efforts to illuminate it. Idealist versus materialist arguments aside, both Marx and Hegel are interested in the phenom-enological question of how reality and subjectivity *appear and are given form*. For Althusser, these are questions of ideology and of knowledge and they must be shorn of all reference to subjectivity. Althusser will claim this as Marx's own project, and the former will seek to elicit the conceptual system necessary for such a venture that will necessitate a return to Spinoza rather than Hegel (see Chapter 2). Nonetheless, in the *Paris Manuscripts*, Marx was very much concerned with a *social* ontology, one which immerses the subject in a social world where its existence is mediated in significant ways by its interaction with nature. For Marx, identity and difference, negation and contradiction are always explicitly social in form. Hegel's error, for Marx, was to wedge thought and social being within the realm of consciousness. To echo Hegel's criticism of Spinoza, the emphasis on the concrete universal, the actuality of the subject, and the self-moving structure of being is forever relegated to the domain of ideas. Marx's interest lies in the political rationale for the subject's estrangement from himself and others; this can only be determined by focusing upon the subject's *intercourse* with others. Thus, 'consciousness is, from the very beginning a social product, and remains so as long as men exist at all.'[51] The problem is the status of the *modality* through which philosophy views its own relation to reality. By remaining in the realm of pure thought, the proof of philosophy (and, for Hegel, existence) can only be given by an exposition of its essence whilst the mode of the subject's *real* existence remains, in Marx's view, untouched.

Both Marx and Hegel are interested in the question of the objectification of the subject. Marx claims that Hegel confounds the socio-economic problem of alienation with that of the objectification of thought. Alienation is not an estrangement from the object in thought because thought cannot be isolated from social being. Marx takes up Hegel's dialectic of master and slave and through it emphasizes the externalization of the subject through its labour for another. It is the labourer's alienation and externalization from the object of labour which gives alienation its objective dimension. Under capitalism, Marx argues, this process of externalization is increasingly alienating: the subject departs from species-being, from a symbiotic relation with nature through work. There is also an important existential dimension to alienation: as an objective being, the subject is a '*suffering*, conditioned and limited creature'.[52] It is the task of communism to transcend this negation of the subject's reality: 'communism as the complete and conscious return of man conserving the riches of previous developments for man himself as a social, i.e. human being.'[53] Marx's anthropomorphization of the dialectic is clear. It is the natural subject, man, not the internal disharmony of Substance which is the ground of

Marx's dialectical system outlined in *The Manuscripts*.[54] As for Hegel, this acting consciousness is embodied in history, but its experiences do not hinge upon 'a restless revolving within itself' rather the experience of consciousness emerges out of the activities of real subjects in their historico-materialist becoming.[55]

The relation between Marx and Hegel is one of perpetual tension and it is re-encountered anew by all who pursue it. Does Marx under-estimate the ontological relation of self to world in this early work *and* overestimate Hegel's idealism? The *Phenomenology of Spirit* describes a complex itinerary for the subject, indeed one which recognizes the subject's finitude and suffering. Appearance is not to be subsumed into an abstract dimension; it signifies the ontological disparity between consciousness and world. It necessitates deceit, illusion, uncertainty and disjuncture between being and worldly phenomenon. To subsume the world of appearance *within* the real, indicates that Marx inverts the problem of the social subject: now it is the sensuous subject of nature which becomes the ground without which social life cannot be understood.[56] The return to Hegel alluded to in the introduction to this section was a return to alienation viewed not solely as a socially mediated relation but also as an ontological relation. The Hegelian motifs of the unhappy consciousness and the master–slave dialectic were adopted by Hyppolite and Kojève in order to develop an ontology of the subject's existence. The question became, in other words, *the mode of existence of alienation*. Could alienation be objectified in the social as Marx maintained in the *Manuscripts*, or was it a relation intrinsic to self and world? If the former, then what could be the political solution (Kojève)? And, if the latter, was there a structure of existence which could still be conceptualized dialectically (Hyppolite)? The form of these questions was to have a profound effect upon the reception of Hegel's conception of subjectivity and the thinkers that were to be read against him as a supplement, notably Heidegger and Nietzsche.[57] This *new mode of questioning* regarding the subject enabled Hegel's philosophy to be interpreted as 'an anti-thetics without synthesis or reconciliation, a play of opposed terms within a unity that continually subverts and divides itself.'[58]

Kojève and Hyppolite: subject, history, structure

Kojève's central thesis is that the movement of self-consciousness and subjectivity in Hegel's *Phenomenology of Spirit* is first and foremost an *anthropology*. History and knowledge, historical becoming and the subject's gradual acquiring of *a truth* for self and world, are given temporal movement only by the human act of making history. Like the early Marx in the *Paris Manuscripts*, Kojève places being and becoming, negation and negativity firmly within the historical field of human action where it becomes subsumed by the act of *labour*. There can be no acting self prior to social interaction with others. In the natural state, being can only be a being-for-itself. Natural consciousness may achieve an isolated, singular self-certainty; it may generate a certain knowledge of objects, and thus produce a simple unmediated identity with itself. However, consciousness of the other is reduced to a function of its own self-consciousness: the other becomes a mere thing. In contrast, for Kojève, the subject who desires recognition of the other and external reality has transcended the 'animal-being' described above; its desire for transformation assimilates, negates and absorbs animal or given-being[59] and hence creates and reveals the I. Thus, 'Man is negating *Action*, which transforms given Being, and, by transforming it, transforms itself.'[60] The subject is the ground, the movement of history; it is not the passive, contemplative behaviour of *natural* being which transforms reality for Kojève, but the active, humanizing desire (as negativity) of a subject seeking self-recognition through the recognition of the other. Kojève places desire at the centre of what it means to exist and it is the centrality of this concept to the humanist *problématique* which Lacan appears to take from Kojève – although not without it undergoing a significant theoretical transformation.

Kojève's philosophical discourse utilizes Hegel's discussion of the master–slave dialectic. Here, his discourse risks, for some critics, turning the duality which Hegel emphasizes as both an interior relation between the self and itself (perhaps most clearly expressed in the 'unhappy consciousness'), and a social relation between self and other, into a dramatic account of two distinct, clashing subjectivities.[61] For Kojève, it is the master who represents consciousness existing for itself, that is, a given-being. The slave's reality, on the other hand, is constituted both by a recognition of the dignity and superiority of the master, which imparts on the slave a sense of contingency, loss (in short, the spectre of death), and by the object of its labour, which remains a negative act. However, whilst the master is fixed in his pure negativity, viewing desire of the object as an end in itself, the slave is ready for transcendence and transformation of the negative. The slave's is a non-essential activity. Desire, or negativity, as work, modifies the natural world and in this process its own relation to the slave. As Michael Roth observes, whilst 'Hegelian time is the temporality of desire, the master's time is the rhythm of satisfaction.'[62]

Work *is* time for Kojève; it exists within time and requires time; by working, the slave creates human temporality as human history, halting the evolution of nature and exceeding slavish consciousness.[63] Furthermore, the creative dimension of desire *as* action is expressed in speech. Knowledge is at once the expression of the experience of the acting subject in discourse, and a transformation and revelation of nature *as* human knowledge of the real.[64] This interpretation of subjectivity and desire is grounded upon an inherent dualism between the natural and the human which Kojève insists he finds in tacit form in the *Phenomenology*.[65] Following Kojève's distinction between the natural and the human world, knowledge is always made manifest in human action. Ideas *appear as the products* of objects and projects mediated by work and action.[66] Truth as Totality (read absolute knowledge) can be gleaned by the subject only with the culmination of the dialectic, with the synthesis of action and history, and the recognition of man as free individual.[67] However, the dualism between nature and history poses a problem for the dialectical sythesis of these two elements. Kojève's anthropological reading of Hegel thus appears to have a dual significance. First, it allows desire to be humanized and tied to the agency of the subject so that it may, in turn, order the dialectical movement of history; second, it generates the conditions of possibility for truth/absolute knowledge in the enunciating subject. In this way, Kojève collapses the problem of the subject into its historical becoming and humanizes the constituent parts of the dialectic in much the same way as that of the early Marx. Through this humanist reading, Kojève has also humanized the conditions of possibility of knowledge and *contained the fissure underlying subjectivity* closely within the human subject.

In sharp contrast to Kojève, Hyppolite's reading of Hegel's conception of the subject emphasizes the tragic component of human existence and whilst he (like Kojève) also focuses upon the historical dimension of the subject, that is, the subject's temporality, this philosophy of history has no humanist component, and no interpretation of the subject as historical actor. Hyppolite does read the condition of human experience to be the struggle for recognition, and views this struggle as fixed on desire: desire for the other and recognition by the other.[68] However, there can be no dialectical recognition of these experiences by the subject. As Hyppolite writes, 'the accomplishment of the absolute is forever deferred.'[69]

Whilst, according to Hyppolite, Hegel privileges a retrospective point of view in the *Phenomenology*, which describes the different figures of knowledge and the journey of consciousness from sensuous certainty through perception towards understanding, Hyppolite asks whether there is not a *logic* of consciousness, structural conditions of experience, which are constant for every historical situation.[70] This structure would not be 'the appearance of a unique subject but an original ensemble, a totality of a quite different type from Hegel's spiritual principle.'[71] If, then, Hyppolite maintains a focus on the existential plight of the subject in the social world, this ontology is not to be viewed anthropologically, but rather in terms of the conditions which structure the possibility of self-consciousness and its experience of truth. Hyppolite writes, 'it is not a question of man considered as a biological species, but of the emergence in the very heart of life of a being who becomes conscious of this life as a condition of his existence.'[72]

The being of life is 'the disquiet of the self',[73] the anxiety, suffering and alienation of a subject which will never coincide with itself 'for it is always other in order to be itself'.[74] This experience is one of inadequacy, infinite non-correspondence with the truth of the object; the subject always fails to reach unity with itself. However, because consciousness always exceeds itself in its reflection it is doomed to oscillate forever on the brink of self-discovery: 'this feeling of disparity within the self, of the impossibility of the self coinciding with itself in reflection [the unhappy consciousness], is indeed the basis of subjectivity.'[75]

Negativity is at the centre of being for Hyppolite; it is immanent in all content and is therefore the condition of possibility of any subject whatsoever.[76] 'This is why', Hyppolite notes, 'the individual is the "absolute impulse", rather than merely the tendency of being to remain in a given state, and it is this in virtue of an internal contradiction.'[77] In his essay 'The Human Situation in the Hegelian Phenomenology', Hyppolite considers the mode through which this impulse of life, that is, subjectivity, may be authenticated in human history. The dislocating force of negativity is the desire on the part of the subject for unity and recognition by the other. In the activity of work/labour, the subject negates itself and shapes and refashions the object; labour humanizes nature and conveys a sense of coherence and universality upon human existence.[78] In other words, it grounds *reason* as a human event. Despite the implicit references to Marx here and the evident parallels with the Kojèvean account above, it is important *not* to subsume Hyppo-lite's conception of the subject within this philosophical perspective. This conception of desire is not secured by a dualist ontology, rather it is an original structure of experience. The humanizing of desire is closer to the structure of recognition as an imaginary movement. Indeed, elsewhere Hyppolite describes the desire for recognition which structures the master–slave dialectic as '*a mirror play*' which recalls Lacan's discussion of the mirror stage in the accession of subjectivity.[79] Furthermore, Hyppolite posits time as the concept which supersedes all other categories; it is the condition of all human reality and it places a limit upon the subject's creative possibilities.[80] This really makes the subject's encounter with the object of labour a *missed encounter*; contra Marx and Kojève, labouring on nature offers no resolution for the unhappy consciousness, just as desire in its infinitude can only find an imaginary satisfaction in the object. For Kojève, time, desire and knowledge were all humanized; they could only gain meaning within a theory of human action. Hyppolite's philosophical discourse is markedly different: it is time which gives birth to the subject; tem-porality which is the basis of all existence. Time is the condition which structures life. It is 'the middle term which makes it possible to con-ceptualize life and the living relation and *the means whereby the problem of knowledge and the problem of life are identifiable.*'[81] Time, moreover, cannot be annulled by the subject by whatever means; its destiny is not to be 'vindicated by Spirit' as Hegel asserts in the final chapter of the *Phenomenology*[82] and Kojève interprets as the end of History. Rather, it is the disquiet of the self (or the 'unhappy con-sciousness') which Hyppolite continues to emphasize: a subjective state of temporal disjuncture with the world. This precludes an identity between being and knowledge and ensures that the fissure between forms of knowledge and their linguistic expression/enunciation by the subject will be ceaselessly re-encountered and re-thought.[83]

Thus the labour of contemporary thought works upon the question of the subject, pursuing the project of re-thinking the possibilities, the movement, the very space of subjectivity, and encountering anew the echoes of past philosophies. Of course, the matter of philosophical inheritance remains a complex one. There is, as we have noted above, no single precursor to contemporary French philosophy (Nietzsche, Husserl, Heidegger remain as important as the thinkers considered in the preceding exercises of thought). Furthermore, whatever be the

philosophical genealogy of contemporary thought, it must also remain
tied to the political effects such thought generates. This latter point is
particularly pertinent in the positions of Lukács and Althusser. It is to
Marxist conceptions of subjectivity that the attention of the next
chapter will turn.

2

MARXISM AND SUBJECTIVITY

FROM LUKÁCS TO ALTHUSSER

The question of the subject has haunted Marxism since its inception. It has often been shrouded by more antinomic discussions around idealism and materialism, yet many of the central preoccupations of Marxism have ignited the fundamental question of the subject. Debates regarding the relative status of theory and practice, reform and revolution, agency and structure, and the respective roles of science and history, all presuppose if not a certain conception of the subject then at least some reflection upon its form. Marxism is a political philosophy of transformation as well as critique and thus the subject will always be infused with a political significance. However, given the multiplicity of interpretations and positions within the Marxist perspective, both the question of the subject and related problems of agency and political praxis are highly contested ones.

The positions considered in this chapter are those of Georg Lukács and Louis Althusser, both of whom introduced new modes of thinking about the question of the subject into Marxism. Their two central, most widely known works, *History and Class Consciousness* and *Reading Capital* stand as two opposed treatises on the relationship between knowledge, consciousness and politics, although both works share in common a rejection of the economic positions associated with the dominant schools of classical Marxism. Neither the mechanistic positions of the Second International nor the piecemeal, evolutionary position of the revisionists were able to develop an account of the subject, or of knowledge, adequate to the needs of a Marxist philosophy. For Perry Anderson, both Lukács and Althusser, along with a host of other Western Marxists (Adorno, Benjamin, Della Volpe and Sartre), were guilty of a gravitation towards philosophy and away from revolutionary practice.[1] For Western Marxists, however, such recourse to philosophy did not imply a rejection of political activity, but rather signalled an attempt to solder the relation between consciousness and knowledge, the recognition of which had largely escaped the political consciousness of the Second International. The realm of philosophy was not viewed as a discrete, self-contained dimension of knowledge. Instead it weaved the fabric of political reality; it constructed the sense of the human subject and hence contributed to an understanding of *political consciousness*. For both Lukács and Althusser, philosophy as Marx proposed in the eleventh thesis on Feuerbach becomes *explicitly* normative. It must be seen not only to interpret the world but to direct and inform the revolutionary transformation of political and social structures. Significantly, it was the broken links between knowledge and consciousness, theory and practice, and being and knowing, that Western Marxists sought to repair and advance.

There are important philosophical precursors to Western Marxist perspectives. Along with Korsch, Gramsci, Sartre and Merleau-Ponty, and indeed Kojève and Hyppolite, Lukács and Althusser return to Hegel, whose *Phenomenology of Spirit*, in particular, forms the background for the philosophical analysis of subjectivity and history. Of course, this relation to Hegelian philosophy is not always of a positive form, as we shall see in the position adopted by Louis Althusser, for whom it is always attached to a reduction of thought to *ideology*. It is to the philosophy of Spinoza that Althusser turns for an understanding of the subject as a complex effect of social structure, and for an epistemology shorn of all subjective referent. Indeed in the reading of Althusser's construction of the subject in Section III, the recently available posthumous works will be utilized to respond to the dominant view of Althusser as a structural determinist without a distinct theory of subject. In fact, Althusser's effort to account for the persistence of the subject matured into a number of incisive philosophical observations that throw the problem of the subject into fresh relief. The case of Lukács' philosophical antecedents is similarly multifarious and Section I will explore their effects upon Lukács' conception of the subject. It will be argued, however, that Lukács' rigorous and critical dissection of the philosophical conditions of possibility for subjectivity and his endeavour to historicize the subject do not ultimately transcend the dualisms of modern philosophy. Specifically, our interrogations of both thinkers will show how the philosophical resources brought to bear upon the conception of the subject risk subverting their Marxist characteristics. Such a diverse philosophical inheritance, then, may bring inconsistencies to their positions, inconsistencies which may infiltrate and subvert the logic of subjectivity. Neither Lukács or Althusser escape the tensions and frictions wrought on the conception of the subject by modern philosophy and discussed in the previous chapter. The question of how to negotiate the history of the subject in order to excavate and refashion the relationship between subjectivity, epistemology, philosophy and politics becomes an important, arguably intractable, question in the work of these two writers. Let us then turn to the position of Georg Lukács and examine his construction of the subject.

I. RETURNING TO LUKÁCS

Lukács' writings, particularly his influential *History and Class Consciousness* (1923), are often viewed as a prime example of Western Marxism. Indeed, the philosophies of Adorno and Merleau-Ponty and, for Lucien Goldmann, Heidegger too, are fully explicable only with reference to the writings of Lukács.[2] However, Lukács' writings of 1910–1923, which include *Soul and Form* (1910) and *The Theory of the Novel* (1915), as well as the aforementioned text, were also contemporaneous with the phenomenological thought of Edmund Husserl, with whom *History and Class Consciousness* has been seen to have a common focus.[3] In 'Philosophy as a Rigorous Science' (1911) Husserl also offered a critique of the empty formalism of much philosophical and scientific thought and proposed an investigation of consciousness of the kind for which Lukács must have had – at the very least – an intellectual sympathy.[4] This broad, neo-Kantian *milieu*, often named the Heidelberg school, included amongst its members not only Lukács and Husserl but also Dilthey, Weber and Simmel. It was their discussions around neo-Kantianism that reinvigorated an interest in Hegel, an interest which had been dormant for some time.[5] The discussions of this school centred on the questions of the validity of positivism as a method for studying social phenomena, and the role that subjectivity should play in theories of knowledge and history. These questions were to be given critical attention and development in *History and Class Consciousness*.

Thus Lukács brought to his analysis of Marx, and to the question of the subject, a critical sense of the Kantian tradition in which he was immersed intellectually, as well as a burgeoning interest in Hegelian phenomenology. It is this diversity of approach which is the source of Lukács' enduring importance. The phenomenological and dialectical reading of history which Lukács brings to Marxism also has a number of commonalities with the Kojèvean interpretation of Hegel discussed in Chapter 1. However, the philosophical discourse developed by Lukács does not equate the Hegelian slave with the proletarian subject. Lukács introduces some important philosophical, methodological and existential reflections on the concept of the subject, *some* of which may be seen to precurse – in very general and incomplete terms – Derrida's critique of metaphysical dualisms. In these and other areas, Lukács' philosophical perspective will be seen to offer up a number of important insights which have a conceptual bearing on constructions of subjectivity considered in later chapters.

The subject and the tragedy of estrangement

> For the proletariat to become aware of the dialectical nature of its existence is a matter of life and death.[6]

For Lukács, as for other Western Marxists, philosophy and existence are closely bound together. However, the problem is one of their possible coincidence or identity: can philosophy become a form of *self-knowledge*? Can the subject overcome the contradictions both within existence and within knowledge to reach a higher state of accordance with truth? The mode of presentation of this problem is clearly a Hegelian one. However, it should be clear that the anxiety of its achievement, the creation of adequate concepts and the articulation of modes of thought which can themselves perform the task of producing unity between the subject and knowledge *is a problem which haunts all philosophies of the subject and not solely its dominant Hegelian formulation.*

In *The Theory of the Novel* Lukács offers an account of the modern self-contained subject, a subject who, through self-reflection on the external world creates the object (however much distorted) in the image of itself. Lukács notes how this 'elevation of interiority'[7] leads to a disjuncture within the subject, and between subject and world:

> as the objective world breaks down, so the subject, too, becomes a fragment; only the 'I' continues to exist, but its existence is then lost in the insubstantiality of its self-created world of ruins. Such subjectivity wants to give form to everything, and precisely for this reason succeeds only in mirroring a segment of reality.[8]

Indeed, this existential self-estrangement of the subject, this absence of a 'life-totality'[9] and a coincidence between life and being, is due largely to the temporal distance of self and world. 'Time can become constitutive', Lukács writes, 'only when the bond with the transcendental home has been severed.'[10] Given the philosophical language of this problem of estrangement, it is of no surprise that Goldmann claims Lukács as one of the fathers of existentialism.[11]

In both *The Theory of the Novel* and *Soul and Form*, Lukács is unable to account for the tragic existence of the subject in socio-historical terms, nor resolve this disjuncture metaphysically. Rather, life, as for Simmel, is a state of 'permanent crisis'.[12] Whilst Lukács views the art-form as representing and expressing the tragedy of life, it can offer no respite, being merely an illusory, sentimentally lived, and hence partial solution.[13] The rift, or the *duality* between the tragic existence of the subject leading an inauthentic, ordinary life, and life and history expressed as a total relation is both paradoxical and unsurpassable: 'History', Lukács writes, 'appears as a profound symbol of fate.'[14] If there is a dialectical logic which can understand this contradiction, it lacks the conceptual means of expression at this stage in Lukács' philosophy. Existential and historical relations cannot be soldered together by any creative action on the part of the subject.

The interpretations of the subject's estrangement identified above are often aligned with the views of the 'early' Lukács whose writings are viewed as lacking a normative dimension which may render concrete the praxis of the subject. However, the *structure* of the crisis identified by Lukács in his early writings remains the central theme of *History and Class Consciousness*. Consequently, Lukács' 'conversion' to Marxism in 1918 should not appear as a definitive break in his intellectual development; rather it must be seen as a practical solution to the problems that had occupied all his writings to that date.[15] It must be emphasized that the concern in the present chapter is with the conceptual structure of the subject and its changing mode of theorization, and not Lukács' intellectual genesis *per se*. What is important to note here, in the light of this interpretation, is that in his earlier works the theoretical concepts were either absent or insufficiently articulated within the problematic, leaving Lukács with no resolution (despite his clear debt to Hegel in *The Theory of the Novel*). The tragedy of estrangement was that it could find no resting place within metaphysical categories which could only evade life, but neither could it come to terms with its historicity, lacking as it did an adequate methodology of history. Commenting in *History and Class Consciousness* on this plight of the modern subject, Lukács repeats the fissure identified above: 'The freedom (of the subject) is neither able to overcome the sensuous necessity of the system of knowledge and the soulessness of the fatalistically conceived laws of nature, nor is it able to give them any meaning.'[16]

However, despite the similarity in philosophical style of this quotation with the earlier works, in this text of 1923 Lukács develops a perspective on Marxist philosophy which re-orders the formulation of the problems of cultural crisis and distorted consciousness which leave the subject unable to *recognize* and compose a knowledge adequate to this crisis. The account of alienation and contradiction in a Marxist vein imbues Lukács' position with a new radicalism. It opens up the possibility of reading the Hegelian conception of history in terms of the Marxist subject of praxis. We have already encountered the range of problems this may raise in our earlier analysis of Kojève, particularly the anthropological construction of the subject as actor. Whether Lukács' problematic of the subject contains the theoretical resources to move beyond this humanization of subjectivity, history and knowledge is a question which we must now address.

Subjectivity and reification

In *History and Class Consciousness* Lukács develops a social ontology of the subject rather than a pure ontology that delineates its abstract conditions of existence. For Lukács, following Marx and Hegel, all modes of thought are historically constituted, although the extent to which this process of social constitution is tied to a materialism, as it is for Marx and Althusser too, can be questioned. History and existence, like knowledge and consciousness, cannot be separated.[17] Given the interconnectedness of social existence, historical movement and forms of knowledge, Lukács classifies the social world as a *totality*. This crucially important concept tends towards an understanding of society as a series of expressive relations which circumscribe yet do not determine absolutely concrete social existence. However, the disjuncture between concrete social existence and the subject's experience or knowledge of it ensures that in *practice* the totality is not experienced as a holistic unity but is rather experienced in its distinct parts, as an abstract, inert, fixed and limited form of life. The process of history in turn becomes static and its temporality is hidden from the subject. The task that Lukács, as a Marxist, sets himself is to understand precisely how subjective praxis, that which *moves* history, that which is its *genesis*, can be redeemed for the revolutionary project. The focus is, in Lukács' words, '*the problem of the subject of the action, the subject of the genesis*'.[18]

The conception of the subject must be viewed in terms of the expressive totality described above. Lukács' focus is upon two dominant relations: the *epistemological* and the *social*, the latter relation being inclusive of political and economic relations. For Lukács, these two dimensions are always intricately linked (epistemic relations are underscored by social ones), although they may not be experienced as such within consciousness. Under modern capitalism, abstract thought and concrete existence cannot correspond in their given forms. Rather they are experienced as fragmented and without necessary connection. Capitalism requires that these facets (which will hold within their essences, for Lukács, the possibility of a unified, expressive totality) be represented in knowledge and experienced by consciousness as separate and unconnected. It is in this context that Lukács coins the term *reification*. This term indicates the dimension through which social, economic and political life is lived. Reification describes a whole range of different phenomena:[19] the consciousness of the subject (specifically but not exclusively, the proletariat); relations between workers and the commodities they produce; the extension and wider rationalization of the commodity relation identified by Marx in *Das Kapital* to all aspects of social life;[20] and, finally, the form of knowledge which predominates in capitalist society, namely bourgeois philosophy.[21]

Reification is most prevalent at the work-place where the real potential of the worker becomes hidden and distorted in its commodity-form. Given that reification requires 'that a society should learn to satisfy all its needs in terms of exchange',[22] the social relations set up around labour-power are likewise seen solely in terms of exchange. Reification mystifies the relation between labour-power and wages; inherently unequal relations appear as a kind of 'second-nature', and as analogous to the 'given-being' of animal-life described by Kojève and discussed in Chapter 1. In short, reification is the universalization of the commodity relation and this implies, Lukács writes, drawing upon Weber's insights upon rationalization, that 'the principle of rational mechanisation and calculability must embrace every aspect of life.'[23]

Reification indicates an interconnectedness of epistemological and social relations; Lukács illuminates their symmetry in *History and Class Consciousness*. Here, the social (proletarian) subject is presented as fragmented: 'a mechanical part incorporated into a mechanical system'.[24] The unauthentic subject of *Soul and Form* becomes the reified subject of capitalism. The subject is atomized and contemplative, inward-looking and without a temporal relation to history, or to the process of capitalist production because reification reduces temporal relations to ones which are purely spatial. Commodities are viewed as objects with forgotten histories; they seem to have lost their origin in the act of human labour. Subject–object relations appear hardened, disembodied and consequently unchangeable. This is how the reified consciousness of capitalism experiences relations of inequality: it is unable to penetrate their essence and move beyond this world of fetishized appearances.

Unsurprisingly, this abstract structure of consciousness repeats itself in *epistemological* relations where a particular conception of the subject grounds the investigations of philosophical thought. Lukács offered an important reading of modern philosophy which examines its *antinomic* basis as that which prevents philosophical thought from achieving unity between the subject and object of knowledge. Specifically, he considers the philosophical limitations of the concept of subject in relation to the constitution of objective knowledge. This discussion is important for two reasons. First, it elaborates the conceptual structure of a subject that Lukács rejects, therefore pointing towards the content of his own concept, formed in its wake. Second, Lukács' critique of forms of metaphysical rationalism, and his discussion of the dualisms inherent in modern thought, embrace wider questions which are central to the project of deconstruction developed in Chapter 4.

The reified structure of philosophical thought

In a discussion entitled 'The Antinomies of Bourgeois Thought'[25] Lukács investigates the objectification of consciousness within the realm of philosophical reason. 'The source of modern critical philosophy', Lukács writes, 'springs from the reified structure of consciousness.'[26] The rationalization of thought and production extend to the sphere of philosophy; this much is indicated by the inclusive concept of totality developed by Lukács. Thus, as rationality in production seeks its realization in a means–end calculus which must abstract from the concrete experience of the worker, so modern philosophy interprets the realization of knowledge as achievable only through formal categories which must transcend the problems of existence. At the centre of all the methodological problems surrounding the concept of rationality (that is, its theoretical form within science, ethics and philosophical knowledge, and its practical form within the sphere of production and social life itself) lies the question of the subject. Rationality *separates* itself from concrete existence; it is unable, therefore, to consider adequately the conception of the subject which underpins its own position. Lukács' analysis aims to explore precisely how this abstraction from existence has come about. Like Derrida after him, Lukács argues that the metaphysical root of the concept of rationality is itself riven by contradictions; this inevitably renders all which is built upon its edifice (particular rationally ordered truth claims) contingent and prone to break down.

Lukács' reading of philosophy draws upon some classical components of the tradition as well as critical (Kantian) philosophy. In particular, Lukács draws a parallel between the centrality of the knowing subject in modern philosophy and the rise of scientific principles within knowledge. The problem of the subject is a distinctly modern dilemma: 'Modern philosophy sets itself the following problem: it refuses to accept the world as something that has arisen (or e.g. has been created by God) independently of the knowing subject, and prefers to conceive of it instead as its own product.'[27]

According to Lukács, the subject which is constituted through this re-ordering of the problem of knowledge is a contemplative self, stripped of particularity and concrete content. The rational method which predominates in modern philosophy, moreover, generates natural laws that remain blind to the contingent event. Significantly, such systematic, ultimately scientific, forms of knowledge claim to be universal in their application. As Lukács notes, this claim can be established only by labelling as irrational that which it is *unable* to account for. Thus, both the dislocations of concrete existence and the contradictory nature of consciousness remain unrecognized. In other words, existence is separated from philosophical knowledge. Lukács writes perceptively of 'the inevitability with which every rational system will strike a frontier or barrier of irrationality'. Indeed, he observes how 'the character of this existence [viewed as irrationality] is revealed at least as clearly by what philosophy does *not* find problematic as by what it does.'[28] Both of these reflections certainly *structure* the problem in a manner not dissimilar to that of deconstruction. Even when philosophy claims to deal with the problem of existence and concrete content, it attaches these so firmly to the formal conditions which may delineate their possible role that its solutions appear empty and devoid of all significance. Thus reification could be described more aptly as a process of containment and delimitation of subjectivity, and as an interpretation of social 'facts' as rigid objects of investigation. In other words, reification performs the act of metaphysical closure *par excellence*.[29]

For Lukács, Kant's critical philosophy is the highest exemplification of the antinomy between form and content even as the latter tries to resolve this dualism on a transcendental level. However, Kant does recognize the impossibility of constructing knowledge as a pure or absolute form because the thing-in-itself (the *noumena*) remains unknowable to the conscious subject immersed in the world. The conditions for the possibility of knowledge are given by experience itself, hence introducing into knowledge the spectre of contingency. The subject (and of course the validity-claims of knowledge) still come up against the unknowability of the thing-in-itself. Of course, Kant understood this: if the subject was not to produce a partial, unreliable and contingent form of knowledge, it had to think transcendentally according to rational categories and eliminate the irrational elements of subjective existence. For Lukács, this effort to transform knowledge into a law-like rational enterprise, if not wholly predictable, then at least freed from certain disruptive tendencies, 'transforms knowledge into ... laws which function in – objective – reality *without the intervention of the subject*.'[30] The Kantian system is viewed as unable to tackle the problem of existence in relation to philosophy:

> its efforts to weed out ruthlessly from its own outlook every subjective and irrational element and every anthropomorphic tendency ... strives with ever increasing vigour to drive a wedge between the subject of knowledge and 'man', and to transform the knower into a pure and purely formal subject.[31]

For these reasons, critical philosophy cannot resolve the dualisms between subject and object, freedom and necessity, form and content. Instead, it reinstates these dualisms. This problem is an inescapable one given that bourgeois philosophy is itself tied to the conditions of capitalist society: rationality in one sphere is transposed onto the other. The problems of critical philosophy mirror the stagnant position occupied by the bourgeoisie. The significance of Kant's philosophy, for Lukács, is that it thinks through the contradiction of social life solely upon a philosophical plane. The irresolvable form of the dualisms, experienced by this mode of knowledge as an antinomy, is inevitable given that the bourgeoisie is unable to achieve a stand-point in knowledge which can reveal how its own conditions of existence are, in fact, inscribed upon the surface of modern philosophy. The impenetrability of the thing-in-itself is viewed 'as no more than the illustration of a reified consciousness incapable of recognising itself in its products.'[32] This argument allows Lukács to develop a two-pronged argument (epistemological and social in structure) which can challenge the philosophical foundation of the modern subject of knowledge and allow for the development of a concept of subject which can generate a solution to the antinomies prevalent within knowledge and social life.

How is the argument framed? Lukács claims that the concept of rationality cannot have universal application because its founding principles (those which ensure deduction, predictability and calculation according to general laws), are built upon a rigid interpretation of objects and the reduction of the subject to a contemplative being that can think only when it obeys the rational laws which allow it to transcend its contingency. This construction of subject and object *subordinates* the concrete form of social existence and fails to recognize that the objects of investigation are reified products of a reified social world. For Lukács, in contrast, 'matter always seeps into the identity of the system'[33] and it is this material substratum that frustrates the coincidence of subject and object, and the separation of form and content, which rational systems strive towards. This concept of matter is important to the development of Lukács' argument. It is folded into the different dimensions of reality that are identified, particularly the realm of nature, which is paradoxically always a human construction. It also indicates that which may best be rendered as the dynamism or flux of material reality (that is, its mobility and becoming), which points to a profounder reality beneath the givenness of capitalist society. This second dimension owes something to Henri Bergson to whom Lukács refers in his correspondence.[34]

For Lukács, this material substratum of reality is always bound to human praxis. This ensures that the interest in the interpenetration of form and content is never simply reduced to a philosophy of naturalism. Lukács remains critical of all attempts to search for an essence which corresponds to nature, precisely because the concept of nature is overlaid by the social construction of reality.[35] He therefore rejects the Schillerian/Rousseauian account of the true essence of man; there can be no *natural* authentic humanity. Natural relations are always inscribed within a social totality. If it may be argued that the content of objectivity is heterogeneous and fluid prior to its formalization in knowledge, it is the construction of social reality as an expressive totality which allows for this deeper understanding and links the material substratum to human action. The interrelation of object-formation and subjective praxis is of capital importance to Lukács' account of the possible overcoming of the objectifying forces of social life.

Lukács' argument derives from the failure of classical philosophy (and Lukács includes Kant in this criticism) to connect the *genesis* of concepts to the movement of history. For Lukács, the problems identified here must return us to an analysis of the historical realm. We have already noted that it is the praxis of the subject that moves history. Thus, when Lukács recognizes that the subject of bourgeois philosophy is a purely contemplative, transcendental ego deprived of action, he is also describing a mode of philosophy which purports to be an ahistorical account of knowledge. However, the *origin* of all forms of knowledge is historical for Lukács, just as the subject of history is, in essence, an integral part of the social totality. What is required here is a methodology which can reveal the (presently distorted) essence of the historical actor within the expressive totality. For Lukács, it is a *dialectical* account of knowledge and history which may best perform this critical task of rethinking the foundation of subjectivity.

Locating the subject of knowledge

It is only in history, in the historical process, in the uninterrupted outpourings of what is qualitatively new that the requisite paradigmatic order can be found in the realm of things.[36]

Lukács' debt to Hegel in the construction of this argument is enormous. Indeed, as he claims in the 1967 Preface to *History and Class Consciousness*, it is also an attempt to 'out-Hegel Hegel'. It must not, therefore, be assumed that Lukács draws upon Hegel uncritically. Lukács is circumspect about the form of a pure ontology which risks evading the concrete-historical by submerging it within a mythology of World Spirit: 'this inappropriate and inconsistent approach to history deprives history itself of that essence which is so important precisely within the Hegelian system.'[37] Lukács tries to rectify what he views as the formalism implicit in Hegel's system which may come to the fore if dialectical movement is viewed as a 'blind dynamic' where the praxis of the subject loses its concrete significance. The historical genesis of the social totality is activated *only* by the praxis of a self-conscious, creative subject. Furthermore, cautious as Lukács is of developing an ontology which loses its social component, he is similarly wary of viewing Hegel's *Logic* as separated from social existence, where the process may become more important than the driving force which fuels logical developments. In his later work *Ontology of Social Being*, Lukács writes of Hegel's distortion of ontological facts, and the discrepancy between logic and ontology in his work.[38] Here, it is important to note Lukács' claim that it is the socio-historical rather than the logical dimension which is central to his own dialectical analysis.

Clearly, Lukács' central aim when elaborating his concept of the subject of history is to avoid recourse to an essentialist conception of the subject. As Merleau-Ponty notes, 'Lukács is trying to preserve ... a Marxism which incorporates subjectivity into history *without making it an epiphenomenon.*'[39] Lukács' distance from Romanticism's search for a natural human authenticity has already been pointed out. In *History and Class Consciousness*, Lukács shows his awareness of the vacillation inherent in humanism: on the one hand it risks degenerating into a crude empiricism, which ends up replicating the condition of the subject in society, on the other hand it may fall into a form of voluntarism, which assumes that the subject is *already* a social actor in its essence.[40] For some of his critics discussed below, particularly Althusser, Lukács does not fully escape these theoretical problems and remains hostage to a form of humanist-historicism.

Let us first return to Lukács' construction of the subject. Thus far we have seen how the interconnections between philosophical knowledge, social existence and historical movement are effectively unified in an expressive totality (in both an existential and social sense) which activates itself via the praxis of a historical subject. The reduction of this totality to a static, reified and 'petrified' social form under capitalism results in the objectification of social relations and the abstraction of class-relations to 'thing-like' qualities. Extending likewise to the realm of consciousness, bourgeois and proletarian both experience reified relations and social forms as *immediately* given. However, whilst the class-consciousness of the bourgeoisie is also the *objective limit* of capitalist production, the proletariat is the *historical embodiment of the limits of capitalism*.[41] The proletarian subject is not abstracted from the object, rather it is objectified in all areas of social existence. This subject lives under the weight of reification as concrete-immediacy. In contrast, the bourgeois subject (and correspondingly the abstract metaphysical subject) is detached from the weight of contradiction precisely because it experiences the world as self-made, as the result of *its action*; the relation to objectivity is of a different order altogether.[42] Lukács does not reduce the proletarian subject to a slavish consciousness in the manner of Kojève, for the slave 'can only attain to knowledge of an object which happens "accidentally" to be himself.'[43] Lukács prefers to give greater weight to the objective possibility of the subject's rise to self-consciousness, a move which underscores his faith in the coincidence of subject and object within history and philosophy.

How then can the proletarian subject become the subject of history? Drawing on Hegel's concept of the dialectic, the antinomies of bourgeois thought and the rigidity of socio-economic life are seen to be part of an 'immanent [dialectical] process'[44] which may (under the right conditions) draw the totality into a synthetic unity. The instrument of this genesis is the (Hegelian) category of mediation; the force and the source of its motion is the proletarian subject. To some extent, the two dimensions are interrelated; without mediation to show the *real tendencies* of the objects themselves, the subject would not be able to act and would remain a contemplative observer of immediacy. The role of mediation is not to abstract from objects but to separate the immanent meanings which adhere in objects from their immediate givenness to consciousness in a reified social world. This has two important effects on the consciousness of the subject. First, it draws attention to the gradations of reality, i.e. between the levels of thought, existence and lived-reality,[45] hence allowing an opening between the given and the possible; second, it brings the point of contradiction closer to the consciousness of the proletarian subject. Thus, for Lukács, the dialectical totality, which is as much part of the internal structure of the subject's consciousness as it is of the structure of the social whole, may lead to greater self-knowledge, providing that new mediated relations between subjects and objects do not once again freeze into a new rigidity.[46]

It is important to remember that these dialectical movements are attached to historical genesis which can only gain meaning through the action of a self-conscious subject. However, this conception of historical knowledge, which becomes a truth only via a synthesis with self-conscious praxis, must not be collapsed into a form of voluntarism. Lukács recognizes that, where the dominant mode of being is reified on all levels of existence, the concrete synthesis of (historical) knowledge and action may *appear* to be impossible. Kojève tried to avoid this apparent dualism between knowledge and action, by tying negativity, or the desire for recognition and transformation, firmly to an anthropological subject for whom action was an essential quality. In contrast, Lukács may seem more sceptical of human action. He notes the *disparity* between empirical, immediately given consciousness, and the already-inscribed possibility of transformation existing in the contradictions of the totality of capitalist relations. What is needed here is for the proletarian subject *as a class*, to realize the mediated identity of the social totality as an *element of self-consciousness*. The category of objective possibility, which Lukács takes from Weber[47], must be utilized 'so as to isolate the conditions in which this illusion [i.e. the unconsciousness of class-position] can be exposed and a real connection with the totality be established.'[48]

In his book *Marxism and Totality*, Martin Jay notes that the distinctions between empirical and ascribed consciousness, and between objective possibility and lived-relations, admit to a gap between the ideal and the real, hence reinstating a Kantian dualism between freedom and necessity, theory and practice and, of course, self-consciousness and historical knowledge, a dualism which Lukács' dialectic of consciousness hoped to avoid.[49] Why might Lukács' conception of the subject lead to a reinstatement of the problem of duality? Is this conception of the subject tied irrevocably to idealist positions? Is it bound to mimic the dominant motifs of subjectivity? These are difficult questions which can only be unravelled in the course of the following chapters. However, it is clear that Lukács undertheorizes the complexities of subject formation which may not always be amenable to dialectic construals. He risks equating consciousness with an essence present within the dialectical system *even before it is actually comprehended in consciousness*. The result is an artificial unity between knowledge and action, a unity which is possible only with recourse to a level of ideality in consciousness which must ultimately intuit its own conditions of possibility.

This criticism of Lukács' idealism of method penetrates his work on many different levels. In his efforts to overcome the so-called 'vulgar economism' of the Second International, Lukács claims that 'what is customarily called the economy, is nothing but the system of forms of objectivity of real life.'[50] Similarly, Lukács equates alienation with a form of objectification which seems to lack a material component and, *contra* Althusser, he appears to privilege the realm of ideas and the interrogation of philosophical formalism over an analysis of the institutional superstructure of modern capitalism. However, it must also be emphasized that Lukács was tackling head-on a problem that had largely been ignored by Marxist theory, namely the relation between philosophical knowledge and the concrete realm of class-consciousness. Perhaps his mistake was to *presuppose* the possible identity between subject and object. This philosophical and political identity is not easily constructed or maintained. Indeed, the coincidence of subject and object occurs only at a cost: those elements likely to distort its achievement are banished to the realm of 'unknowables' (illustrated by Lukács in his discussion of antinomies). A *possible* solution, according to Lukács, is to collapse the distinction between history and philosophical knowledge; this places the subject's action in dialectical exchange with theory (knowledge) and practice (consciousness). However, in the case of Lukács, this also places the subject in the extraordinary position of appropriating its own essence in history.

These difficulties arise, in part, because the concept of the subject is *undertheorized* in Lukács writings. The constitution of the subject and its profound relation to reification is not developed in its full complexity. Lukács notes that the antinomies of modern philosophy are also internalized *within* consciousness when he writes, in criticism of Kant: 'even the subject is split into phenomena and noumena and the unresolved, insoluble and henceforth permanent conflict between freedom and necessity now invades its innermost structure.'[51] This point is not, however, developed as a *conceptual* problem which may have an effect upon the theory of class-consciousness. Certainly, there is reference to a class-conditioned *unconsciousness*, and of course the formal consciousness of the philosophical subject, but Lukács does not develop an analysis of reification as a process which may affect profoundly the constitution of the human subject. It is knowledge of reification alone which will demystify the effects of reified political forms. Lukács' analysis appears to produce a universal (class) subject with the essential attribute of self-consciousness who need only recognize the philosophical *effects* of objectification in order to take up the privileged stand-point within history and the realm of (absolute) knowledge. The next section of this chapter will consider the structualist conception of the subject developed by Althusser. According to Althusser, Lukács reduces knowledge to the realm of historical necessity. By constructing a theory of knowledge upon a humanist–historicist foundation, where the subject is the universal essence which activates history, Lukács jettisons the emancipatory potential of knowledge which remains forever tied to a problematic of subjectivity and consciousness. Before moving to evaluate Althusser's anti-humanist perspective, the relation of structuralism to the question of the subjectivity must be sketched out and clarified.

II. THE ENCOUNTER BETWEEN STRUCTURALISM AND SUBJECTIVITY

The theoretical positions and conceptual resources which have developed within a broadly structuralist framework have had an indisputable impact – sometimes distant or indirect – upon the conceptions of the subject considered in the following three chapters of this book. Lacan, Derrida, Foucault and, of course Althusser, were all deeply influenced by structuralism. However, this alliance with structuralism is often an uneasy one punctuated by relations of tension and ambiguity. For example, whilst Althusser's anti-humanist perspective may have some affinity with the displacement of the subject initiated by structuralism, a more careful reading reveals his position as drawing upon very different traditions of thought. The same is true of the other three thinkers, who confront the structuralist problematic with quite different, competing philosophical perspectives. Much passes under the banner of structuralism (and post-structuralism) and the readings here will always be qualified ones, sensitive to the *diversity* of reflections upon structuralism as well as drawing attention to the manifest similarities in position.

Most texts on the movement, philosophy and conceptual base of structuralism emphasize its theoretical variety, its 'family of methods', and the contestability which has arisen in the concept of structure itself.[52] There is, however, one factor which can enframe this diversity, namely the central role of language in the construction of the subject and knowledge and, for some, in the constitution of modes of social life. Of course, the centrality of language to methods of interpretation has long been common to analytical and continental philosophy alike. Where the structuralist focus upon language begs to differ is in the *autonomy* it wishes to give language as a structure with its own rules of operation, application and possible modes of signification. The structural linguist Ferdinand de Saussure divided language into two constituent parts: *la langue*, the rule-governed component of language, the underlying structure which makes speech possible; and *la parole*, the actual instances of speech in day-to-day usage by subjects. For Saussure, and those who took on the ideas which became associated with structural linguistics, the constitution of language and the sign (i.e. the level of meaning imparted on language) was part of an objective structure that required no recourse to the enunciating subject. As Paul Ricoeur puts it, 'the notion of signification is placed in a different field from that of the intentional aimings of a subject.'[53] No longer can language be viewed as manipulable and its content determined by the creativity of consciousness; the density, instability and sheer range of language's possibilities makes the imprint of consciousness on language faint and without weight. It draws attention, therefore, to the *chasm* between experience and the content of the subject's speech. For structural linguistics, moreover, language is part of a quasi-scientific, objective study, which could focus on the division within signification, between the *signifier* – the sound-image, the material attribute of language where sequences, relations and codes are established – and the *signified* – the concept of a particular sign, the dimension where meaning and reference is determined. However, structural linguistics finds no natural relation between signifier and signified. The signifier is the realm of possible determinations of reference, and it may have numerous effects on a whole range of signified words or concepts. Language, for Saussure, is an arbitrary system, based upon the difference rather than the simple coincidence between signifier and signified. As Vincent Descombes summarizes:

> Language is in no sense a *medium*, a means of expression, a mediation between interior and exterior; for the code precedes the message ... The message is not the expression of an experience, rather it expresses the possibilities and limitations, in comparison with experience, of the code employed.[54]

The challenge to the philosophy of the subject is clear: no longer can the subject be viewed as the author of speech and the origin of all linguistic expression.

Structural linguistics privileges the objectivity of the linguistic system which can search for the properties, permutations and mutual characteristics of signifiers. This rather formal method is directly counter to the *anti-formalist* position of Lukács, who takes as his central motif the praxis of the human subject. A structuralist method also challenges the representationalist structure of philosophical language which contains subject and object in a relation of reciprocity and opposition. However, it must be emphasized that structuralism does not *abolish* the subject *tout court*. Structuralism had a radical agenda: to challenge the existential and phenomenological accounts of the subject of history, and the assumed identity between self-consciousness and philosophy. This certainly brings into question Lukács' humanist–historicist method but it does not imply that the subject is rendered an inert determinant of structure. In fact, there is a perpetual risk that structuralism can masquerade as a subject; in other words, by a process of inversion structuralism can effectively take over the subject's function, role and status by becoming the determining origin of all content and form. If its exponents can avoid such risks, then the structuralist project may contain a creative moment of analysis. As we shall see, both Foucault in *The Order of Things* and Derrida in *Of Grammatology* take up this challenge posed by the anti-subjectivist logic of signification.

For structuralism, all constituent elements must be considered in terms of their relation with other elements, without which their own properties and functions are meaningless. This totality is not expressive of an original essence; rather, it has a complex structuration and is determined by the specific elements which compose it. The movement of subject and object can evoke no identity between the elements of the structure, instead *subject and object are structured in relation to other elements which may determine their own (unstable) identity*. In this way, the subject is *displaced* from its function of determination and a system of objective relations are understood to underpin and construct subjectivity. In effect, the function of the subject is dispersed in a system of differential relations. Far from announcing its wholesale abolition, structuralism reconfigures the subject in such a way as to call into question its metaphysical properties. According to Althusser, it is these metaphysical properties which tie the subject to empiricist and idealist conceptions of knowledge, and to individualist and voluntarist forms of politics. In structuralism then, as anticipated in Spinoza and Nietzsche, we encounter a fundamentally anti-humanist gesture that repositions the subject and introduces a new mode of analysing social forms and constructing knowledge.

III. ALTHUSSER AND THE REPOSITIONING OF THE SUBJECT

It is impossible to *know* anything about men except on the absolute precondition that the philosophical (theoretical) myth of man is reduced to ashes.[55]

If both Althusser and Lukács may be described as Western Marxists it is surely an indication of the elasticity of the label which can be seen to fit Althusser in name alone. Althusser's Marxism shares no obvious similarities with that of Korsch, Lukács and Sartre, although Althusser draws quite significantly on Gramsci's distinction between coercion and consent in his theory of ideology. In his own words, Althusser's project is 'to draw a line of demarcation between Marxist theory and the forms of philosophical (and political) subjectivism which have compromised or threatened it.'[56] This certainly indicates that his position will occupy a radically different theoretical space to the one occupied by Lukács, who understood the praxis of the subject to be the source of political transformation and philosophical truth. In contrast to Lukács, Althusser constructs a scientific discourse which aims to *break* with all forms of historicism and all conceptions of the subject. This scientific structure of knowledge, which Althusser claims to recover, in embryonic form, within Marx's later writings and build into an abstract epistemological system himself, will be untainted by subjectivity and indeed by any method which can be found to have a residual component of subjectivism present in its concepts. Althusser's epistemology demands a scientific basis for Marxism which will not collapse into a dogmatic materialism, insensitive to the contingencies of an advanced capitalist socio-political formation, or a naive idealism which takes as its guide to understanding political appearances none other than the essence of the self-conscious subject.

This quest to develop a science for Marxism may appear redundant in the light of the totalizing critiques of science by contemporary theorists. In one of his final published interviews with the Mexican philosopher Fernando Navarro, Althusser qualified this turn to theory: 'in order to change our world we must first change our way of thinking.'[57] It was a new apparatus of thought that Althusser endeavoured to bring to Marxism by generating an epistemological break between the ideological form of some of Marx's texts and the scientific form latent in certain others. Althusser aims to read Marx *symptomatically*, that is, beneath the letter of Marx's texts. Marx, he claims, abandoned the anthropologism inherent in the Hegelian problematic, in order to embrace a series of non-subjective concepts.[58] This theory of knowledge, constructed without recourse to the subject, offers an important philosophical and political challenge to many of the problems encountered in Chapter 1 and continued in our study of Lukács above.

However, it is wise to maintain a degree of caution regarding this radical proposal to transform the very mode of thinking. The introduction to this book has pointed out that whilst the subject may be reinscribed within – or indeed deemed extraneous to – another theoretical register or perspective, this subject may remain tied to its previous conceptual formulations. This is the problem of philosophical inheritance to which all philosophers must maintain a certain assiduity and a degree of vigilance. Althusser appears to recognize the urgency of this problem when he writes of the need for 'every philosophy to make a detour *via* other philosophies in order to define itself and grasp itself in terms of its difference: its *division*.'[59] Similarly, he notes the imperative 'to work on the phantasms of philosophy (which underlie its categories).'[60] It was precisely the phantasm of the subject which Althusser strove to eliminate in *Reading Capital*. Subjectivity is associated with all that is ideological and this deems Hegel, and all those who draw upon his philosophical construction of the subject, redundant. Whilst Althusser is perhaps better known for his construction of the political subject of ideology, the discussion in this chapter will turn first to consider ideology's *other*, namely science. In mapping out a terrain of science opposed to ideology and the latter's tendency towards subjectivism, Althusser's flirtation with the impossible purity of science can be encountered and his own vigilance towards the risks of the subject, even in its absence, can be assessed.

Althusser against Hegel

We are all caught up in the decomposition of Hegel ...[61]

In Marxist circles, the problems which are understood to pervade philosophy and history, namely the status of consciousness, history and truth, are given clarity by the dialectical movement of inversion of idealism into materialism. Any inversion of conceptual system, in this case the privileging of a materialist conception of the idea over an idealist conception, will always carry the logic of the oppositions or the differences which define its own identity *within* its theoretical problematic. It is this complex relation between opposing positions which will be of interest when considering Derrida. In his earliest essay on Hegel 'On Content in the Thought of G.W.F. Hegel' (1947) Althusser acknowledges this conceptual failure when he draws attention to the *circularity* of the Hegelian system which obviates against a reading of idealism and materialism as self-contained opposites. Althusser claims that Marxist practice 'has not yet grasped its own structure, because it has not yet clearly conceived the place Hegelian truth occupies within its own reality.'[62]

Althusser's critique of Hegelianism is at the same time a critique of forms of humanist–historicist Marxism. An exploration of this critique also affords an insight into Althusser's own scientific account of knowledge and of the denial of any role for the subject in this process. Althusser wishes to untie the dialectic from its historical affiliations. For both Hegel and Lukács, the subject of the dialectic is also the historical subject who constructs a form of knowledge ultimately adequate to itself and to its own conception of the world. Althusser's critique of Hegel rests on two axes: first, a reading of the latter's conception of history and the mode of political analysis which emanates from it; and second, a reading of Hegel's philosophy of knowledge and the role of the subject in the construction of the object. It is important for Althusser to be able to separate the epistemological and the historical, given that his aim is to establish a realm of knowledge distinct from concrete history.

The recent publication of the collection of Althusser's early writings affords a more colourful picture of his negotiation of Hegel, drawing attention to a much more receptive though critical reading of the Hegelian project than a focus on his 1960s works alone would indicate. Althusser's aforementioned first essay on Hegel, together with the 1947 review of Kojève and the 1950 essay 'The Return to Hegel' all point to a very early engagement with Hegel and the French philosophical scene. In particular, the first essay illustrates a careful working through of some central Hegelian themes. Indeed it was also around this time that Althusser attended a lecture on Hegel given by Lukács. Hegel's system, for Althusser, cannot be simply panlogicist, theistic or anthropological because 'the universality attained without detour is a universality that brooks no appeal.'[63] This detour must pass through the concrete empirical, the historical *and* the subjective, but it must not forgo the logical, or the objective pole of analysis. This, according to Althusser, was Kojève's mistake and the resulting existential reading of Marx collapsed the role of substance into the dialectical reversals of history.[64] Marxism also comes under fire in this essay for its limited grasp of the structure of Hegelian truth to its discourse. It remains necessary to determine the relation of Marxist epistemological categories (science) to the socio-economic categories that command them, in other words to reconsider the dualism between truth and reality. The mode of couching this problem offers the seeds for Althusser's later reflections upon the science/ideology opposition. It will mark out what is, for Althusser, a philosophical limit in Hegel, and it further inaugurates the second, more critical readings of Hegel in *Reading Capital* and *For Marx*.

This later critique of Hegel makes three central points. (i) Hegel's system is seen to correspond to an *expressive totality* where the dialectical movements of the relations of the totality are inseparable from their own genesis as concepts. The totality is therefore circular; even if it is recognized that Hegel's concept of origin is split in its moment of essence by negativity, the auto-genesis of the system seems to restore the logic of origin to the totality. As Althusser writes, somewhat telegraphically: '(Origin = ((Subject = Object) = Truth) = End = Foundation)'.[65] In other words, the Hegelian system is inseparable from its goal which is *given* in the dialectical structure of its conditions of becoming. It is the *aufhebung* which structures the movement of the dialectic, ensuring it will always continue in the same mode. It implies, as Ricoeur similarly notes 'a substantial continuity; the first term returns as the third through its negation.'[66] (ii) This dialectical conception of totality moves according to a linear time sequence, what Althusser calls the 'homogeneous continuity of time'.[67] This mode of temporality anticipates the future in the simple immediacy of the historical present, in the 'contemporaneity of time'.[68] Thus, 'the structure of historical existence is such that all the elements of the whole always co-exist in one and the same time, one and the same present, and are therefore contemporaneous with one and another in one and the same present.'[69] This leads to the co-presence of each of the elements of the totality to their essence (in other words, the essence of subject and object are reflected in history), and establishes a specific conception of knowledge which Althusser labels empiricist. (iii) The concept of history that pertains to this expressive immediacy of the dialectical elements to one another is teleological or circular; the historical process moves according to the genesis of its concepts, particularly the subject. Knowledge is generated through the hidden movement of essences; in other words, knowledge, whether philosophical or scientific in character, is always gleaned from the historical process itself.[70] Furthermore, this Hegelian problematic also extends to the theoretical field of Western Marxism even as it is reinterpreted by them. Hegelian concepts which have not been rigorously reconsidered on a different theoretical terrain always haunt the concepts of Western Marxism. We have seen above that Lukács distils the essence of knowledge from the praxis of the historical subject. Althusser recognizes that Lukács' historicism links him unwittingly with many of the problems raised above. Thus, in Lukács, 'the proletariat, the human essence in revolt against its radical negation, became the revolutionary affirmation of the human essence: the proletariat was thus *philosophy in deed* and its political practice philosophy itself.'[71]

The theoretical lesson to be drawn here, according to Althusser, is that, however much Marxist conceptions of totality try to counter Hegelian idealism by appealing to history, the component parts of this totality are 'flattened out ... into a variation of the Hegelian totality.'[72] Furthermore, by collapsing the theoretical field of knowledge into the movement of real history, that is, by *historicizing knowledge*, Marxist forms of knowledge, like those associated with Hegelianism, are subjected to the ideological idiosyncrasies of the historical process. A form of Marxism which follows Hegel and is steeped in historicism cannot escape the realm of ideological knowledge. To put this in more rigorous terms, the ideological conception of knowledge that arises confuses the relation between *knowledge and being*, or the relation of the object to the concrete-real. Western Marxism is thus equated with an *empiricist ideology* – a form of thought which views 'the relation between real history and philosophy as a relation of expressive unity.'[73] Althusser's objective throughout his writings is to banish these ideological remnants of subjectivity, empiricism and idealism from his theory of scientific knowledge. It is to the construction of this new epistemology and its debt to Spinoza that we shall now turn.

In Spinoza's wake: constructing the object of knowledge

Althusser's anti-humanist credentials are well documented. Less well known is their source, which is often attributed to structuralism rather than Spinoza's anti-Cartesianism.[74] Althusser himself notes in his *Essays in Self-Criticism* that his Spinozism was often mistaken for a form of structuralism. *Reading Capital* is peppered with references to Spinoza and many of Althusser's posthumous publications indicate explicitly the Spinozist affiliations of his epistemology.[75] Like Althusser, Spinoza was critical of the authority imparted on the subject as the creator of knowledge (an authority which was, of course, guaranteed by religious faith). This led Spinoza towards a theory of knowledge that departed from a simple correspondence between the subject and the real, and from an uncritical account of the role of representation (of both ideas and images) in the formulation of knowledge. Thus, according to Althusser, Spinoza constructed a theory that reflected on 'the difference between the imaginary and the true.'[76] He recognized, in other words, that the empiricist construction of the object gave rise to an *imaginary* or ideological formulation of knowledge. Thus:

> Spinoza's 'theory' rejected every illusion about ideology, and especially about the number one ideology of that time, religion, by identifying it as imaginary. But at the same time it refused to treat ideology as a simple error, or as naked ignorance, because it based the system of this imaginary phenomenon on the relation of men to the world 'expressed' by the state of their bodies.[77]

This same quotation will be our focus later when ideology is considered in its political dimension. Here we will concentrate upon the difference between the imaginary and the true, and the distinctions alluded to here within Spinoza's conception of knowledge.

What shape does Althusser's epistemology take and what, precisely, does it owe to Spinoza? Our discussion of Althusser's critique of forms of Hegelian Marxism has already established the central target of his epistemology, namely empiricism. Furthermore, in *Reading Capital*, Althusser links empiricism with what he calls a 'philosophy of vision'.[78] This is described as 'the logic of a conception of knowledge in which all the work of knowledge is reduced in principle to the recognition of the mere relation of *vision*; in which the whole nature of its object is reduced to the mere condition of a *given*.'[79] The dominant metaphors of empiricism are those of transparency and reflection; these metaphors underwrite an 'epistemological contract'[80] between the activity of perception and empiricist method. Empiricism requires a conception of a knowing and perceiving subject (the two are mutually dependent as they will be for Derrida), who *identifies* the object and extracts the essence of the object as form of self-knowledge.[81] As Althusser observes, this process of extracting an essence must itself identify a dimension of the real which can be freed from the contaminated sensory perception of the subject. Empiricist method thus imparts a distinction *within* the real itself: 'it [the real] is structured as a dross of earth containing inside it a grain of pure gold, i.e., it is made of two real essences, the pure essence and the impure essence, the gold and the dross.'[82] All that is required for knowledge to be unearthed, according to empiricist method, is for the real essence of the object to be dislodged from the impure dimension of the object. The grain of knowledge unearthed is, however, *already present within the object*. The formation or structure of knowledge here requires no separation from, or dislocation with, the ideological impurities of the object because the object of knowledge is intrinsic to the real, empirical object. Empiricism invests in the kinds of dualisms that contravene its own efforts to isolate the kernel of objectivity. Quite clearly, it upholds a conception of a divided subject, split between mind and body, thought and affect. Similarly it relies upon dualisms between essence and appearance, the visible and the hidden. All of these dualisms, particularly the sovereign antinomy between truth and fiction, are *wholly internal to the structure of ideology*, according to Althusser. Empiricism then, is resolutely attached to the *givenness* of reality and its critical distance from the concrete-real, for Althusser, the ideological, is henceforth denied.

Althusser shares this critique of empiricism with Spinoza. For the latter, the subject must be destabilized of its position as the source or foundation of knowledge; it is not the creative agency of knowledge or a faculty of autonomous experience which, opposed to the object, creates the conditions of possibility for knowledge. Spinoza's anti-anthropomorphism precludes these forms of philosophical subjectivity. The reading of Spinoza in Chapter 1 emphasized that the subject is not self-caused; rather mind and body are different attributes, different modes of existence of substance (or structure). Body and mind are not understood in a dualistic fashion where the first, through an inward-turning (and, of course, a religious guarantee) can oppose itself to the passions of the body. For Spinoza and Althusser, the form of knowledge built upon such dualisms is one which gives full power to the imagination. Knowledge of the 'true' is not the result of a philosophy of reflection, whose mast is always empiricist, rather it is derived according to *conditions internal to the production of knowledge*. To recall, once again, Spinoza's conception of 'knowledge of the third kind' (discussed in Chapter 1, Section II), it is the intellect (itself an attribute of substance and not to be confused with the active intentional thought of the subject) which is able to think reflectively body and mind as *ideas* of substance and hence produce the conditions for an immanent knowledge.

Althusser's epistemology *almost* mirrors Spinoza's derivation of a knowledge of the third kind. Both positions dislocate the subject from its primary role, both postulate a form of reflective knowledge which is able to surpass (but not simply in a transcendental sense) the real world of objects, and both understand the idea of an object in *thought* to be distinguishable from a conception of the real object gleaned through bodily affects. Thus Althusser announces in *Reading Capital*,

> Spinoza warned us that the *object* of knowledge or essence was in itself absolutely distinct and different from the real object, for, to repeat his famous aphorism, the two objects must not be confused: the *idea* of the circle, which is the *object* of knowledge must not be confused with the circle, which is the *real object*.[83]

Althusser develops this important distinction in his own formulation of the real object, utilized by empiricism, and the object internal to thought which is produced by a form of knowledge that has no stake in the everyday world of objects. Furthermore, for Althusser the form of knowledge has three modes or levels which again appear to echo Spinoza's three gradations of knowledge. Generality I consists of the raw material or brute facts upon which scientific theory labours. These facts are never pure and uncontaminated but always carry conceptual residues from previous ideological interpretations. Science must manoeuvre a path between this dimension of the real, Generality I and Generality III, namely the theoretical field where science produces and practices a distinct mode of knowledge. Generality II is 'an extremely complex and contradictory unity';[84] sandwiched between these two regions, it will always contain their ideological residues and their scientific possibilities. Generality II is the *problématique of knowledge*; it is the set of related concepts which must be worked upon by science, and it will take markedly different forms depending upon the degree of development of knowledge at a specific point in its history. In order for an ideological practice to become a scientific one, *the mode of framing the questions asked of knowledge must be transformed.* According to Althusser, and Heidegger and Derrida too, all of modern Western philosophy has formulated the problem of knowledge retrospectively, that is, in response to answers or solutions already posed. Thus ideological knowledge performs the kind of political function examined by Lukács and considered in Section I above.[85]

Althusser's epistemology has some difficult paths to negotiate in its journey away from ideologies of historicism and humanism. It seems unclear – at least following the reading of Spinoza developed in *Reading Capital* and *For Marx* – whether the theoretical resources necessary to counter ideology have been developed adequately within this epistemology. Althusser is well aware of these problems: 'there is not one side of theory, a pure intellectual vision without body or materiality – and another of completely material practice which "gets its hands dirty".'[86] Or, as Pierre Macherey writes 'every science, in the relation it has with the ideology it emerged from, can only be thought of as a "science of ideology".'[87] Whilst Althusser's three levels of 'generality' seek to dissolve the dualism between science and ideology, in practice, a residual dualism reemerges. In Chapter 5 we will encounter this problem once again in Foucault's *Archaeology of Knowledge*, specifically in the latter's distinction between discourse and the non-discursive realm.

Althusser pursued various ways of countering this infectious problem. For Althusser's critics, the problem led him back to idealism, specifically to the containment of science and the divorce of theory from any extra-theoretical referent.[88] This problem remains in Althusser's epistemology as a consequence of his rather limited development of Spinoza's philosophy. Althusser's epistemology *almost* mirrors Spinoza's construction of knowledge, as was noted above, because there remains one central problem outstanding, *namely the formulation of the subject not just as a complex effect of knowledge* but also as a *point of interconnection of ideas and things*. Spinoza, it will be recalled, established an identity of connection between body and mind, a parallelism which is also, as Deleuze points out, an epistemological parallelism between the idea and its object.[89] This implies that knowledge is intricately connected to greater knowledge of the socially constituted body. If the intellect is equivalent to the 'thought' of science in Althusser's schemata, then there must be a way in which science may act upon (and be *acted upon*) and affect (and be *affected by*) the wider structural whole. If this dual activity of scientific knowledge can be established, an activity immanent with itself, and with/against ideology, it *may* save Althusser's epistemology from many of his critics who accuse him, somewhat superficially, of determinism. Indeed, the collection entitled *Sur La Philosophie* and other later writings indicate that Althusser moved a considerable distance towards a formulation of parallelism which returned to the thorny problem of the subject and gave his epistemology a more nuanced Spinozist form. Before turning to these enigmatic last thoughts, that *other* of science which, in an unrelenting venture tries to tame and incorporate science, fix and discipline the subject, must be considered for its deep political resonance.

'Like a planet revolving around the absent sun': ideology and the real

The theoretical terrain of Althusser's theory of ideology is much more familiar to his readers. However, the central essay of 1972, 'Ideology and Ideological State Apparatuses', rests upon the prior epistemological work carried out in Althusser's earlier works. Indeed, it is in the context of his discussions around the form and structure of ideology that the concept of the subject, being an ideological concept *par excellence*, is most fully developed. Althusser's rejection of the subject as the foundation, origin or essence of a theoretical concept precludes him from establishing an overly simplistic account of ideology as false-consciousness where the subject's experience becomes the source of knowledge necessary to transcend ideology. Likewise it should be clear from Althusser's critique of empiricism that a definition of ideology as an inversion, or mystification of the real, as presented by the metaphor of the *camera obscura* in Marx and Engels' *The German Ideology*, is rejected. Althusser is not concerned to investigate what particular subjects may think, or even *how*, by what means, they carry out the act of thinking, rather he is concerned with the *ideological mechanism* according to which thought, perception and subjectivity are produced.

For this position, ideology is not to be associated with the realm of ideas; it is material and relational precisely because of its *structural existence*. Ideology is an element of the social totality and functions in a complex relation to the other 'levels' of the structure (for example, the legal, political, economic, cultural and philosophical and scientific levels). These levels are not hierarchical; there is no direct causality between infra- and super-structure. They are viewed according to a model of *structural causality* which allows each structural mode a degree of autonomy from the rest, although it may in practice, under certain political and social conditions, become a dominant mode of being. To delineate this more sharply from the notion of expressive totality discussed above, and from the logic of contradiction, which attributes effects according to a single cause, Althusser borrows from Freud the concept of overdetermination. In Freud's psychoanalytic discourse, this concept refers to the multiplicity of dream-thoughts contained, by the censorship of psychic agency, within a single dream-image.[90] This concept performs a considerable theoretical labour within Generality II, for Althusser. The concept of overdetermination recognizes that where a specific level may appear to determine the general form of the structure, it is 'also determined in one and the same movement, ... by the various *levels* and *instances* of the social formation it animates.'[91] Overdetermination ensures the absence or deferral of a pure origin, unity, or uniform causality. For Jacques Derrida, it is a concept that may return to haunt or threaten the logic of the structural whole.[92] Arguably, this is its function in Althusser's structuralism which recognizes the contingent nature and the socio-historical specificity of any structure. The concept of overdetermination thus allows for the disruption of notions of goal, end, origin and centre by emphasizing the complex, uneven structuration of the social whole.[93]

Seen within this framework, the concept of ideology is not simply superstructural, or merely an epiphenomenon of an economic base. Ideology does not just mask reality; there is no brute social reality because it too is always overdetermined by the material forms of ideology. Just as Althusser argued that empiricism tarnishes the real object through its method, so ideology is, to paraphrase Lacan's reflection on the real, the net cast over reality. Ideology is also a modification of structure. It has, like other elements of the structural whole, its own modality, its own *modus operandi* or function, which follows the logic of the economy only in the always deferred moment of the last instance.[94] The function of ideology is to reproduce the relations of production, to ensure that individuals are constituted as subjects ready to take up their allocated position within the dominant discourse. To this end, ideology operates principally through ideological state apparatuses (ISAs), which include institutions like the church, school, family, political parties, etc. The repressive state apparatus (RSA) secured by force when necessary the conditions for the reproduction of the relations of production, and hence the conditions for the action of ISAs.[95] During his time in captivity (and as a Catholic), Althusser deliberated somewhat balefully on Pascal's advice to would-be atheists trying to reckon with their lapse in faith: 'Kneel and pray'. Little did he know that the command would come to have central importance in the apparatus of ideology. Consequently, in his example of religion, Althusser notes the modalities of kneeling, the discourse of prayer, the sign of the cross, the gaze of the Absolute, all of which insert the subject into the materiality of religious ideology.[96] It is significant that these practices work not only to tame and discipline consciousness but they also, as Spinoza anticipated too, aim to normalize and subject the body according to certain models of behaviour. Althusser may have underplayed this latter function of ideology but it is clear, nonetheless, that an analysis of the concrete *practices* of ideology renders incomplete all accounts which digress to an analysis of the distortion and mystification of consciousness with little regard for the practice of constructing particular modes of consciousness.

Unsurprisingly, given Althusser's epistemological argument, 'there is no ideology except by the subject and for subjects', and there can be no subject that is not ideological. '[T]he category of the subject', Althusser writes, 'is only constitutive of all ideology in so far as all ideology has the function ... of constituting individuals as subjects',[97] or as in the more often noted formulation, 'ideology represents the *imaginary* relationship of individuals to their *real* conditions of existence.'[98] In contrast to Lukács, for whom the concept of reification was understood as an objectifying distortion of social totality, Althusser understands the subject's perception of their lived-relations to be *anchored* resolutely to an imaginary relation. The concept of the imaginary is invested with allusions to Spinoza, and the psychoanalyst and philosopher, Jacques Lacan. From Spinoza, Althusser takes the view of the imagination as a source of deception and illusion; from Lacan, the view that the imaginary is a necessary form of misrecognition; it deceives subjects as to their relation to the social world, which Lacan calls the symbolic, the place of the law and the only possible place for speaking and acting subjects. According to Lacan, however, the imaginary only partially constitutes the subject with a fantasy of wholeness and containment. It leaves a dimension of experience, the *real*, which is forever foreclosed and cannot be represented in the symbolic social order except through its effects. We will take the opportunity to investigate the complementarity of Lacanian concepts to Althusser's construction of ideology in Chapter 3. Here we only draw attention to Althusser's reliance on Lacanian themes for his theory of the ideological construction of subjectivity.

How does Althusser account for the constitution of the subject by ideology? Contra Lacan, Althusser's explanation for this process of constitution is the much more inclusive notion of *interpellation*. This is the *structure of recognition* by which the 'concrete individual' finds its place and in doing so becomes a subject. The theory of interpellation performs a vital function of identification for Althusser, enabling subjects to recognize themselves in the dominant ideology. That such a structure of recognition remains forever on the level of misrecognition is a necessary and essential counterpart to the receipt of consciousness, belief, action and speech by the subject. In this way, *méconnaissance*, or the imaginary structure of ideology, is constitutive of the subject seemingly without remainder or residue.

The theoretical problems which emerge from this event of constitution of the ideological subject are significant and deserve attention. Nevertheless, some reference must first be made to the development of psychoanalytic themes in Althusser's writings collected in the recent work *Essays on Psychoanalysis*.[99] In the period leading up to the essay on ideology, Althusser produced two important essays, 'Freud and Lacan' (1964) and 'Trois notes sur la théorie des discours' (1966), as well as another significant essay 'Marx and Freud' in 1976. In these essays, Althusser pursued, in different ways and to varying degrees, the relationship between interpellation and the unconscious. The central objective of the first essay was to situate what Althusser viewed as Lacan's scientific reading of Freud alongside his own reading of Marx and the general theory of historical materialism. Like Marxism, psychoanalysis must conduct a battle with anthropological conceptions of the subject. It must negotiate philosophical forms of knowledge which tempt psychoanalysis towards a humanist psychology. This interest in the unconscious as a dynamic structural agency is consistent with Althusser's 1976 essay 'Marx and Freud' which also stresses the need for a psychoanalytic supplement to Marxism. Thus, for Freud, the subject 'is not a *centred unity* but a complex of agencies constituted by the play of unconscious repressions. ... the ego, formerly the sole seat of consciousness, itself becomes in large part unconscious, fully participant in the conflict of unconscious repression in which the agencies are constituted.'[100] Correspondence between Althusser and Lacan over the years 1963–1966 further indicates that Althusser recognized an affinity between Lacan's own project, and the latter's intellectual marginalization, and his own.[101]

Of greater significance however, is the importance Althusser attached to the relationship between the unconscious and ideological discourse, specifically the unconscious as 'the absolute place [in each human being] where his particular discourse seeks its own place, seeks, misses, and in missing, finds its own place, *in the imposition, complicity and negation of its own imaginary fascinations.*'[102] 'Three Notes on the Theory of Discourse' extends this to a broader concern with the relation between the psychoanalytic mode of signification (that which Althusser considers in the notes as a 'general theory of discourse'), the unconscious and ideological subjectivity. This series of notes anticipates the proceeding account of interpellation found in the influential essay on ideology, although there is very little evidence of any sustained development of this linguistic dimension of interpellation in the work that followed these notes. Certainly by the late 1970s Althusser's enthusiasm in the Lacanian project had waned, culminating in a critical speech to the conference which voted to disband Lacan's school.[103]

For Althusser, the function of ideology is inseparable from the constitution of the subject. If the subject comes retrospectively to view itself as the origin of its consciousness, beliefs and actions (and Althusser cannot, it seems, depart from the *validity* of this correspondence because it is ideology's *function* to impart this logic of correspondence), then the status of this origin must be rethought. Paradoxically, Althusser still has recourse to a residual language of subjectivity despite the fact that he wishes to decentre the subject and reduce it to an effect of ideology. We will encounter this paradox of the subject repeated in each of the thinkers considered in this work. Caught by the labyrinthine question of the subject, Althusser's philosophical aim to displace the problematic of the subject is compromised perpetually by his desire to account for the constitution of the subject. According to some commentators, these residues of the subject dilute the radicalism of Althusser's claims.[104]

Let us turn to the thorny problem of the constitution of the subject of ideology. The most repeated criticism levelled at this conception of ideology is that the constitution of the subject as subjected being is absolute. A single spectacle, a single event of constitution, and subjects 'seem to work all by themselves'. Whilst it is apparent that Althusser wishes to protect his analysis from the risks of subjectivism, this anti-humanist theoretical manoeuvre stops short of an analysis of exactly how material practices constitute particular forms of subjectivity (or even Spinozist bodies), that is, the degree to which ISAs *succeed* in their task of normalizing and disciplining individuals.[105] Here we can antici-pate Foucault's consideration of the physical processes of subjection in *Discipline and Punish* which was influenced surely by Althusser's 'Ideology and Ideological State Apparatuses'.[106]

In his 1972 essay on ideology, Althusser seems to presume rather than interrogate the sense in which the process of interpellation must be continuous if it is to produce and maintain self-disciplining subjects. There is no focus upon the *perpetual* process of interpellation; no account of the link between ISAs and the constitution of the sub-ject; no sustained development of his earlier references to the role of linguistic articulation in the theory of interpellation which can bring about the subject (i.e. 'It is I, the subject of recognition'), and no consideration of the possible relation between ideology and the unconscious.[107] As Althusser admits in an undated letter to a friend, 'I stopped short (quite clearly) before the question that interests you about the "relations" between ideology (or concrete ideological formations) and the unconscious ... there is a limit that has not been crossed.'[108] If it is the case that Althusser's discussion of signification in 'Freud and Lacan' and 'Three Notes on the Theory of Discourse' at least *begin* the consideration of these problems, particularly in noting that all lived-relations are built upon a specific, regional relation (both abstract and material) to the order of language, and that ideological discourse/signifiers also construct the unconscious 'subject', such considerations are not extended in any thorough sense to the analysis of ideology.[109] Hence, the nascent account of the subject as a complex production which is never fully constituted, and always unstable and disruptive of theories which retrospectively view it as such is not adequately developed by Althusser. This is precisely where *Discipline and Punish* may exceed Althusser's formulations. Whereas Althusser pushed the problem of the internalization of ideology to one side, preferring to consider the mechanism of interpellation as an imaginary recognition or a *méconnaisance*, Foucault continues the focus on the physical processes of subjection, the way in which the subject inscribes within itself the principle of subjection, and the body as a transmogrifying site of disciplinary power.

A similar kind of absence is also notable in Althusser's discussion of the *real* which is distanced conceptually from Lacan's own rendering of the term. Despite the assiduous construction of the real in his epistemology, there is no parallel development in relation to ideology. Thus the *real* conditions of existence described in the essay on ideology seem to have a functional relation to the form of capitalism rather than being understood as overdetermined by ideological institutions and practices. Must it be concluded, therefore, that the relations between language and representation, signification and subjectivity remain aporetic in form and will have to await the analyses of Foucault, Lacan and Derrida in the following chapters of this book?

It could be argued that many of these difficulties present themselves in Althusser's theory of the subject because the latter is seemingly isolated from science and tied too closely to ideology. Althusser seems reluctant to consider any construction of subjectivity in relation to knowledge precisely because the subject is equated with all that is ideological. However, the philosophical rejection of subjectivity does not have to signal the wholesale abandonment of the relation of social being to the object of knowledge. All of the philosophical positions considered in this work take part in the dislocation and repositioning of the subject. If a dominant form of subjectivity has been questioned, this does not entail that the *problematic* surrounding the question of the subjectivity must be abandoned although its conceptual residues must be negotiated carefully. For example, Spinoza continued to operate with a quite novel conception of body and mind no longer as distinct facets of an originating subject, but as modes of substance. According to Althusser, the problematic of the subject and the concept of ideology are explicable fully only in the context of the rupture which divides them from scientific knowledge.[110] Hence the resources available to inter-rogate the subject are delimited from the start. Derrida and Ricoeur both speculate as to whether this opposition between science and ideology is established in order to reduce the role of philosophy and the possible constructions of the concepts of subject and object.[111] In particular, Derrida questions whether ideology and science may be 'cut off ... from their history, from semantics sedimented within it, etc., as if one could obtain a non-ideological, uncontaminated, scientific concept of ideology.'[112]

Of course, we cannot assume that Althusser was unaware of ideol-ogy's tendency to wish for its own absorption by its opposite num-ber, truth. Like Derrida, he was equally aware that ideology could strengthen its hold by swallowing up its adversary, or that the two could become locked into a dualism which was *wholly internal to ideology*. This was Althusser's political worry as well as one that beset his epistemology and yet he endeavoured to stay within the limits of both fields rather than entering the void outside of them.[113] Never-theless, this attentiveness to the fluidity of boundaries between ideology and science cannot mask the fact that the subject has been theorised solely on the terrain of ideology. What of the relation between *science* and subjectivity, or some creative formulation of the latter? Might the logic of interpellation be revised to produce anything other than a uniform conception of an individual subject? Can this logic of inter-pellation be extended to the realm of science, or must ideology and science remain doomed to oscillate uneasily between the possibility of scientific knowledge and its ideological denial? Perhaps we can seek answers to these questions in Althusser's return to Spinoza and his later reflections upon materialism.

Crossing the limit?

To search for answers in Althusser's later works is an immensely rewarding if disconcerting exercise. It is rewarding because we find that Althusser continues to negotiate the problem of the subject and the possible form that knowledge may take, this time through a refined understanding of materialism. It is disconcerting, however, because some of the central theoretical positions associated with Althusser are transformed. As Antonio Negri points out, 'in any philosophical *Kehre*, elements of continuity and innovation intertwine, but the latter ones acquire hegemony.'[114] It is apparent that Althusser, in this later work, was moving towards a more dynamic conception of the subject that could return a political dimension to his epistemology. At the same time, this epistemology was to be reframed and renewed to deem it adequate to a Marxism of the late twentieth century. If these significant movements were given shape by Althusser's reflections on the form of materialism, what was the basis of this materialism and how was it derived?

Some of Althusser's clearest formulations of what he calls 'aleatory materialism' may be found in his 1984 interview with Fernando Navarro.[115] Here Althusser traces a subterranean materialist tradition beginning with Democritus and continuing with the Epicurean vision of a disorderly fall of atoms through a vacuum causing their free encounter in order to give birth to a world. This materialist path continues by way of Hobbes and Spinoza, it finds its politics in Machiavelli, Rousseau and Marx, and in the twentieth century it finds particular expression in the philosophies of Heidegger and Derrida.[116] Aleatory materialism establishes the radical primacy of materiality over everything else. It is not to be conceived mechanically as brute matter because, as Althusser notes, in Derrida's philosophy 'the primacy of the trace (of writing) can be found even in the phoneme emitted by the voice that speaks.'[117] Materialism can have many different modes of existence but what is distinctive about these *vis-à-vis* a mechanical materialism is that the former has no ontological fixity, no sense of origin, essence or uniform cause. This does not imply that it collapses into formlessness or random chaos. Althusser's gives weight to the spectre of the encounter present in an aleatory experience. If this materialist encounter is tied to an ontological becoming, it is also a nominalist one that is contexualized by the singular historical event and by contingency. It is, to put it in Negri's words, 'aleatory *après coup*.'[118] Althusser draws upon a metaphoric example of the idealist and materialist adventurers to illustrate the distinctiveness of his materialism. Whereas the idealist philosopher knows in advance and plans his train journey always arriving at his destination, the materialist philosopher is an experimental traveller who

> takes the train in motion but without knowing where the train is coming from or where it is going. He climbs onto a train of chance, of encounter, and discovers in it the *factual* installations of the coach and of whatever companions he is *factually* surrounded with, of whatever the conversations and ideas of those companions and of whatever language marked by their social milieu they speak.[119]

Aleatory materialism will always lack a philosophical model, or at least its model will be ceaselessly reinvented to accommodate the contingent, the unexpected and the historically new. What Althusser seeks to evoke through this philosophy of materialism is a thinking otherwise: 'the thought of the new in the absence of all conditions'.[120]

To these reflections on materialism we must add Althusser's later thoughts on Spinoza which indicate the new regard the former has developed for the relation of the body and its powers to the problem of knowledge.

> That one can liberate and recompose one's own body, formerly fragmented and dead in the servitude of an imaginary and, therefore, slavelike subjectivity, and take from this the means to think liberation freely and strongly, therefore, to think properly with one's own body, in one's own body, by one's own body, better: that *to live within the thought of the conatus of one's own body was quite simply to think within the freedom and the power of thought.*[121]

In this quotation we find Althusser thinking about the *power of thought* not as an abstract mechanism of knowledge or as the active intentional thought of a subject. For Spinoza, in order to create a knowledge of the true rather than the ideological, thought must pass through the body and relations between bodies. This entailed a parallelism between the idea-in-thought and the body as the object of an idea; an interconnection between the nature of bodies and the order of ideas. Can Althusser trace, in Spinoza's parallelism, the form of a political practice which can think the body anew and hence beyond ideological conditions? Furthermore, will this reintroduce a more open, underdetermined structure of subjectivity (after its ideological critique) into epistemology? Are the risks of a collapse into ideology too great, or can this project throw the problem of the subject into fresh relief?

These questions must be a topic of speculation given their open-ended nature. Althusser's does not present us with a completed system of thought. These later essays represent the beginning of a new philosophical perspective as much as they seek to correct his past theoretical positions. However, Althusser had broached already the question of the difficult relation between science and ideology in *Reading Capital*. Indeed, the formulation of the 'knowledge effect' purported to account for the mechanism by which scientific objects might pass through their ideological relation to the object upon the plane of experience. The knowledge effect was the mechanism by which the real object was appropriated by scientific knowledge; it is the means by which the ideological object was *converted* into a scientific object-in-thought. It functioned, therefore, in a similar way to the process of interpellation described above, although, unlike Spinoza's account of parallelism, it continued to *bypass* the subject.[122]

Althusser did not compare the knowledge effect to the mechanism of interpellation, although he did distinguish it from the Hegelian category of mediation utilized by Lukács to arrive at the objective possibility of consciousness in relation to knowledge:

> The concepts of origin, 'original ground', genesis and mediation should be regarded as suspect *a priori*: not only because they always more or less induce the ideology which has produced them, but because, produced solely for the use of this ideology, they are its nomads, always more or less carrying it with them.[123]

The knowledge effect is not a concept, and it has no ground; there is no *original* knowledge effect to give rise to *current* knowledge effects. Rather, the form of this mechanism is given by the criteria internal to scientific practice, by what Althusser calls ambiguously the 'systematicity of the system'.[124] In *Reading Capital*, it appears that the knowledge effect is enveloped in a tautology. However, the more explicit awareness Althusser indicates, in his later work, for the interconnectedness of the attributes of substance (for example, thought and body) allows for a deeper analysis of the inter-relation between ideology and knowledge. For Antonio Negri, this new focus of Althusser's later writings illustrate his 'search for an open subjectivity that would construct theory and struggle together'.[125] Perhaps it is only in the later Althusser that we find the means to understand and gain knowledge of ideology in terms of its efforts to ceaselessly reconstitute the subject.

What conception of the subject could be adequate to such a task? In the late twentieth century, ideology and power have achieved such dominance over, and unification of, social life. It is the virtue of Althusser's work to have theorized this system of dominance which was to have such analytic importance in cultural, gender and film studies, as well as social and political theory more generally. The material practices of ideology, varied and singular as their modalities may be, seem to have permeated the social body, rendering it passive and inert. If after Spinoza, however, thought must begin with the body and pass through the body, then Althusser recognizes this significance. The body contains a power as *potentia* (but also as *élan*: opening to the world, free gift) which may exceed ideology's function to dominate and control.[126] Any reading of Althusser's theory of ideology as being premised upon a formal account of structure must be supplemented by his account of aleatory materialism. This chapter has sought to point out the ways in which this rendering of structure is unsatisfactory given Althusser's emphasis upon contingency and overdetermination. This position is given an ontological strength by aleatory materialism because the latter emphasizes *the encounter of ideology with thought*. Of course, ideology will always attempt to cover over this *élan* of subjectivity, and contain the possibility of new forms of subjectivity and social being. The subject is not constituted once and for all by ideology because the limits placed on our dominant mode of being are contingent and historically specific; they can take different future forms and posit new relations between thought and knowledge. There is a clear trajectory between these formulations and Foucault's reflections on power and resistance developed in Chapter 5.

Althusser's *recomposition of the subject* owes everything to Spinoza and very little to dominant forms of French structuralism. However useful the logic of structuralist antihumanism may be in isolating Althusser's position from those of Lukács and other Western Marxists who continued to utilize the principle of subjectivity, it can also lead to inaccurate readings of Althusser as abolishing the subject and the problems which it raises in philosophy and social theory. The journey travelled by the concept of the subject in Lukács and Althusser is a fascinating one, marked by the presence not only of Marx, but also of Hegel and Spinoza. Neither Lukács or Althusser presented solutions to the question of the subject; indeed both thinkers often remained ensnared by the antinomies of modern thought (particularly Lukács) even as they tried to escape them. This chapter has encountered the multiple ways by which the work of Lukács and Althusser is ordered by the problems thrown up by the concept of the subject. Certainly, both try to modify the subject and to release all critique from the latter's dominion. However, whilst Lukács tends to privilege the subject as the self-conscious agent of history, Althusser remains sceptical of such a move. Like Spinoza before him, Althusser recognizes beneath the dominant philosophical motifs of subjectivity, an endless series of effects and *potentia* which cannot be mastered by ideology or knowledge.

3

PSYCHOANALYSIS, SUBJECTIVITY AND THE *VITA LINGUA*

The psychoanalytic conception of the subject developed in the writings of Jacques Lacan has come to occupy a central position in discussions which question the form, structure and indeed the possibility of the subject. Psychoanalysis, in its various schools, purports to examine the structure of consciousness and the means by which the experience of self-hood may be expressed and represented in the speech, action, gesture, emotion and physical–corporeal state of the subject. In all its various forms, particularly Freudian and Lacanian, psychoanalysis identifies a dimension of subjectivity which is *always more* than an underside to the autonomous, rational subject, a dimension that frustrates the subject's efforts to impart meaning upon the social world. The object of knowledge will always be based upon incomplete reflections or construc-tions of the subject's positions in relation to those objects. However, if psychoanalysis posits an unconscious behind, beneath or before the subject, does this not introduce a new dualism into subjectivity, one that merely rearranges other oppositions, for example, the antinomy between mind and body, or inside and outside? Might not these oppositions still presuppose that which they seek to unravel, namely the subject? We have already encountered such problems in relation to Lukács and Althusser in the previous chapter. Clearly we must be wary not just of the 'lie of consciousness' but also of the lie of the *unconscious*.[1]

Lacan's theory of the subject attempts to avoid such dualisms. The subject is decentred by Lacanian psychoanalysis and repositioned across three spatio-temporal registers, which he calls the symbolic, the imaginary and the real. Lacan also recognizes the power of language to produce subjectivity, and what, for him, becomes known as the subject is always overdetermined by a linguistic structure which contests the former's enunciative function. Both of these theoretical moves should immediately cause us to question a dualist account of the subject. In his early formulations, Lacan does construct a model of the *spaltung* of the subject, understood as the wound or gap in being. This appears to *split* the subject in two pieces and inaugurates a structure of alienation which marks the subject in a fundamental, ontological sense. However, it is important that we paint the whole picture of Lacan's account of the subject and bring the philosophical background (his many influences) into the psychoanalytic scene. This account of the subject is primarily psychoanalytic but it is informed deeply by philosophical conceptions of consciousness and subjectivity. Lacan's writings cover a vast period, from the mid-1930s to the early 1980s. His thought passed by way of phenomenology and structuralism, but it also drew upon surrealism, anthropology, theories of science, and of course structural linguistics. It is this diversity and creativity in method which yield the novel conception of the subject associated with Lacan's position.[2] However, these diverse influences often sit together uncomfortably in his work and they are sometimes responsible for inconsistencies in his positions. For some critics, notably Jean-Luc Nancy and Phillipe Lacoue-Labarthe, Lacan does lapse back into a philosophy of the subject; this may indicate that he fails to overcome the problems, and dualisms, inherent in all discourses of subjectivity. However, it should also draw our attention to the paradox of the subject that we have already come up against in earlier chapters.

Lacanian psychoanalysis situates itself right at the heart of the paradox of subjectivity. The connection between subjectivity and psychoanalysis is an inescapable one because the conditions of possibility of psychoanalysis are linked, by necessity, to the experience of the individual subject. In fact, it is almost impossible to imagine a discourse of psychoanalysis, as a mode of knowledge of the subject, existing prior to the subject as self-consciousness inaugurated with modernity. Whilst psychoanalysis may not *be* a philosophy in any straightforward sense, its concepts are formed within the same metaphysical horizon. Thus, Lacanian psychoanalysis occupies a paradoxical position in relation to subjectivity: it both *requires* the subject as the focus of its analysis (indeed psychoanalysis seeks to unravel the question of consciousness), and yet it seeks to *depart* from the subject, for example, by seeking to subordinate the latter to a conception of structure. The presence of this paradox does not reduce the significance of psychoanalytic discourse for the elaboration of the question of the subject. Instead it announces

the centrality of psychoanalysis to questions regarding the structure of
the subject and the latter's epistemological and political significance.
The aim of this chapter is to investigate the paradox of the subject and
its effects within the discourse of psychoanalysis.

In his correspondence with Lacan, Louis Althusser alludes to a com-
monality in their respective projects. In their readings of Freud and
Marx, each made a detour via other philosophies, each sought to develop
a scientific basis for Marxism and psychoanalysis, and each conducted
a symptomatic reading of the texts in order to discover their latent
scientism. However, things are more complicated in the case of Lacan
because his re-reading often attributed to Freud innovations which really
belonged to himself or originated with those from whom he borrowed or
smuggled.[3] If Althusser was often reticent about the influence of Spinoza
upon his formulations, Lacan is deliberately opaque about those who
influenced his perspective on the subject.

Lacan can be described as a philosopher as well as a psychoanalyst.
He engaged with philosophers throughout his work especially those
which devoted attention to the *subversion* of thought so that the unconscious could be approached. He remained convinced that a psychoanalytic knowledge of the unconscious could show philosophy its own
blind alleys.[4] However, the re-ordering of Freudian concepts according
to very diverse philosophical positions (Hegelian, Kojèvean, Heideggerian, Saussurean, amongst others) is often carried forth by a theoretical sleight of hand hence ensuring that the psychoanalytic basis
of Lacan's Freud continues to be a topic of fervent debate. Nevertheless, Lacan's reconstruction of Freudian psychoanalytic discourse
challenged the dominant analytic paradigm by arguing that psychoanalytic concepts assume their full significance only when orientated
in the domain of language, that is, only when ordered in relation to
the function and structure of the subject's speech.

Lacan's critique of the psychoanalytic community was directed
towards the so-called revisionists who utilized the Freudian concept of
the ego as a largely autonomous structure which could be strengthened
against the effects of the unconscious id. 'The progress of an analysis',
Lacan writes, 'does not consist in the enlargening of the field of the *ego*, it
is not the reconquest by the *ego* of its margin of the unknown'.[5] The ego
is viewed as acting as a mediator between the claims of the external
world and the subject's internal world; it is seen to have *privileged* access
to external reality and can be built up as a defensive structure against
the subject's internal fragmentation. It is this kind of development that

Lacan refers to when he describes the crisis which has arisen in Freudian technique. The subject, Lacan argues, cannot be *centred* by the ego,
because of what he identifies as a gap in the being of the subject, a gap
for which the analytic community has shown nothing but disdain.
In his essay 'The Ego and the Id', Freud noted that the unconscious
does not coincide with what is repressed by the ego; it is something
more.[6] The unconscious is not *contained* by the ego; it has its own
dynamic and desires which punctuate the ego's actions. Part of the ego,
Freud speculates, may itself be unconscious. Using the analogy of the
horse, Freud writes: 'Often a rider, if he is not to be parted from his
horse, is obliged to guide it where it wants to go; so in the same way the
ego is in the habit of transforming the id's will into action *as if it were
its own.*'[7] The mastery and autonomy that the ego assumes can only be,
Lacan argues (along with Freud here), an *imaginary* autonomy; the ego
is not in control but is 'disorientated in its practice'.[8] Furthermore, by
misperceiving the structure of the subject and the binding of the ego to
the unconscious, the dominant analytic technique has failed to direct
attention to the *linguistic* composition of the unconscious which Freud
presented in his analysis of dream-work.

For Lacan, language, subjectivity and knowledge are intrinsically
related. This may also be noted as a guiding thread of structuralism and
its ill-named child, *post*-structuralism; neither relinquish their focus
upon the linguistic composition and structuration of the objects of
knowledge. This is particularly the case for Derrida's deconstruction
of the subject discussed in Chapter 4. For Lacan, the Freudian discovery
'puts truth into question'.[9] If the construction and perception of objects
by the subject are also residues of memory and unconscious traces, the
representation of objects may be affected by *something other* than
the knowing subject, who, as ego, maintains only an outer-autonomy
by default. In 'Psychology of Dream-Processes', Freud points out that
'all thinking is no more than a circuitous path from the memory of
a satisfaction (a memory which has been adopted as a purposive idea)
to an identical cathexis of the same memory which it is hoped to attain
once more through an intermediate stage of motor experiences.'[10] The
neurological language of this early text should not detract from its central point: the thinking subject, so easily equated with human reason,
cannot constitute truth, but is part of a dynamic process which always
escapes consciousness. In other words, the subject is not the author of
discourse; discourse is constituted by a process that exceeds the subject.
For Freud, it is the motion of the pleasure principle which sets the

subject upon a search for catharsis with the object. What is important to note here is that Freud's account of the movement of the subject's thought embraces a *non-referential* view of knowledge which is likewise adopted by Lacan, but predictably according to a different theoretical register.

This chapter will develop two main themes, the first epistemological, or more broadly, philosophical, and the second political. Together, these themes will flesh out the major concerns of Lacan's theory of the subject. We will keep in mind the paradox presented above. Of all the thinkers considered in this book, Lacan is probably most vulnerable to critique because he draws so heavily from such a myriad of philosophical positions. Inconsistencies abound in his writings as first a quasi-Hegelian reading of the subject is developed, followed by a more widely recognized staging of the structuring role of language which pushes subjectivity into the wings. It has been argued convincingly by Jean-Luc Nancy and Phillipe Lacoue-Labarthe that Lacan risks reintroducing precisely what he seeks to question: the subject of representation. Does the unconscious depend upon a structure of representation for its articulation? Might we conclude that Lacan's theory is an uncritical reception of the subject? Is the subject reduced to a linguistic structure, or does Lacan theorize a *different* mode of existence which exceeds this structural logic? Before these questions can be broached properly, the different presentations of Lacan's theory of the subject must be explored and evaluated.

I. LACAN'S THEORY OF THE SUBJECT[11]

In his early writings, Lacan makes an important distinction between the subject as ego or 'I', that which may achieve an elusive sense of wholeness, and the subject as primordial being, which lies in a place beyond the ego-subject and may be approached through analysis. The structure which has come to represent this dynamic process of creating the 'I' or human individual is the mirror stage, a phase in the constitution of the individual located between the ages of six and eighteen months. For Lacan, it is this structure, rather than the Oedipus complex described by Freud (which occurs later in the development of the subject's life), that necessitates the birth of the self and its primary identifications. The experience of the formation of the 'I' is opposed 'to any philosophy directly issuing from the *Cogito*.'[12] There is no thinking subject prior to the recognition of the 'I'; this ego *requires* an identification with an image before it can *function* as subject, and before it can become a distinctly social animal. The event of the mirror stage, through which the subject perceives an image which is other than the largely mute, discordant being that it is, offers the subject its *first apprehension of bodily unity*. It allows the fragmented being to become an 'I' and to be harnessed to an ontological structure according to which the ego or Ideal-I may think, perceive and recognize itself as a permanent, coherent structure. In short, the mirror establishes that which Laplanche and Pontalis call 'the first roughcast of the ego';[13] it allows the still powerless and largely uncoordinated human being to anticipate its future wholeness by identifying with another, in this case, the reflection of its own image.

It is important that Lacan's structure of the emergent ego is not reduced to a genetic, biological or developmental moment; much more will be shown to be at stake here. The unification perceived by the subject has an imaginary form. The mirror-stage situates the instance of the ego in a line of *fiction*, of alienation; a function of *méconnaissance* is thus seen to characterize the ego in all its structures.[14] In this stage of narcissistic identification, where the subject is its own double more than itself, and where the image of plenitude forever alienates the subject from itself, both the *form* and the *energy* which henceforth govern the subject, are secured. These two functions of the imaginary ego will be elaborated below in the wider context of Lacan's discussions of the subject. What must be noted here is how the imaginary ego becomes the support for a division or split, *Spaltung*, of the subject, who is forever divided between a coherent self and a mode of being which is always *other* to the subject. The imaginary ego attempts to solder the discordance created within the subject who remains ignorant of its alienation. Thus begins the chronic cycle of misrecognition of self and the causal chains that determine the structure of human existence.

A developmental account of this event, whether biological or genetic, cannot appreciate the 'epistemological void'[15] which characterizes the reality of the mirror stage. Neither can it understand why the subject remains captivated by the mirror's alienating function as both trap and decoy.[16] Furthermore, such an account cannot consider the experience of this event, with Lacan, in terms of 'a temporal dialectic that decisively projects the formation of the individual into history'.[17] This mode of temporality cannot be reduced to the linear development of the individual subject or the historical process because the subject brings an existential experience of time which will give rise to different temporal horizons that remain distinct from a linear view of historical development. For Lukács, such discordance is the result of the reification of social life and philosophical form which underlies the subject's historical experience. How does the Lacanian subject experience this discordance?

One cannot easily speak of experience in psychoanalytic discourse. The activity of experience clearly presupposes an experiencing subject able to register effects and actions and rationally articulate and account for those experiences. Psychoanalytic discourses view the experience of the subject as radically fissured; for Lacan, experience is always mediated by the trauma of misrecognition and relations with others (both the other as Ideal-I and the others with whom the subject interacts). The mirror-stage, in so far as it gives rise to the subject, also introduces two important drives in the subject. These drives are not reducible to biological instinct, for Lacan, they gain significance only in relation to language. The first drive, aggression, is the 'correlative tension of the narcissistic structure in the coming-into-being (*devenir*) of the subject'.[18] Aggression is a necessary instrument through which the subject may experience itself as a unified self. In order to maintain its coherence and sense of mastery, it is necessary for the subject to impose this idealized image upon others. The characteristic of aggression is essential to the interaction of subject and other; it qualifies recognition and seems redolent of Hegel's description of the master–slave dialectic as much as it may be attributed to the Freudian death-drive. For Hegel, however, the master–slave dialectic also has a positive function; it contributes to the historical development of consciousness and it beckons self-knowledge; for Lacan, in contrast, the mutual recognition of subject and other is always forestalled. Lacan's dialectic of the mirror stage is a formal one and there is no role for consciousness in transforming the dialectic. Instead this role is reserved for the *determinants* of subjectivity rather than the human agent itself. Aggression must also be attached to the subject's experience of finitude, that which Lacan calls the *lack of the subject*, its impossibility of achieving correspondence with its ideal-image. In other words, it is precisely because the subject is *never quite whole* that aggression, as a defence-mechanism and a mode of reassurance, is brought into play with the other and upon the self. The death-instinct, for Lacan, is thus an aporia 'which lies at the heart of the notion of aggressivity'.[19]

The second drive that is brought to bear upon the subject as a result of its newly found, though at this stage, roughcast, wholeness is the propensity to desire. The concept of desire occupies an important space in Lacan's writings and it will be developed and interpreted in the course of this chapter. If aggressivity may be viewed as tied to the death-instinct, desire must be viewed as operating in accordance to the pleasure-principle. It too, is a drive for wholeness and plenitude, but now via specific objects of fulfilment and satisfaction. For the little being prior to the event of *méconnaissance*, desire is subsumed by a few basic biological needs (for food, warmth) easily satisfied by the object of the mother's breast; need and desire are thus equivalent and the possible tension created by desire is easily satiated. However, desire as experienced by the subject of the imaginary 'takes shape in the margin in which demand becomes separated from need.'[20] Desire, according to Lacan, is at the origin of every human act. However, it is not a biological instinct in the manner of need; desire is bound to the *Spaltung* of the subject. It arises 'as a presence from a background of absence'[21] which guides the subject towards the primal experience which has been foreclosed by the visual economy of the mirror-stage. Desire always points to the past even as it instils a vision of a fulfilled future in the subject; it reminds the subject of that which it lacks, but can never return it to an ideal state of primal harmony. There is no vision of wholeness, self-realization or absolute knowledge in Lacan's structure of subjectivity. This pessimism is illustrated in a remark upon the tragedy of Oedipus by one of Lacan's students: 'It was lucky that Oedipus did not know too soon what he knew only at the end, for he still had to fill out his life.'[22]

Thus far the discussion has been limited to drawing attention to the *structure of the subject*, the narcissistic form of the ego and the alienation of the ego in the imaginary. Lacan's turn to structural linguistics follows the temporal shift of Althusser, Derrida and Foucault. However, we have pointed to the rather amorphous form of structuralism. To what extent is Lacan's reading of the subject structuralist? Can Lacan transcend the risk inherent in all forms of structuralism, namely to replace the subject with some other determining form? Before these important questions can be considered, Lacan's structuralist formulations require clarification and critical evaluation.

From subject to language: 'everything emerges from the structure of the signifier'

Freudian psychoanalysis has always attached great significance to the structure of the subject's speech as Freud's work *Jokes and Their*

Relation to the Unconscious testifies.[23] By listening to the form of the subject's speech, slips of the tongue, misplaced speech, as well as the recollection of dreams noted above, a point of access to the unconscious of the subject can be found. Lacan's theory of the subject is first and foremost an effort to explore this linguistic schema in greater detail. However, this linguistic turn requires that the speaking subject be brought under closer scrutiny, and the structure of language be subjected to critical analysis. Both of these moves must be situated within Lacan's reading of structural linguistics. For Lacan, language is an *a priori* autonomous structure. It is also, in compliance with the Kojèvean motifs in his work, a medium of self-recognition. However, in accordance within structuralism's anti-humanism, Lacan's focus becomes the formal structure and rules which organize the possibilities of discourse and communication between subjects. As we shall see, this introduces a certain structural limit upon the subject's speech or enunciation.

Drawing upon the linguistic theory of the sign developed by Saussure, Lacan claims that the structure of language and the construction of meaning is the result of a constitutive algorithm: the signifier, as sound image, material attribute of language, and the signified, the concept of a particular sign.[24] According to Saussure, the signifier and the signified exist in a relation of reciprocal difference and language is itself an arbitrary system where meaning shifts endlessly between different referents. However, language does settle or fix its terms of reference according to certain signs because the signifier and signified are 'indissolubly joined'.[25] Only the fixing of the linguistic system makes it possible to have signs which, although arbitrary, are not free to take on any form. Signs then, must be seen to have a reciprocal *inter-dependence* within a linguistic system; they cannot be separated from their inter-relation with other signs. The synchronic system of laws fix the sign or referent in place and make signification and speech possible. As Saussure notes, 'without language, thought is a vague, uncharted nebula. There are no pre-existing ideas, and nothing is distinct before the appearance of language.'[26] To summarize this position: the structure of language may contain unlimited *possibilities* for signification; these however, will be limited by the system of inter-relations between signs.

Lacan agrees with the Saussurean perspective: the structure of language is a material support behind speech, and 'no signification can be sustained other than by reference to another signification.'[27] Language, moreover, is a *logos*, a fundamental, rational order which imparts conditions of possibility upon speech. However, Lacan departs from

Saussure in one significant respect, namely by loosening the noose of signification and widening the scope of its structural effects. Significa- tion is borne progressively from a permanent dialectic. Lacan establishes what he calls the 'incessant sliding of the signified under the signifier',[28] he *unfixes* the reciprocal relation between signifier and signified estab- lished by Saussure, and erodes the distinction between referent and meaning. This 'aporia of reference',[29] or the non-correspondence be- tween word and thing, destroys the representational function of the sign. On Lacan's reading, the algorithmic bar between signifier and signifier resists meaning: the signifier seems to take over the role of the sign in Saussure's theory, and the signified is no longer associated with the concept of the object, but seems closer to the dominant social meanings, norms and prejudices which occupy a cultural community. As a result, the signifier is diachronic and polysemic; it operates with a certain auton- omy, in separation from the process of signification. As Malcolm Bowie notes, the signifying chain is 'mobile, sinuous and able to loop back upon itself; any one of its links can provide a point of attachment to other chains.'[30] When the subject takes up a position in language, in the symbolic order, it is as heterogeneous as the signifier. Furthermore, as *speaking* subject (which is the only possible identity for the subject in this register), the subject *becomes* a signifier: 'the signifier is that which represents the subject for another signifier. This signifier will therefore be the signifier for which all the other signifiers represent the subject.'[31]

Lacan's structuralism has radical implications for the conception of the subject. Language is made up of a network of elements and rela- tions operating according to a synchronic structure which can be known only in its general form and not via specific signs. Language is anterior to any experience of the subject, and it is this structure which confers meaning on the subject's speech.[32] Thus, 'the form of language defines subjectivity.'[33] The subject therefore, is not the *enunciator* of discourse, but the *enunciated*. In line with structuralism's reduction of the subject, Lacan claims that only signifiers exist. It thus appears that the subject *tout court* is lost within the mobility of signifiers: 'the signifier causes the subject to arise [in the symbolic], but at the cost of becoming fixed. What was ready to speak there disappears, being no longer anything more than a signifier.'[34] However, the focus of psychoanalysis upon the subject refutes the easy containment that structuralism offers. It has been been argued above that Lacan's method is, at various points, struc- turalist, his elaboration of the registers of subjectivity upon whose surfaces the subject is caught, ensures that a dimension of subjectivity continues to disrupt the process of signification. It is the central task of psychoanalysis to analyse this disruption.

Dislocating the subject: symbolic, imaginary and real

When the subject makes its entry into language as a signifier, it is also scattered across three registers: the symbolic, the imaginary and the real. These are neither mutually exclusive nor fully constitutive of the subject. Together however, they form what Lacan calls a 'Borromean knot': structurally related, their properties press continually upon and call into question the stability of the others. The *symbolic order* is the order of language, 'an order of interdependent signs bound together by specific laws.'[35] It is useful to make an initial distinction between Lacan's use of the *symbol* and symbolic *order*. A symbol is *not* a signifier, although it may be evoked, transmuted or mediated by language. Symbols are elementary, primordial forms, pacts, myths, which envelop life and the body prior to signification; they may depend as much upon visual and corporeal resemblances as upon the universal laws they may well engender. Lacan refers to the planets as symbols, but he privileges the understanding of the symbol as primary pact or law, taking the anthropological studies of Lévi-Strauss rather than Freud's studies of myths, as his central reference point. Lévi-Strauss's structuralist analysis of culture identifies the prohibition of incest as a socio-symbolic law. Relations of kinship and marriage ties are symbolic systems of exchange which have universal significance identical to a law of language. Lacan adopts this understanding of a primary symbol which finds permanence in a signifier only by becoming a petrified symbol in the subject's unconscious. As for Freud, symbols thus come to have special significance in psychoanalysis. However, Lacan's structuralism allows for no phylogenetic analysis of history like the one developed by Freud in *Moses and Monotheism*.[36] Symbols, we may note, in so far as they rest within the unconscious, can play a dynamic role in relation to imaginary and real structures of existence.

The symbolic *order*, on the other hand, contains symbols only as mediated by language and overlaid with social convention. It is, moreover, a rational *logos*, and as a space of signification and communication, it is social and intersubjective. Lacan often refers to the symbolic order as the field of the Other, the Other in this instance being language itself. The symbolic order signals the eclipse, suture, or *fading* of the subject, who takes up a place in this order only by losing itself in the process.[37] The subject, it will be recalled, only enters the symbolic order through the structure of the signifier. This order is described by Lacan as governed by the Name-of-the-Father, a term used to describe the symbolic law of the Father. This conception of sexual and social relation follows the form of the Freudian Oedipus complex, but it is not to be reduced to concrete biological relations; the importance for Lacan of this symbolic law is its linguistic *effects* at the level of the subject's speech.

The imaginary realm has already been described as the field wherein the illusion of individuality maintains itself. The imaginary thus becomes the holder of contradiction. It is associated with the genesis of the libidinal drives, desire and aggression; if it can be seen to *represent* anything, it would be the primordial lack generated by the birth of the subject as signifier. However, given the differential structures of imaginary and symbolic, the former is experienced and represented only phantasmatically through a fictional union with an (imaginary) object, or via a fixation by the ego of the state of *méconnaissance*.

What of the real? The Lacanian real is not to be confused with conceptions of reality. It is not the historical representation of the world.[38] It is not the discursive construction of reality. Neither is it the *réalité humaine*, the subject's lived relation to the world described by existentialists. Rather, this register, according to Lacan, is unrepresentable by discourse. It is that which always remains foreclosed in the experience of speech, that element of speech which can never be grasped as signification. It is a dimension beyond and behind symbolization, but it is resistant to symbolization. The real is rather like a reserve or residue 'before which the imaginary falters and over which the symbolic stumbles.'[39] When Lacan says 'man is not entirely in man' he is attending to the unthinkable space of the real.[40]

Lacan cannot help taking a philosophical detour in his discussions of the real. It is clear that his interpretation of this concept changed with parallel transformations in his philosophical position. Whilst the content of this concept shifted, allusions to its incompleteness and its impossible representation continued. The symbolic can try to bind it, the imaginary can create fantasies which claim to fill it out, but the real will always remain outstanding and subversive. The challenges to epistemological accounts of truth should be clear. Bits and pieces of the real (itself the site of the *lack* of the subject) will always infect the purity of perception and burden the subject with an excess that must be transformed and contained somehow within identity and within representation. The materiality of the real will be considered below in Section II.

Thus far, the Lacanian subject has been described as an imaginary ego (in its mirror identifications) and as a signifier (in its accession to language), a distinction which generates a rift within the being of the subject ensuring that it will always be split in form rather than whole. Such a description may invite a definition of the subject as dualist in structure; a body repressed and a self-consciousness which comes to predominate in discourse. Quite clearly, for Lacan, and Freud, it is the subject of the unconscious (what is often called the subject of desire) that disrupts any dualist structure of the subject. It lies *between* the signifier and the signified, and it flaunts all three registers outlined above. The unconscious can be approached by psychoanalysis because it is structured like a language. This formulation has become an aphorism in Lacanian studies and it raises as many problems as it does degrees of understanding. At worst, it gives rise to the view of the Lacanian schema as a form of linguistic reductionism.[41] However, once the subject of the unconscious is viewed as making a mark upon each of the registers above, it will become apparent that the *materiality* of language can ward off such claims to reductionism.

For Richard Boothby 'the unconscious is both something ideally inaccessible, something quasi-real, yet it is also realized by the symbolic.'[42] What is clear however, is that the unconscious is not, for Lacan, reducible to the drives; it is neither primordial nor instinctive in form, and 'what it knows about the elementary is no more than the elements of the signifier.'[43] If Lacan's recourse to structural linguistics performs one crucial function, it is to obviate all reference to the unconscious as 'the seat of the instincts'.[44] The unconscious is the *gap* in the subject, that which Lacan often refers to as 'another scene'. It arises in the separation of the being of the subject from its spectral formation. As such, it is pre-ontological but not pre-discursive; it co-exists with language and may be appropriated by it, but it also mediates the subject's *lack* of being (represented by its alienation in the symbolic) and its desire is a desire for plenitude and recognition. In this way, the unconscious may be seen to send the subject on false trails towards an absolute place, where objects may coincide with the subject and represent the real. Lacan calls such an unobtainable object, *objet petit â.*[45] For Lacan, there is no *aufhebung* of Hegel's unhappy consciousness, or of the 'discontents of civilization' described by Freud.[46]

The unconscious thus occupies a space within all three registers. It haunts the subject-as-signifier, who must live within the Law of language, a patriarchal law which forces the subject into masculine and feminine identities and sets the phallus in the place of transcendental, albeit illusive, signified.[47] This structuring element of language acts as a *point-de-capiton*, it sews the process of signification together, and orders the possibilities of language. The symbolic order operates as a *scopic* economy, the ego synthesizes the perceptions of the subject, defining identity solely in terms of the image. The ego operates, Lacan writes, 'solely with a view to covering the displacement constituted by the subject with a resistance that is essential to discourse as such.'[48] However, whilst the subject is constituted as a signifier in the symbolic order, this can not ensure that it *will* speak in the designated intervals of discourse. Indeed, 'every signifier of the subject of the enunciation may be lacking in the statement.'[49] If the unconscious may be structured like a language and speak in the gaps within discourse, it is through metaphor and metonymy that the social censure of the symbolic order may be circumvented by the unconscious. These two rhetorical tropes (linguists may claim that Lacan ignores, amongst others, synecdoche, catachresis and allegory) are understood to break up, subvert the signifying chain and disrupt speech. They further extend Freud's own account of condensation and displacement constructed in relation to dreams. Condensation arises from the simple fact that the dream is much shorter and more compressed that its verbal representation (i.e. the dream 'text'); condensation is the nodal point of the dream which is always open to multiple interpretations. Displacement, on the other hand, is a form of distortion more difficult to define. It is represented indirectly in dreams and can cover any form of diversion from thought.

In Lacan, these functions are given much wider significance in relation to everyday speech. They expose the symptoms of the subject caused by its division (through metaphor) and the flux of desire (through metonymy). Psychoanalysis thus approaches the unconscious hermeneutically; its language makes present the *absence* of being and the lack of the subject.[50] Lacan has referred to the language of the unconscious as 'a net over the totality of the real'.[51] It is the unconscious function in speech that appears to inscribe the effects of this elusive register of the real upon the form of the symbolic.

However, we have also identified the unconscious as linking the experience of desire to language and articulating the subject's drive for recognition. The concept of desire thus has a dual significance. It is linked to the origin of every signification and it translates the subject's demand for recognition. Desire contains a *structural* moment in relation

to language, and a subjective, *experiential* dimension drawn from
Hegelian phenomenology. In other words, there is a duplication of the
concept of desire according to two distinct and largely incompatible
philosophical positions. Can Lacan's conception of the subject carry the
weight of these two, incompatible positions? Will they reveal a faulty
structural logic and return Lacan's subject to the status of that which he
sought to displace, namely the *cogito*, or can the two positions be synthesized? The philosophical root of the concept of desire is frequently
traced to the writings of Alexandre Kojève and it is at the intersection
of desire and the subject of the unconscious upon the three Lacanian
registers that Kojève's formulations of the key concepts of Hegel's
philosophy is often noted. This relation will now be considered within
the wider philosophical framework of psychoanalysis.

II. THE PARADOX OF THE SUBJECT:
BETWEEN PHILOSOPHY AND PSYCHOANALYSIS

Lacan's psychoanalytic project of reframing the subject is clearly also a
philosophical project. Whilst Lacan spoke of his own recourse to philosophy to be of propaedeutic value only,[52] references to philosophical
figures are scattered throughout his writings, particularly to Descartes
and Hegel. Indeed, it is at the intersection between psychoanalysis and
philosophy that the paradox of subjectivity can be encountered most
directly. Section I of this chapter has emphasized Lacan's *repositioning* of the subject in relation to linguistic structures. Does Lacan call
the modern, post-Cartesian, conception of the subject into question?
Lacan's adoption of philosophical motifs of the subject – critical as it
may be – ensure that he continues to be preoccupied by the questions
thrown up by the concept of the subject. *If the subject is dislocated by
psychoanalysis, its presence is sustained by the form and structure of
these questions.* Let us investigate Lacan's diverse philosophical borrowings and consider their significance for the concept of the subject.[53]

In his essay on the mirror stage, Lacan opposes the formation of the
subject to any philosophy beginning with the cogito, a form of selfhood
which he associates with the birth of the modern ego. The Cartesian
problematic of the subject is the point of departure for psychoanalysis.
In *The Four Fundamental Concepts of Psychoanalysis*, the spectre
of Cartesian doubt is understood as a sign of the *resistance* of the subject to transparency and truth.[54] In 'The Agency of the Letter in the

Unconscious' Lacan inverts Descartes famous description of the *ego cogito ergo sum*:

> it is not a question of knowing whether I speak of myself in a way that conforms to what I am, but rather of knowing whether I am the same as that of which I speak. ... I am not wherever I am the plaything of my thought; I think of what I am where I do not think to think.[55]

Set within the linguistic structures which make the Cartesian subject of enunciation possible, the subject of certainty gives up its metaphysical place to the structure of language. Lacan, it may be argued, decentres the *cogito* and in so doing takes the philosophy of the subject to its limit. No longer is the subject the *author* of meaning, insecure as this status may be, rather, the subject is authorised by the signifier which *appears in its place*.

Lacan's utilization of Hegelian concepts is also apparent throughout his writings but what is more important is his *interpretation* of Hegelian phenomenology in relation to his conception of the subject.[56] Our discussions of Hegel in Chapter 1, in particular, the reading of Kojève, focused on the concept of desire. Desire, as negativity, was viewed as a tension within the subject in much the same way that the *Spaltung* of the subject in Lacan is experienced as a wound, a gap, a lack of being. Depending on the theory of history and knowledge underlying Hegelian positions, negativity might be overcome by the desiring subject who labours for recognition within history (Kojève), or remain a limit, an aporia to fulfilment (Hyppolite). Lacan finds a natural ally in this Hegelian problematic.[57] Like Lacan, Hegel also endeavoured to re-situate the primacy of the knowing subject and to understand the object in relation to the movement, development and transformation of subjectivity in time. Indeed, Lacan's account of the mirror-stage often reads like a commentary on Hegel's own depiction of the master-slave dialectic. As Hegel writes in *The Phenomenology of Spirit*,

> self-consciousness is faced by another self-consciousness; it has come out of itself. This has a two-fold significance: first, *it has lost itself, for it finds itself as an other being*; secondly, in doing so it has superseded the other, for *it does not see the other as an essential being, but in the other sees its own self*.[58]

What is not to be found in the mirror for either Hegel or Lacan, is the subject's self-recognition; it is an imaginary wholeness that is experienced here. Both Hegel and Lacan agree that the mirror cannot reflect the subject's desire. The life and death struggle leaves the desire for recognition in the subject unsatisfied. However, Lacan *limits* the scope and meaning of desire to the dominant themes of law, language and their relation to *méconnaissance*. Hence it becomes important to question the possibility of a dialectical synthesis of desire with the subject.

In his book *Lacan in Contexts*, David Macey notes that one should refer not to Hegel, but to the Hegel–Kojève matrix in Lacan. 'To return to Kojève after reading Lacan is to experience the shock of recognition, a truly uncanny sensation of *deja vu*.'[59] Lacan attended Kojève's lectures on Hegel between 1933 and 1939, and it is therefore likely that Lacan's concept of the desire for recognition repeats Kojèvean formulas.[60] This may also account for the Heideggerian conceptual motifs in Lacan's writings which may have been filtered through Kojève's reading.[61] Nevertheless, such a straightforward assimilation of Lacan to Kojève may risk producing a philosophical simplicity in Lacan's position. The resemblance to, and the influence of Kojève's Hegelian perspective upon Lacan's own conception of the subject is certainly evident. However, the interpretation of Kojève in Chapter 1 aligned his thought with an anthropological reading of the subject and a theory of the *culmination* of history which, despite its sensitivity to the groundlessness of knowledge, remained attached to a form of anthropological humanism. It is precisely this philosophical reading of Kojève which would be incompatible with Lacan's structuralism.

Lacan's psychoanalytic theorization of the subject attempts a philosophical marriage between an account of subjectivity which must remain non-subjective in formulation, and a structuralist account of language and the social world. Lacan's Hegelianism, therefore, must be tempered by his structuralism. Such a theoretical synthesis is complex and not without contradiction. It does point to a more critical reading of Hegel than the one often noted by Lacan's commentators and critics. Indeed, a comparison of the *Rome Discourse* of 1953 where supportive references to Hegel abound, with the 1977 essay, 'The subversion of the subject and the dialectic of desire', illustrates that by the time of the later essay, Lacan was beginning to adopt a more critical position on Hegelianism. Lacan now draws attention to the teleology implicit in the Hegelian system. It is now viewed as a 'permanent revisionism, where truth is continuously reabsorbing itself.'[62] For Lacan, a dialectical synthesis aims to bring about a resolution of the real and the symbolic, a synthesis which is theoretically and practically impossible.[63] Truth may be searched for for ever in the images of others, but it will never be attained.[64] Lacan notes that the real, for Hegel, is 'a subject fulfilled with his identity to himself', a subject 'always already perfect'.[65] Lacan's subject, in contrast, is always divided and this disjuncture is *perpetual*; the experience of subjectivity and the *real* content of its concept are radically different. Lacan's concept of the real is equated with the unrepresentable. It is the residue of the subject's linguistic structure, confined and repressed in the unconscious. The contents of the real furnish an element of experience which can never be fully disclosed to the subject. Its channel is the vehicle of language itself. The paradox of the subject is that consciousness is unable to account for discontinuity with recourse to itself, because this discontinuity is part of the ontological structure of the subject.

Taking into account these views, it may be the case that Lacan's conception of the subject is much closer to Hyppolite's reading of Hegel than the Kojèvean position often linked with his conceptualizations.[66] For Hyppolite, and Lacan too, 'the self never coincides with itself, for it is always other in order to be itself.'[67] Moreover, the project of attaining identity and reconciliation between the subject and the objects of its desire are always overshadowed and doomed to collapse. Lacan's understanding of the *objet petit â* is indicative of such a position. The *objet â* of desire will always deceive the subject; its meaning will always dissipate in the light of the subject's experience of it. Desire, therefore, may be viewed as having a two-fold significance. First, it is a relation of being to lack; the experience of desire is a reminder of the subject's lost relation to itself which, arguably, cannot be reclaimed. Second, desire is always the desire of the Other; it is linked to language and the law of the symbolic order. It is articulated within a linguistic framework which has always, in effect, *crossed out* the subject's significance before signification occurs. Quite clearly then, desire, in so far as it is constructed through language, fails to reach the being of the subject. Hyppolite's own emphasis upon the Unhappy Consciousness quoted in Chapter 1, evokes a similarly tragic account of the subject: 'This feeling of disparity within the self, of the impossibility of the self coinciding with itself in reflection, is indeed the basis of subjectivity.'[68] It was Lacan's aim to explore this ontological rift which constitutes the subject.

The theoretical parallel, with Hyppolite's anti-humanism rather than Kojève's impending anthropomorphism, can be extended further with reference to Lacan's interpretations of history, the possible end of analysis, and his views on the realization of the truth of the subject. Hyppolite, Kojève and Lacan all subscribe to a Heideggerian account of temporality. Human temporality, for Heidegger, cannot be represented by a uni-linear time sequence. *Dasein,* the order of Being, is caught up in past, present and future temporal modes; to be human is to be divided between these three dimensions. As Bowie writes, 'Being is borne forwards on a composite tide that pulls it towards the utmost fullness of being and, concurrently, towards death, its ultimate loss.'[69] Time is seen to structure human existence; the discord which Lacan describes as a primary characteristic of the subject is mediated by these different temporal modes. The subject becomes a subject-in-time as soon as it takes up a place within language and tries to signify absence. The oft-quoted example of this temporal and linguistic moment is found in Freud's account of the *Fort/Da* scenario, where the small child tries to represent absence and its desire for the mother using a cotton-reel. By throwing the object out of sight (*fort*) and then reclaiming it (*da*), the child comes to terms with the temporal absence of the mother through the presence of language. According to Lacan, these two phonemes together encapsulate the mechanism of alienation. The child learns to separate the thing from its name, in effect producing a division between the real and the symbolic and creating the basis for subjective meaning. Furthermore, this setting up of signifiers in a binary rela-tionship, creates the rupture and consequential *fading* of being which is effectively excluded from the temporality of the symbolic order.

Lacan's psychoanalytic discourse thus establishes three temporal registers (symbolic, imaginary and real) which present the structure of subjectivity in markedly different ways and can never be actualized as a singular, self-bounded experience. Whilst the Kojèvean account of time – itself a reading of Heidegger with Hegel – recognizes the tem-porality of desire and its relation to language and speech (which is, of course, emblematic of Lacan's own terminology), time is linked to authentic human action and is realized with the *end* of historical time. However, in Lacan's psychoanalytic account, the subject's history exists in bits and pieces, strewn across these temporal registers, and often hidden in the form of (repressed) memory, fantasy and alienation. The role of analysis is not to demystify or merely reveal the subject to itself. Such an act is radically impossible given the structure of social existence and the ontological form that subjectivity may take. Psycho-analysis can only *forge links* between the different temporal registers.

The closest the subject may come to 'authenticity', according to Heidegger and Lacan, occurs with being-towards-death where authenticity is itself foreclosed. It is here that the finitude and historically contingent form of the subjectivity is most dramatically exposed. As Lacan writes 'when we wish to attain in the subject what was before the serial articulation of the word, and what is primordial in the birth of symbols, we find it in death, from which his experience takes on all the meaning it has.'[70]

The philosophical problems of the relation of time and desire to a psychoanalytic conception of subjectivity have important consequences for the interpretation of Lacan offered within this chapter. There is no end of analysis, if by which we mean the realization of the subject, because the end-point can only be reached with the obliteration of the human subject. If death is experienced as a 'tending towards' as implied in both Heidegger's and Lacan's readings, as well as in Freud's presentation of the pleasure-principle, then the termination of analysis becomes impossible. Despite this claim, it is often argued that Lacan seeks the *truth* of the subject. It is the Heideggerian notion of full as opposed to empty speech adopted in *The Rome Discourse* which is the source of such views. Certainly, speech imparts presence within language, but this does not align the subject's speech with truth. The unconscious after all, as Lacan points out, cannot be made continuous with language. Discourse has no criteria of truthfulness unless it is that of conjoining the subject with its desires and introducing an awareness of this limit to the subject's speech. A distinction must therefore be made between a correspondence theory of truth which appeals to a substantial definition of reality, and a view of truth which is always partial and delimited, what Lacan has called a 'limping truth'.[71] What must be emphasized here is that there can be no end-state which may restore plenitude to the subject, or mend its division. Lacan denies that it is possible to speak the truth of the subject. Here he shares with many other philosophers, including Spinoza, Nietzsche, Heidegger and Derrida, an awareness of the disjuncture between being and language. Psychoanalysis, whilst orientated towards the future, can have no hold upon the direction that its path may take. Psychoanalysis has, in other words, no metaphysical warrant to totalize experience, or limit and contain knowledge.

Let us summarize the argument of this section: psychoanalytic discourse presents the subject as constituted with a fissure which may be only partially represented by discourse, a fissure that remains forever outside the frame of representation and without ontological form. How can this dimension of subjectivity (if we may still call it by this name) be understood in relation to the political and how may it alter the horizon of our questions concerning the political? Before turning to these important questions, we must reckon with an argument which presents Lacan's problematic as caught forever within the trap of representation. Will this discredit the structure and form of the above questions? Will it, moreover, return the subject to its role as *subjectum* and distance psychoanalysis from its critical function: to contest and restructure the foundations of such a conception of the subject?

Subjectivity and representation

In their book *The Title of the Letter*, Nancy and Lacoue-Labarthe endorse Lacan's critical reading of Descartes:

> Lacan not only takes issue with the psychological depth that a certain tradition thought possible to retain (after having imported it into the Cartesian *cogito* from elsewhere), but also with the pure self-transparency of transcendental subjectivity, insofar as it maintains the subject within the horizon of presence-to-self in general.[72]

Furthermore, Lacan's *subversion* of the subject, its displacement and replacement by the structure of language, also introduces an element of deception into knowledge because 'every emission of speech is always, up to a certain point, under an inner necessity to err.'[73] If the attributes of knowledge and subjectivity were, for Descartes, permanence, identity and substantiality, in Lacan's reading, these become associated with provisionality, uncertainty and contingency.

Nevertheless, Nancy and Lacoue-Labarthe also take issue with Lacan's theory of the subject which still remains, on their reading, attached to a classical, Cartesian conception of the subject, and the structure of representation which in turn supports its significations. This textual analysis is a deconstructive one which owes much to Derrida's interrogation of the subject; it explores and locates the conditions governing the possibility of conceptualization. In the case of Lacan, their reading opens up the ontological site of the subject and it finds that Lacan has remained attached to a certain metaphysics of the subject. In other words, by identifying the Cartesian *cogito* as 'at the centre of the mirage that renders modern man so sure of himself even in his uncertainties about himself',[74] Lacan's theory remains tied to a conception of the subject of certainty even though he constructs this identity as the *méconnaissance* of the subject. For example, in the essay on the mirror stage, the subject of the imaginary is *still* equivalent to the metaphysical subject who *thinks* that its articulations upon the plane of representation are autonomously driven. Whilst all meaning is distilled from this subject, who remains split and alienated within language – and strewn across the symbolic and the real, it is still this structure of subjectivity which forms the ground of Lacan's construction of the linguistic inscription of the unconscious. Thus,

> not only is the Cartesian foundation indispensable to measure the gap introduced by psychoanalysis, but ... the excentricity which Freud sought to exhibit in the relation of the subject to itself, is in fact only formulable in linguistic terms - namely in terms of the difference between the subject of enunciation and the subject of the statement.[75]

Against this position, Lacan's theory of the subject can be viewed as dislocated and as reduced to a function within a theory of the sign, which can in turn challenge the philosophical basis of representation. Nevertheless, the subject is understood to borrow 'the *material support of its discourse* from the structure of language.'[76] The subject is not so much displaced as reinscribed upon another (linguistic) register where it is represented as a signifier for another signifier. Contra Nancy and Lacoue-Labarthe, it could be argued that this mode of representation cannot be viewed as the total assimilation of the being of the subject into the *subjectum* because the subject is *absent* and divided. Rather, it is *through* the subject that the sounds of another scene may be expressed in the subject's discourse, and upon the plane of signification. This speech presents a *truth*, according to Lacan, but it is presented in a disorderly and confused fashion because it, too, must encounter the deception of language. The language of the unconscious passes through the subject as signifier but it is anterior to the subject of consciousness and often remains inaccessible to consciousness.

However, for Nancy and Lacoue-Labarthe, this account of the unconscious *still relies* upon the structure of representation. If the unconscious is hidden, repressed and forbidden, it nonetheless 'forces the inscription of its very refusal [within discourse]'.[77] Even if desire cannot *speak*, it can still find its way into language through the signifying chains of metaphor and metonymy as well as via its manifestation as symptom. By identifying the unconscious with metonymic desire in language, *and* with truth, Lacan *risks* equating truth with the representation of language and subjectivity in discourse. This conflation is seen to result from Lacan's faulty reading of Heidegger's thoughts upon *logos* and speech. Lacan shares with Heidegger an ontological regard for the finitude of the subject, but whilst the latter tries to decipher the unthought of philosophy, the former, it is claimed, wishes to locate and compartmentalize it within the structure of language.[78]

Lacan's thoughts on truth and its possible manifestation within discourse have their indispensable source in Heidegger's essay 'Logos' which the former translated in *La Psychoanalyse* in 1956.[79] In this essay, Heidegger acknowledges the distortion and destruction of the possible definitions of *logos*, viewed not only as a logic and a law (the significance often attributed to it by Lacan), but also as a gathering, a laying-forth of existence, an opening for thought and speech. Heidegger captures the distance which separates language as *disclosure*, as an appeal to the order of Being, and language as *expression* of subjectivity, as 'externally contrived representation'.[80] Modes of signification which are tied to representation impose limits upon what may be laid forth in speech; they conceal, for Heidegger, 'an essential dispensation of Being to men'.[81] Paradoxically, speech as a laying forth of Being (anterior to signification) is *also* concealed when it tries to present or disclose itself. Heidegger's conception of truth as *aletheia* expresses this unsettling of truth and the web of disclosure and concealment which characterizes the hidden nature of truth. This may be described as truth as impossibility; truth caught forever in the trap of presentation and the chance of disclosure. Lacan's conception of truth draws its philosophical shape from this Heideggerian formulation. It has no relation to adequation or correspondence; rather it is identified with the deception, the error inherent within speech itself. The language of the unconscious, for Lacan, is closely bound to Being in the Heideggerian sense, and the *logos* is the possibility that unconscious speech may be 'brought-forth'.

Nancy and Lacoue-Labarthe view Lacan's reading as a simplification of Heidegger's interpretation of truth. Instead Lacan hypostatizes *logos* as signification and refuses to reconstitute a theory of truth as inaccessible and deferred.[82] This reading is also symptomatic of Lacan's broader aims to systematize psychoanalysis. Lacan's discourse requires a logic, a *telos*, a pedagogical *guarantee*, a scientificity, all of which require, in turn, a closed theoretical system. The linguistic appropriation of Freud can be achieved only by adopting philosophical motifs which return Lacan to the general concerns of a philosophy of consciousness. Ultimately, Lacan's reliance upon the classical conception of the subject can be understood as re-enclosing his discourse within a traditional theory of representation and language.

The question of the structure of representation and its capacity to enclose all dimensions of subjectivity through the many properties and constituting functions of language (as home for being, as vessel of desire, as law, as symbol, as Other) is of fundamental importance to the contribution that psychoanalysis can make to a critical theory of the subject. If Lacan's concept of the subject is attached so firmly to an account of linguistic *representation*, and if his discourse can no longer insist that this structure of representation is anathema to form of the subject theorized, then Lacanian psychoanalysis must be understood as a form of linguistic reductionism which can only do so much work for the concept of the subject by displacing and reconfiguring its primary attributes upon the plane of language. This risk pervades all forms of structuralism and both Derrida and Foucault will remain wary of its totalizing, reductionist possibilities.

What is the status of Lacan's dislocation of the subject and its linguistic reinscription? Does Lacan resolve this paradox of the subject, namely that its adoption generates an attachment to a host of philosophical problems, of which representation is only the most recognizable? Does Lacan's use of the subject draw him, irreparably, into these metaphysical quandaries? The answer must be a qualified 'yes'. *Every* theory of the subject is attached to the *historicity* of the subject, to its philosophical genealogy and to the problems which, in their questions and their metaphysical reversal, *still sustain the concept of the subject.* This situation is not unique to Lacan but plagues every position which attempts to reconstruct the subject. Hence Lacan's Cartesianism is inevitable but its degree is also a matter of reading and a question of interpretation. Some weight must be given, therefore, to Lacan's influential effort to rethink the subject.

This chapter has argued that the Lacanian concept of the subject must be understood as a topographical structure which is unevenly distributed across three overlapping registers: the symbolic, the imaginary and the real. The concept of the real is an understated dimension in Nancy and Lacoue-Labarthe's interpretation of Lacan; it is not articulated in their argument despite the importance this concept may have both to a critique of traditional theories of representation and to an elaboration of a theory of truth.[83] Might the concept of the real produce a materiality of subjectivity which cannot be located on the plane of representation, or communicated in language?[84] If the real does have such a structuring function, its importance lies not within the representative function of language as Nancy and Lacoue-Labarthe maintain, but elsewhere in the corporeality of the subject. The real has a certain density, affectivity and movement which exceed representation. Michel Henry prefers to view affectivity not as an *abridgement* to language but as a self-immanence sufficient in itself. No theory of representation can contain it, and it has nothing to do with subject–object relations. The real may be discharged in language, but a language which is its servant rather than its adjudicator, and it will always remain out-standing of signification. Lacan's concept of the real resonates with this primordial state of life. If the law is that which 'safeguards the rigour of the existence of the real',[85] it can do so only because the efforts of the law of language to reform the real will always distort its form.[86] According to Henry, psychoanalysis, through its proximity to affectivity, has an important role in a philosophy which looks beyond representational forms of knowledge and being.[87] Arguably, the concept of the real can offer up these possibilities. Unfortunately, they are not adequately pursued within Lacan's discourse; perhaps because its dense, unmarked theoretical path and its tendency towards the accumulation of diverse and uninterrogated philosophical positions act as a barrier to such analysis. Certainly, Lacan shies away from any detailed consideration of this structure of being;[88] what we can know of it is only that which may be translated into the subject's speech.[89] If the real is undertheorized, it is nonetheless the concept most utilized by those writers exploring the relation of Lacan's construction of the subject to the political and social field. Let us turn, finally, to the political significance of Lacan's theory of the subject.

III. PSYCHOANALYSIS, SUBJECTIVITY AND THE POLITICAL

> The slightest alteration in the relation between man and the signifier, ... changes the whole course of history by modifying the moorings that anchor his [the subject's] being.[90]

Psychoanalysis and the political stand in close relation, particularly if we regard, with Lacan, 'a study of languages and institutions as necessary to an understanding of the text of our experience.'[91] If it is through the dual structure of language, *langue* and *parole*, that the form of the subject may be seen to take shape, then the modes of signification, the rituals, myths and symbols that underlie and found a social community and its language, must become a resource for psychoanalytic theory. However, psychoanalysis cannot be a simple retrieval or recollection of history; both the subject and the symbolic order are constructed temporally and spatially to the past in a complex manner. Certainly, a genealogical account of the symbolic structure of language and culture is *not* Lacan's aim, however interesting such a project may be. It can only be the social *effects* that resonate *within the subject* that may engage the attention of psychoanalysis. For some critics, notably Cornelius Castoriadis, this limits the scope of Lacanian psychoanalysis for political intervention. Furthermore, Lacan's structuralist method isolates signification and reduces it to a linguistic law which is then understood to account for the form of the subject. This formal approach to language jettisons the *irreducible uniqueness* of the subject.[92] For Castoriadis, there can be no given structure or law which can constitute the subject because there is a productive, creative element of any structure which is ungraspable. Castoriadis shares this space of critique with a number of other commentators who paint a picture of Lacanian psychoanalysis as producing an ahistoricist, universalist account of the subject ignorant of both praxis and contingency. For both views, the structure of signification is viewed as fixed and the possibilities for speech and action are viewed somewhat statically and pessimistically as unchangeable, offering up no possibility for the transcendence and transformation of the dominant symbolic community which remains tied to the patriarchal Law-of-the-Father.[93] Thus, conservative and radical readings of Lacan appear to sit uneasily together: the first position affirms the presence of a universal symbolic, the second questions the significance of this forever instituted symbolic law and emphasizes the openness, irreducibility and perpetual institution of the symbolic order.[94]

Is there a role for history, for the radical historicity of the subject and the political in Lacan's account? How far does Lacan's conception of the subject embrace a structuralist problematic which leaves no room for historicity? Surely the ruse of language is precisely that it *cannot* equip, or support, the subject with a system of meaning. For Giorgio Agamben, it is this double articulation between language and speech, that is, the coexistence between the structure of enunciation and the discontinuous experience of subjectivity which cannot be spoken, that constitutes the specific structure of human language. Thus, for a being whose experience of language was not always split into language and speech – in other words, a primordially speaking being ... there would be no knowledge, no infancy, no history: he would already be directly one with his linguistic nature and would nowhere find any discontinuity or difference where any history or knowledge might be produced.[95]

For Lacan, this aporetic experience is reflected in the temporal disjuncture between synchronic and diachronic conceptions of language. It is precisely this dual structure of language which makes the closure of the political an impossibility because no political community can truly mend this rent in being and contain the subject. Without this difference or residue of *unappropriated subjectivity*, there could be no history or politics, 'no modification of the moorings that anchor the subject's being' (Lacan), only a total system where subjectivity would be pure sameness incorporated as a mere reflection of the already given social world. Agamben and Castoriadis develop very different accounts of the significance of history to language and subjectivity. The former is certainly more sensitive to Lacan's own theory of language. Both thinkers, however, are united in their understanding of an unappropriated dimension of subjectivity, something other than the subject-as-signifier (the *experimentum linguae* for Agamben, the radical imagination for Castoriadis) which disrupts and resists the order, the logic and the ideological closure of political form. It is this dimension of uncontained subjectivity which ceaselessly negotiates signification, releasing something other than the subject into the space of history and creation.

It may be argued that Lacan's psychoanalytic account of the subject, in so far as it remains sensitive to this *experience* of language, can afford to place emphasis upon the linguistic constitution of the political. Such a position challenges the overly formal reading of Lacan's theory of language; it further recognizes the creative and disruptive space within language wherein an unappropriated dimension of subjectivity can have effect. Signification *sustains* the form of the political by placing representational limits upon the possibilities of meaning-construction available to the subject. Thus it may also be viewed as *creating* modes of identification of the subject with the structure of the political.[96] At the same time, language must be viewed as frustrating the order and cohesiveness of the political, rendering its form uneven and fractious. Social bonds are founded by discourse and its power of presupposition; institutions maintain themselves to the precise degree to which they are able to maintain their founding symbols and signs.[97] It is here that founding moments of origin and emergence are created and it is here that they are simultaneously fissured and called to account for themselves. Like Derrida's deconstruction of the representational structure of language and its subjective counterpart, developed in Chapter 4 of this book, Lacan's analysis points to a conception of the political – and the subject – as radically incomplete and always overdetermined by the complexities of identity which not only resist incorporation but is also *unrepresentable* within the linguistic precepts governing political order and community. As Agamben points out, a community, and a subject, born of the *experimentum linguae* cannot take the form of a presupposition.[98]

If Lacan's theory of the subject opens up this relation to history and transforms itself in the process, what of its relation to historical materialism, and to the idea of aleatory materialism discussed by Althusser in his final writings? Despite Althusser's claim to the contrary, psychoanalysis is not easily conjoined with historical materialism. Can Marx and Lacan be usefully synthesized? We have already observed the rather partial utilization of Lacanian concepts by Althusser in the latter's theory of ideology, and there is certainly very little attention given, in Lacan's writings, to what is overtly social.[99] However, this relation between materialism and psychoanalysis deserves attention in spite of the difficulty that it poses, particularly in view of the exploration of psychoanalysis and the political alluded to above. The previous chapter has presented two Marxist perspectives on the question of the subject. Both explored the social construction of the subject in relation to history and knowledge. Lukács developed the concept of reification to account for the atomization of the social subject who lives a one-dimensional existence. Althusser endeavoured to explore the ways in which ideology constructs particular forms of subjectivity. Indeed, the latter's theory of ideology and the mechanism of interpellation resonate with Lacan's construction of the subject through the mirror stage. As with all positions that transpose concepts from one problematic to another, some elements of a problematic may contaminate another. Althusser grappled with such a difficulty in his consideration of the conceptual distance between ideology and science. Let us recall Althusser's central formulation of ideology: 'ideology represents the *imaginary* relation of individuals to their *real* conditions of existence.' These two Lacanian concepts are utilized and applied with undue attention to their conceptual specificity. The crucial concept of the real, that which remains distinct from any theory of representation, is equated by Althusser with actual conditions of existence. Similarly, the concept of the imaginary is undertheorized and aligned with a process of *recognition*, rather than its inverse, and the mode of experience of alienation, *méconnaisance*, is not considered in any detail. Furthermore, Althusser's Spinozist critique of empiricism and his rejection of phenomenological thought – particularly its Hegelian formulation, make his deployment (and misuse) of the concept of the real seem inconsistent with his anti-empiricism. His use of Lacan is certainly uncritical in view of the traces of Hegelian philosophy in the latter's discourse.

In Chapter 2, the problems inherent in Althusser's construction of the subject as an effect of ideology were also considered. Significantly, Althusser offered no account of the link between the materiality of ideological state apparatuses and the constitution of the subject, that is, how ideology is internalized and how it produces the effects of sub-jectification. Mladen Dolar notes the 'empty gesture' of subjectivation in Althusser: 'there is a part of the individual that cannot successfully pass into the subject, an element of "pre-ideological" and "presubjective" *materia prima* that comes to haunt subjectivity once it is constituted as such.'[100] Leaving aside for one moment the status of this *materia prima* for Althusser, Dolar's point plays upon a description of interpellation as perpetual and immanently productive of subjectivity. There can be no single event of constitution of the subject because there can be no abso-lute fixing of the subject according to any symbolic law. It is not possible then, to view the subject according to the positions and functions which the subject may come to occupy within ideology. Following Lacan, this is viewed as masking the lack inherent in the subject and the political, a lack which underlies all ideological mechanisms of incorporation.[101] The play of the symbolic cannot simply *coopt* the subject in a singular relation, but must perpetually transform themselves in order to provoke the symbolic incorporation of the real. Hence ideology's relation to the fantastical, the illusive, and the subject's desire. For Dolar, 'there is a kernel of the Real which prevents the self-construction from the inside and disrupts any delicate balance in the relation of the self, the traumatic point around which subjectivity [and the political] is constituted.'[102]

According to this perspective, the real must be understood in its Lacanian construction as puncturing the symbolic. If we wish to investigate and question the logic of the political as a stable order, or as a transparent community, analysis should be extended to the contra-dictory effects of the real. This analysis views the political as always open, contingent, ruptural, an uneven terrain whose closure can never be absolute. The political can only attempt to create and maintain an artificial unity.[103] Thus, ideology must incorporate the effects of the real within it; if it is able to rationalize contradiction and dislocation, then its function of regulating signification in the symbolic order is sustained. Whilst this regulation of discourse is artificial and internally fractured, it is also an act of power, if by power we denote an objectivity whose *arbitrary* construction has already been erased.[104] Such a perspective endeavours to consider more than an understanding of the subject according to the logic of the signifier, and more of what the inevitable failure of this logic demands of the subject of the real. Moreover, it is a perspective which develops certain parallels between the work of Lacan and Althusser, and those who interpret them.

Without doubt, there does exist a number of parallel concepts in the work of these two thinkers. However, we have emphasized many times above, the problems surrounding the utilization of the same concepts across different theoretical frameworks. A similar awareness must apply to the *conflation* of ideas and the identification of similar positions between thinkers. We have drawn attention to this difficulty specifically in relation to the concept of the subject, which is meaningless outside of the problematic within which it is situated. Every concept must be fleshed out, lest its ontological ground be taken for granted or ignored. Remaining cognizant of the risks involved (these risks will become *explicit* and *insuperable* when we turn to Derrida's philosophy), can a similarity be gleaned between what Dolar calls above the *materia prima* of the real, and that of aleatory materialism in Althusser's later writings?[105] Indeed, the trajectories of both of these concepts lead us back to the question of the subject, although this journey is by no means a regressive one.

Aleatory materialism has been described as a materialist encounter which can take many different modes. Materialism need not refer to a brute nature, nor interpret mechanically the movements of a natural order; instead materialism can be an inscription, a voice, an energy, a power, a becoming. Lacan also describes the real as an encounter, although he qualifies it by saying that it is more often a missed encounter within psychoanalysis.[106] What is clear, however, is that the real alludes to a productivity or a surplus in being which is often experienced through its symbolic effects, namely through speech. It is also 'present' (in an illusive sense) in the traumatic kernel of the subject's experience, in desire, in the corporeal experience of the subject. If the real can occasionally and dramatically untie forms, by causing its centre of signification to collapse, it also unravels all attempts by the subject to unify experience and elicit a system of meaning called knowledge.

Althusser was correct to draw attention to a shared project in his own and Lacan's work. The latter's theory of the subject supplements the former's in quite significant ways. The incomplete constitution of the subject in relation to ideology can now be appreciated for its resistance to such ideological construction. At the same time, Lacan's account of the subject has brought with it a philosophical genealogy from Descartes to Hegel that threatens to undermine its formulations. Lacan's structuralism was never a fully qualified one and his reading of philosophy was often eliptical as well as, at times, instrumental. Does Lacan escape the paradox of the subject? Does his conception of the subject presuppose a Cartesian foundation? Lacan has claimed that psychoanalysis builds itself upon the structure of Cartesian doubt. Indeed, without Descartes there could be no Freud.[107] In contrast to Nancy and Lacoue-Labarthe, Slavoj Žižek argues that Lacan exposes the excessive kernel of the *cogito* and the hole in representation.[108] This difference of encounter in reading itself indicates suitably the paradox of subjectivity which engenders all conceptions of the subject.

4

DERRIDA, SUBJECTIVITY AND THE POLITICS OF *DIFFÉRANCE*

The project of deconstruction initiated in the 1960s by Jacques Derrida has had a great influence upon contemporary conceptions of subjectivity. In common with the thinkers considered thus far in the study, Derrida's writings are woven, inextricably, into the philosophical tradition, traversing, contesting and critiquing philosophy's multiple modes of understanding, its methods and directions, its limits and exclusions, its mode of historical presentation. At the same time, this philosophical siting of deconstruction places it firmly within a problematic of subjectivity and language. For Derrida's project is one of re-thinking the boundaries of subjectivity, theory and praxis as conceived throughout the Western philosophical tradition, an activity which focuses upon language as the ordering force of the world. The general value of such an enterprise will be apparent from the discussions regarding the form and structure of language and its relation to subjectivity in the preceding chapters. In Chapter 1, the theoretical analysis of Spinozism identified the *inadequacy* of linguistic signs in the construction of knowledge both of the concrete body and of the thought of the subject. In Chapter 3, Lacan sought to theorize the *effects* of language and signification upon the constitution of the subject. Derrida's interest in this relation is somewhat different and the aim, at this stage, is not to draw parallels between Derrida, Lacan and Spinoza, but rather to emphasize the centrality of language and subjectivity to philosophical discourse.[1] As Derrida has famously remarked: 'there is nothing outside the text.'[2] However, Derrida is not *reducing* the significance of the social to a text as some critics maintain, rather he posits an intricate relationship between language and the world, such that the former, as sign, tries to represent or mirror the world in its fullest manifestations.[3] In other words, the concern with language as a support and vehicle for subjectivity initiated by Jacques Lacan, becomes with deconstruction, a strategic questioning of the foundations of language and the ontological status of the concept of subjectivity. If Lacan may be understood to rearticulate the logic of the signifier in relation to linguistic subjectivity, Derrida, it will be argued here, deconstructs this logic (of both the signifier and the subject) by utilizing *something other than the order of the human subject.*

This mode of deconstruction, whatever its conceptual structure or philosophical form (we have yet to investigate such matters) perhaps requires a *preliminary* definition. Deconstruction may be understood as an exploration, location and questioning of the conditions governing the possibility of conceptualization, together with a consideration of the historicity of meaning and the modes of subjectivity which may support philosophical systems of thought. The conditions which deconstruction may be understood to locate are linguistic as well as metaphysical; these conditions, we will argue, are by no means transcendental in any pure sense.[4] Deconstruction works to uncover the intersection, the inseparability, of language, thought and philosophy. In an early interview Derrida describes the practice of deconstruction in the following way:

> to 'deconstruct' philosophy ... would be to think – in the most faithful, interior way – the structured genealogy of philosophy's concepts, but at the same time to determine – from a certain exterior that is unqualifiable or unnameable by philosophy – what this history has been able to dissimulate or forbid, making itself into a history by means of this somewhere motivated repression.[5]

Derrida's project of deconstruction may also be understood as a new mode of thinking and writing. We can point out immediately that such an understanding of thought will not be an essential characteristic of an originary subject, neither will writing be synonymous with the *written word* – despite Derrida's interest in philosophical *texts*. Both writing and the text, and their broader relation to language, enter into a complex relation with the process of signification and the construction of meaning in philosophical discourse. It is impossible for language to live up to its ideal, namely to act as absolute referent for subject and world (object) and unite both in a single signifier. We have seen that, for Lacan, language and signification are closely bound to subjectivity and the possibility of articulating experience and *marking* the world in the form of knowledge. For Derrida too, philosophical discourse operates under the constraints of language. Indeed, the possibilities for thinking – and indeed for thinking the *limits* of conceptualization – are profoundly affected by the form and structure of language. The form of philosophical language may appear hidden and inaccessible; it is rarely considered as anything more than the communicative surface of discourse. However, if language, or the linguistic dimension of speech and signification, is viewed as *delimiting what may be signified*, then by critically exploring the limits of discourse and considering other possibilities for thinking, the form, the structure and the possibilities of discourse may be transformed. Here Derrida follows Heidegger in his interpretation of the ways in which representational thinking may delimit the possibilities for critical and creative thought within the field of scientific objectivity – a field which binds knowledge, truth and science very tightly together and is closely aligned with secular modernity. Derrida asks 'What is the system and history of representation?'[6] This form of representational thinking defines meaning only in relation to being; it understands the subject as *subjectum*, as the ground of truth-claims, and it also 'constrains us, imposes itself on our thought through a whole dense, enigmatic, and heavily stratified history.'[7]

The concept of the subject must be understood then – at least at this introductory stage in our discussions – in terms of its historicity and inscription upon the plane of meaning. Deconstruction seeks to undo forms of discourse that *centre* the subject in relation to knowledge, using the metaphysical qualifications of reflection and recognition (and all that will be shown to entail from this), in order to ascertain the mode of existence of objects and the production of ideas.[8] Thus Derrida is not abandoning the subject as his critics simplistically assert. Rather, he points out the *futility* of hoping to break with the metaphysical underpinnings of subjectivity in either their Cartesian, Kantian or Hegelian formulations, *without* considering the conditions of possibility that give rise to these conceptualizations of the subject. Even then, complicity with metaphysics remains because the subject has inscribed upon its surfaces the traces of all the conceptual transformations which gave rise to it. This demands that the site of the philosophical subject will be the object of a perpetual negotiation from the clutches of metaphysics. In his early works, *La Voix et le Phénomène* (1967) and *De La Grammatologie* (1967),[9] Derrida shows how the efforts of Husserl, Saussure and Rousseau to dispense with these foundations clearly failed (see Section II below). Deconstruction scrutinizes the conceptual formation of the subject, but it does so *not* from a transcendental position. Transcendentalism is a practice that is produced and named by metaphysics. It relies on a separation and ordering of fields of thought and being. By focusing on the order of the concept of the subject Derrida reframes the mode of questioning about the subject. The kind of the questions posed by deconstruction thus become important.

In the Introduction we pointed out that the mode of questioning regarding the form and attributes of the subject will itself *shape* the concept of the subject. Deconstruction asks the following questions: what conceptual apparatus *gives rise* to the conceptual form of the subject? How is the constitution of the subject achieved and how is self-certainty maintained? What structures pertain to consciousness? These questions do not involve posing the question what/who is (or is not) the subject, questions which already presuppose a certain ontological structure of the subject, and an account of its attributes, function, endurance and metaphysical status. Instead, deconstruction examines the various philosophical positions that try to constitute the subject without remainder, and shows how the assumptions regarding the structure of the subject which stress its qualitative difference from the object are unsustainable. The difference at stake here will be shown to be radically opposed to the dialectical construals of subject and consciousness. It is a difference, moreover, which can only be apprehended, Derrida would claim, by pursuing the spatio-temporal activity which allows the formation of concept and meaning to have definitive representation as sign. For deconstruction, this requires an interrogation of the origin, grounds, and limits of our conceptual, theoretical and normative apparatuses, and their fundamental relation to language and otherness.[10] It is this imperative that informs and structures the mode of questioning of the subject developed by deconstruction and insists on its political significance.

I. SITUATING DECONSTRUCTION: DERRIDA, ALTHUSSER AND LACAN

Derrida's early writings draw critically upon developments within linguistic theory and the discourse of structuralism considered in Chapters 2 and 3. In his deconstruction of Saussurean linguistics,

SUBJECTIVITY AND THE POLITICS OF *DIFFÉRANCE*   **113**

Derrida's writings also partially deconstruct Lacanian psychoanalytic theory (although his writing still draws upon a form of psychoanalysis), and illustrate a theoretical sensitivity to the Marxist project of Louis Althusser. However, many aspects of his work, particularly *Of Grammatology* and the essays collected in *Writing and Difference*, differ from these theorists in significant respects. Derrida considers the constitution of the subject and consciousness neither in terms of their structural interceptions and logical positions, or their unconscious resonances. Certainly Derrida does offer some critical comments on the constitution of the unconscious but this is not to be subordinated to a structure of language and exposed through instruments of metaphor and metonymy.[11] In contrast to Althusser and Lacan, Derrida views social relations and their contradictions as layered into a text without claiming to offer a meaning via the form of its structural organization. The uncovering of a true meaning does not appear to be the aim of deconstruction. If the deconstruction of literary texts has been a repetitive focus of literary theorists, a *methodology* for revealing a hidden logic not apparent on a traditional reading, this only bears witness to some of the ways in which Derrida's work is misappropriated. This reification of Derrida's philosophical interventions acts to conceal his theorization of the text in terms of the metaphysical more generally. In *The Tain of the Mirror*, Rudolphe Gasché notes that,

> the generalized concept of text is precisely that which exceeds the traditional determination of totality. In whatever the terms – empirical, idealist, or dialectical – *text* is defined, it always implies a closure upon itself with a clear inside and outside ... , the generalized text delimits the traditional totalizing concepts of what has been called text, ... [it] is rather that border itself, from which the assignment of insides and outsides takes place, as well as where this distinction ultimately collapses.[12]

In other words, a text does not totalize meaning, instead it is the *locus* of established philosophical, political and historical meanings through which we read and understand the world. A text will have already delineated the world of subjects and objects as an intelligible whole. Textualization then, is a process of signification. Further, if deconstruction subverts the epistemological and ontological centrality of the subject such that meaning is no longer viewed as *constituted by* a subject located outside the text then consciousness must likewise be located in the layers of this philosophical text. Hence Derrida's wider project could be understood to contest the autonomy of the text from the structures which give rise to it, and in the wake of this theoretical analysis to disrupt the primacy of the self-conscious subject. As he writes, 'deconstruction accomplishes itself through the deconstruction of consciousness.'[13]

What is the *status* of philosophical concepts for Derrida? Thus far in our discussions, we have understood concepts as inseparable from their philosophical and socio-political conditions of existence. Derrida's writing here is instructive because it understands that the construction or derivation of ideal concepts via a process of abstraction from the empirical cannot be secured. Concepts are always underscored by philosophical models; they are articulated by, inscribed within this model and their isolation from this philosophico-political genealogy is impossible. Concepts, then, will always bear the marks, not only of their past uses, but also of the dominant philosophical motifs of the epoch in which they are inscribed. This analysis is one which draws attention to the historicity of concepts as 'the condition of an access to science and philosophy',[14] the history of the meaning of being as an insight into the construction of the subject of philosophy and science as essence or origin. The subject is inscribed within various philosophical problematics; its ontological existence cannot be assumed but only constructed. The question of a break or wholesale transformation of epistemological foundations, such as that accorded to the work of Marx by Louis Althusser, assumes that one can rid contemporary theory of the philosophical baggage, the historical signification that comprises the notional meaning of a concept.

> [I]t is more necessary ... to transform concepts, to displace them, to turn them against their predispositions, to reinscribe them in other chains, and little by little to modify the terrain of our work and thereby produce new configurations; I do not believe in decisive ruptures, in an unequivocal 'epistemological break', as it is called today.[15]

When old concepts are transcended, deemed unscientific or ideological, certain power relations are operating on the philosophical terrain. In other words, a certain authority, what Derrida calls a 'logic of exclusion' is present, a logic which claims the superiority of one form of conceptual apparatus over another. Recourse to a *new* epistemological foundation cannot wholly hope to replace, or bracket, in a phenomenological sense, that which precedes it: 'There *is not* a transgression, if one understands by that a pure and simple landing into a beyond of metaphysics, at a point which also would be ... first of all a point of language or writing.'[16] We cannot then, dismiss past conceptual frameworks: 'Deconstruction is not simply a forgetting of the past'.[17] As we shall see below, Derrida is engaged in a form of history understood as the *historicity of concepts*. It is within the new theoretical field of understanding presented by deconstruction that philosophical concepts and their normative significance must be reinscribed.

History, structure, anti-humanism

The theoretical motifs of deconstruction have an ambiguous relation with structuralism. On the one hand, deconstruction exhibits many similarities. It pits itself against humanist discourses, it contests an expressive, totalizing view of the historical, and it closely tracks the questions of essence and origin, be they of history, subjectivity or meaning. On the other hand, deconstruction departs from structuralism in its insistence that 'structures [are] to be undone, decomposed, de-sedimented'[18] and their logic reconsidered in terms of *how* an ensemble may be constituted. Deconstruction demands that attention be given to the historical dimension of structures, to the *historicity* of history. It requires that historical analysis is not jettisoned *tout court* but that the conceptual possibility of the object of history, namely its philosophical bearings in relation to time, the subject, otherness and language are brought to the analysis.[19] Anti-historicism, like forms of transcendentalism, are always folded into language and this ensures that the specificity, the concrete location of text and event are not passed over. This criticism of teleological conceptions of history becomes one of several strategies adopted by Derrida to expose the ontological reliance of metaphysics upon a conceptual framework which strives for completeness, *telos* and finality.[20]

Now, despite his provocations against structuralism, Derrida's reading of the historical shares much with Althusser's. Derrida is similarly critical of a linear view of history and its dialectical formulations: 'Althusser's entire, and necessary, critique of the Hegelian conception of history and of the notion of an expressive totality, etc., aims at showing that there is not one single history, but rather histories different in their type, rhythm, mode of description – intervallic, differentiated histories.'[21] However, Derrida's departure from structuralism is also evident from his commentaries on it.[22] If deconstruction directed its attention to structures, 'to deconstruct was also an anti-structuralist gesture.'[23] Structuralism according to Derrida was guilty of a 'nostalgia for origins, ... a desire for a centre'[24] which in the work of Louis Althusser manifested itself in the lonely hour of the last instance. It is this dimension of structuralism, namely its emphasis upon an ever-present determining instance – even if this centre is always foreshadowed and overdetermined by its wider structural relations – which precluded an account of the *freeplay* of the structure, a play 'permitted by the lack, the absence of a centre or origin.'[25] We have seen above in Chapter 2 that, whilst Althusser rejected the formulation of structure as an expressive unfolding of its constituent parts, a number of dualisms (being and knowing, subject and object, ideology and science) nonetheless found their way into Althusser's epistemology, arguably because of the lack of attention given to the historicity of concepts employed.[26]

Deconstruction does nevertheless *appear* to share a common philosophical space with structuralism's *anti-humanism*. Derrida affirms a freeplay which tries 'to pass beyond man and humanism' and undermines the subject as the constitutive ground of meaning.[27] However, we will argue that Derrida does not abandon the subject, but deconstructs the philosophical positions which support the subject as a particular kind of being that is self-present, identical to itself, and precedes language and the securing of the object. In other words, 'a being who, throughout the history of metaphysics ... has dreamt of full presence, the reassuring foundation, the origin and the end of the game.'[28] Whilst Derrida's early works are written against the dominant backdrop of structuralism in France, as indicated in so many of his interviews, we will see that his theorization of subjectivity does not fit easily into an anti-humanist position. Rather it will necessitate a mode of thinking outside of this humanism/anti-humanism dichotomy.

In his early essay 'The Ends of Man' (1968), Derrida offers an important critique of the form of post-war French philosophy and its trend towards anthropological humanism. This, Derrida contends, is due largely to the humanist reading of Hegel, Husserl and Heidegger. Jean-Paul Sartre, the primary example of post-war philosophy in this text, subscribes to an uncritical use of the concept *réalité-humaine*[29] and fails to bring the history of this concept under critical scrutiny.

Derrida's intervention – which appears to take many of its cues from Heidegger's own 'Letter on Humanism' – is not a local interpretation. Its aim is to draw a much more significant parallel between contemporary humanist philosophy and the wider path of Western metaphysics. The language of metaphysics has not always been couched in terms of the subject 'Man', the consideration of philosophical discourses of the subject pursued in Chapter 1 have illustrated how philosophy is always engaged in a project which tries to seek out the finality, the end of knowledge in the essence or origin of consciousness, often in spite of the insecurities such a project encounters. With Hegel, notes Derrida, this metaphysical *complicity* between philosophical anthropology and the theological, comes to understand the subject as the vehicle of spirit or absolute knowledge: 'Consciousness is the truth of man inasmuch as man appears there in his being-past, in his having-been, in his surpassed and preserved, retained, interiorized (*erinnert*) and taken over (*relevé*) past.'[30]

Thus, the realization or *end* of man relies as much upon its original eschatological foundations as upon the dialectical movement which can give rise to pure knowledge. The stable referent of origin is thus essential to every claim to truth. Even Hegel's concepts of negativity and difference, as marks of finitude and contingency at the heart of dialectical movement, will not enable his speculative system to escape this onto-theological structure of metaphysics. Derrida's critique shares much with Hyppolite's reading of Hegel, producing a questioning of the dialectical mapping of history and the derivation of a self-conscious subject. Hence in 'The Ends of Man', Derrida points again to the fragility of the subject: 'The transcendental end can appear to itself and unfold before itself only in the condition of mortality, of relation to finitude as the origin of ideality. The name of man has always been inscribed in metaphysics between these two ends. It has meaning only in this eschato-teleological situation.'[31]

These criticisms pertaining to the centrality of consciousness within the original problematic adopted by Western metaphysics (and extended to include its contemporary existential and phenomenological formulations), have also been developed by Nietzsche and Heidegger. Derrida draws upon and develops these earlier positions. He joins Heidegger in questioning the alliance between a philosophy of consciousness as the ground of being and the onto-theological frame which contains it: 'the unity of man is not in itself called into question ... the history of the concept of man is never questioned. Everything takes place as though the sign man had no origin, no historical, cultural, linguistic limit, not even a metaphysical limit.'[32]

Heidegger's reading of the growing centrality of the subject in relation to knowledge and being-in-the-world (everyday existence) is also a *subjectification* of Being or *Dasein* as that which lies outside, beyond and before the subject as being. In his essay 'The Principle of Identity', Heidegger follows the pre-Socratic philosopher-poet Parmenides in understanding thought and Being as 'belonging together'.[33] Being can only be approached by thinking *differently*, more specifically, by thinking the ontico-ontological difference (the difference between Being and being). The origin of this difference, for Heidegger, is Being itself and it is the belongingness to being that is obliterated within metaphysics. However, Being is not to be interpreted as the hidden foundation of subjectivity; this would entail a metaphysical ontology which would stifle the ontico-ontological difference that allows difference-as-origin to be thought. 'Being, since the beginning of Western thought', Heidegger writes, 'has been interpreted as the ground in which every being as such is grounded.'[34] Metaphysics 'persists in the oblivion of Being'.[35] Its modern 'world picture' is one which privileges representational thinking, where Being is *reduced* to the assertive thought of the Cartesian *subjectum*. Its dominant *techne* has, for Heidegger, abandoned all sense of responsibility to Being. It is content with maintaining its scientific claim to truth, desiring the presence of the object to thought and it has abandoned thinking, if that 'thinking is of Being, belongs to Being, listens to Being'.[36] Language, too, has come to embody the structure of metaphysics; it objectifies the propositional mode, and casts its questions always within a deterministic frame; to speak and name is to erase Being. Metaphysics denies us both the essence of language as 'the house of being in which man dwells',[37] and its poetics which are able to think Being in its authentic formulation as the ontico-ontological difference.

Sharing a position which has been attributed to Lukács and Husserl in Chapter 2, Heidegger views the metaphysical subject as forever distorted by the technique of modern rationalism. The philosophical and historical narratives of both Husserl and Lukács drew attention to the closure enacted by the metaphysical formalism of modern thought and the reification of consciousness that ensues. For Heidegger, however, Being is an essential substratum existing prior to subjectivity; the history of metaphysics as humanism impedes and distorts the question of Being because it does not recognise or understand its primary call.[38]

Heidegger's *destruktion* or dismantling of metaphysics seeks to *unveil* the original, authentic sources from whence it arose. This begs the question as to what constitutes authenticity. How does one become an authentic being? How do we place value upon this notion of authenticity that is bound up historically with the ontological? For Heidegger, man is never a mere subject that receives recognition of consciousness and existence in a subject–object relation: '. . . before all this, man in his essence is ek-sistent into the openness of being, into the open region that lights the "between" within which a "relation" of subject to object can "be".'[39] It is the nature and form of this return to origins and its claim to authenticity that Derrida will deconstruct.

Derrida recognizes many important elements in Heidegger's questioning of the history of being; the careful historicization of philosophical concepts and their relation to difference as the unthought of metaphysics; the focus upon language as the erasure of Being and the prevalence of a linguistic form which seeks to rationalize existence and, perhaps most significantly, the thinking of difference *as* origin, a move which subverts the *telos* as well as the ground of metaphysics. However, in 'The Ends of Man' Derrida considers Heidegger's understanding of the absolute *proximity* of Being to Man[40] as illustrative of his recourse to metaphysics on three levels. Firstly, Heidegger risks privileging a form of presence-to-self which gives rise to identity rather, than opening the possibility of ontico-ontological difference. Secondly, the understanding of *Dasein* (as a thought of man) serves as an *ontological determinant* which requires only its unveiling.[41] Thirdly, Heidegger's recourse to metaphoric language, *Dasein* as home, homeland, shelter etc., further authenticates his position and sets his philosophy within the linguistic structures of Western metaphysics and seems to leave Heidegger revalorizing its dominant humanist motifs. This deconstruction of Heidegger's thought allows Derrida to use some of the former's own insights against him. In particular, it offers Derrida the possibility of considering the relation of *presence* to the structure of subjectivity and metaphysics more generally. Before turning to consider this theoretical infrastructure of deconstruction and its significance to the repositioning of the subject, Derrida's theoretical relation to Nietzsche must also be brought into the present discussion.

Like Heidegger, Nietzsche also rejected the conception of the subject founded by metaphysical humanism, and the echoes of a rationalist language that follow from it. Rationalism, and indeed subjective consciousness, are also viewed as the *consequences* rather than the cause of metaphysical form. Nietzsche posits an intricate relationship between metaphysics and language, between the existence of things and the structure of concepts and thus, for Derrida, 'contributed a great deal to the liberation of the signifier from its dependence or derivation with respect to the logos.'[42] Nietzsche questions the adequacy of linguistic expression to make sense of reality and remains suspicious of all claims to a single truth. He problematizes the relationship between metaphor and concept: truth is a 'mobile army of metaphors, ... illusions about which one has forgotten that this is what they are.'[43] Further, our grammar has privileged a certain metaphysical relation between subjectivity (particularly the 'I think' of the *res cogito*) and truth. If we discern the subject behind our ideas, our truths and our morals then we forget complex process of becoming which gives rise to all forms, ideas and subjectivities. Many metaphysical systems appear to place the subject in the position of origin, using ideas of thought, reflection and perception to designate and legitimate the emergence of knowledge. Nietzsche proposes to challenge this visual contract, the *ocularcentrism* which orders Western thought;[44] He incites us:

> to *see differently*, ... to think of an eye which cannot be thought at all, an eye turned in no direction at all, an eye where the active and interpretative powers are to be suppressed, absent, but through which seeing still becomes a seeing-something, so it is an absurdity and non-concept of eye that is demanded. There is *only* a perspective seeing, *only* a perspective 'knowing'; the more affects we allow to speak about a thing, the *more* eyes, various eyes we are able to use for the same thing, the more complete will be our 'concept' of the thing, our 'objectivity'.[45]

For Nietzsche, the subject is *multiplicity*,[46] a multiplicity which is also the generation and becoming concrete of a *will to power*. In its desire to rationalize knowledge and order relations between world and truth, this will to truth suppresses what it considers to be dangerous, impure and disruptive – in particular, the body and its affects. Yet the will is a multiple form, a plurality of sensations, forces, drives and affects which cannot be domesticated. The subject is identified as the origin of meaning only via a process of reduction and differentiation of the will which is designated a psychological property.[47] Thus, metaphysical knowledge responds to, reflects and repeats the desires and anxieties of the subject for purity and stability in meaning, its drive to create the world in its own image.[48]

However, the persistent suppression of the body and its affects within metaphysics has consequences which extend far into social and political relations. In *The Genealogy of Morals*, Nietzsche shows us that the concept of morality and notion of good arose not through any objective calculus of utility but out of a 'pathos of distance' from the lowly elements of society, deemed to be, in opposition, evil.[49] The etymological root of 'the good' across various languages is always associated with what is noble, aristocratic, of a higher order. Further, '[it] signifies one who *is*, who possesses reality, who is actual, who is true'.[50] To maintain conceptual and hence political power, the notion of the good must contain its opposite: 'it seeks its opposite only so as to affirm itself more gratefully and triumphantly'.[51] This logic follows for other conceptual oppositions; indeed here, both Nietzsche and Derrida point to the way in which certain privileged concepts are posited as properties of the subject, they come to mirror established norms concerning truth and objectivity, and thus become knowledge. In other words, and anticipating Foucault's view regarding the construction of truth, all knowledge derives from a perspectivism which has at its source the will to truth, mastery and power.

Derrida develops these critical overtures on the status of metaphysics and the subject in *Of Grammatology*. In this text Derrida formulates an interpretation of language and otherness which is used to explore the relation between *logos* and signification. Following Nietzsche, the genealogy of philosophical concepts is shown to be inextricably bound to the structure of language. Moreover, it is the thinking subject who holds together language and worldly object. If thought is assumed to precede language, then Derrida exposes the ways in which consciousness is viewed as acting as a vessel for thought and language. In his readings of Husserl and Saussure, Derrida deconstructs the stability and primacy of the subject who, through a process of self-reflection upon the object of knowledge is also viewed as holding an ontological relation to speech. For many philosophical positions, this speaking subject is placed at the origin of representation and it is the stability of this ontological relation, the 'metaphysics of presence', which deconstruction contests. This dominant episteme is neither ancient nor modern. Its ontological conditions of existence are given by the unity shared by voice (speech), subject and truth, a unity which produces a logocentric structure of

philosophical knowledge.⁵² It is to an analysis of this ontological unity
that we shall now turn.

In *Speech and Phenomena* and *Of Grammatology*, Derrida deconstructs the transcendental phenomenology of Edmund Husserl and the
science of linguistics developed by Ferdinand de Saussure. In these
essays, philosophical thinkers whose primary efforts are to rid their
analyses of psychological and empirical accounts of the subject –
Saussure by a largely synchronic account of the laws of language which
requires no organizing reference to the 'human person', Husserl by a
transcendental reduction of the level of analysis to exclude the communicative and psychological aspects of language and subjectivity – are
shown to have recourse, *by necessity*, to certain residual historico-
metaphysical presuppositions which ruin the theoretical *purity* of their
analyses. The writings of Husserl and Saussure exhibit, on Derrida's
reading, a preoccupation with a linguistic form which produces, in its
wake, a privileging of a subject as self-presence.

Husserl's entire phenomenology is motivated by what he understands as a crisis in the constitution and understanding of meaning, a
crisis which has to extend to the realms of subjectivity and philosophical method. The objective of phenomenology is to return to
philosophy its true beginnings, its sense of rigour, its concern with the
constitution and emergence of worldly things, and its first-order validity,
that is, a fundamental interest in the pure, *a priori* analysis of essence.
Thus phenomenology leaves Hegel and returns, with Husserl, to the
Kantian problem of the transcendental, namely how to derive for
existent, empirical subjects a form of knowledge which can ground itself
within a conception of consciousness which can be adequate to itself.
Contra Kant, Husserl's objective is to locate the origin of experience in a
realm which does not distinguish the abstract and the concrete subject
but understands subjectivity to encapsulate the realm of the ideal alone.
Now, Husserl's philosophical trajectory is vast and multi-faceted and
the concern here is a limited one, namely to point, with the help of
Derrida's deconstruction, to some of the possible limitations of this
transcendental, phenomenological conception of subjectivity. There is
no denying however, that the Husserlian gesture – which never simply

repeats a past philosophical gesture, be it Kantian, Hegelian or Cartesian[53] – brings many questions that are central to the concerns of this study to the fore.

In *Logical Investigations* (1900), Husserl set out the groundwork of what was to become his central preoccupation in his later major works *Cartesian Meditations, Ideas I and II* and *The Crisis of the European Sciences*. In this early text, his project is to construct a theory which could account for an *a priori* structure of language at the level of a transcendental consciousness, hence freeing subject, object and idea from the idiosyncrasies of the empirical, worldly realm.[54] This project involved Husserl taking issue with the concept of meaning employed by Frege which emphasized a distinction between *Sinn*, meaning in its most general extension (ie as referent), and *Bedeutung*, meaning as signification.[55] Husserl endeavoured to replace this duality of meaning with a phenomenological conception of meaning which was founded primarily upon an *expressive* form of *intuitive* signification. This isolation of a pure, ideal realm of meaning comprised two philosophical movements at the level of language and subjectivity. The first involved a bracketing of what Husserl described as the *indicative* aspect of meaning. This signifying dimension of language is forever contaminated by the natural attitudes of psychologism, historicism, anthropologism, biologism, in short, all those quasi-sciences which viewed the existence of the object uncritically and naturalistically. In much the same manner as Althusser after him, Husserl is concerned with the absolute givenness of objects, not the way in which they are thought, felt and described, but their inner-essence as they appear as objects to consciousness.[56] This form of phenomenology shares structuralism's desire to avoid historicism and psychologism and the presuppositions that both embrace, the former by denying history and subjectivity their formal level and reducing all sense and meaning, form and content, to a speculative present, the latter by adopting a naturalistic conception of consciousness tied, irrevocably, to the sensible, empirical world.[57] As Derrida observes, it is as if 'by a strange paradox, meaning would isolate the concentrated purity of its *ex-pressiveness* just at that moment when the relation to a certain outside is suspended.[58] The true foundations of predicative meaning can only be reached, according to Husserl, by grasping consciousness *in itself* as transcendental subjectivity. This constitutes phenomenology's second philosophical movement: the eidetic reduction of subjectivity to a mode of pure, constitutive cognition. In contrast to the sensible sphere, this ideal, intelligible sphere is able to delimit a sensory, primordial, *expressive* aspect of meaning, grounded not through consciousness's communication with reality, but via an interior, pre-discursive, intuitive relation with meaning and the ideality of objects. This pre-theoretical realm produces ideality through original experience; moreover, it does not need to be inscribed in a signifier. Instead, it rests upon a direct, internal, immediate and *natural* relationship between transcendental subjectivity and expressive meaning. Furthermore, it is the *proximity* of primordial intuition to the truthfulness of objects (their ideality) that renders the indicative, sensible, worldly aspect of meaning fictitious and unnecessary.

Husserl's phenomenology is not so much an abandonment of the subject–object dualism as a rigorous rethinking of its mode of constitution. Thus, phenomenology privileges the transcendental sphere of ideality over the sensible world. Intuition, a pure thought, a pure givenness immanent in consciousness is understood to be the objective source of all things. This sphere of ideality becomes the origin of signification and representation. As stated above, language and meaning are tied to this expressive notion of signification where being is present to itself and its immediacy denotes a 'living present'.[59] Thus Derrida argues that Husserl expects language not only to unify life and ideality (the empirical and the transcendental) but also to frame and act as a border to the phenomenological space of meaning itself. This priority of language masks what Derrida will call the 'disquietude of language' as that which inaugurates the very possibility of sense, world and signification.[60] Yet Husserl does not question the structure of language, its possible autonomy, its power and its *insistence*. This transcendental subject (being-as-self-presence) is given a certain permanence by its ability to *repeat* the production of meaning indefinitely and transcend both the spatial and temporal dimensions, and the contingency of empirical existence. This act of repetition, auto-affection, the self-presence of the self to itself, is produced by the primordial unity of speech and subjectivity. It is speech which is able to preserve and contain the sphere of ideality; wholly intimate with its speech, the subject's proximity to language guarantees self-presence and immediacy. Speech and language are immanently related through the intuitive constitution of meaning on the part of the transcendental subject. As Derrida comments,

consciousness owes its privileged status (about which Husserl in the end never asked *what it was*, in spite of the admirable, interminable, and in so many respects revolutionary, meditation he devoted to it) to the possibility of a living vocal medium [*la vive voix*]. Since self-consciousness appears only in its relation to an object, whose presence it can keep and repeat, it is never perfectly foreign or anterior to the possibility of language.[61]

Nevertheless, if, for Husserl, the voice is able to represent a non-present future as well as a non-present past in the immediate, atemporal identity of presence as self-presence, this is a philosophical move that cannot be contained. The punctuality of the subject as self-presence is achieved only by excluding past and future dimensions of temporality and their effects upon the unity of consciousness and speech, and by reducing the order of representation so that it excludes the realms of non-presence and non-identity which are also, for Derrida, constitutive of speech and language. Much hinges upon whether the purity of the phenomenological reduction can maintain itself, and it can only maintain itself, according to Derrida, via an essential affinity with metaphysics.[62] What is the relationship between language, the ideality of objects and self-presence? Upon what conceptual order do these relations stand? What is the relation between Husserl's conception of the sign and his construction of the subject to the history of metaphysics, a metaphysics identified 'under the rubric "voice" as a value of presence, presence of an object, ... self-presence in so called living speech and in self-consciousness?'[63] What moreover, is the relation of *writing* to this rubric? Each of these questions will deconstruct the order of language, assumed by Husserl to have a certain immanence and immediacy to consciousness. Each also deconstructs the unity assumed between voice and subjectivity, and the opposition between indication and expression, empirical and transcendental.[64] Both of these pre-suppositions are ontological *decisions* which mask complex interdependencies. Might not these relations each be irreducible and ceaselessly productive of difference and otherness? Are they not marks and traces of language that will fissure and destabilize phenomenology's contract with a (hidden) philosophy of the subject?[65]

Of Grammatology extends these same questions concerning the metaphysical foundations of language and subjectivity to Saussure's theory of language and signification, and Rousseau's account of the origin of language. In many ways, Saussure may be considered to challenge the centrality of *logos* to the order of signification by proposing that the relationship between the object of investigation and the means of representing that object in knowledge will always fall short of true or necessary correspondence. Saussure thus described the bar between the signifier and the signified (s/S) to be forever shifting and slipping away from its task to represent and conceptualize meaning. The sign is able to salvage its claim to meaning only with reference to a whole range of other signifiers in the language system. Hence, meaning is given *not* via a single identity between signifier and signified, but through a structure of oppositions and differences that characterize language, that is, by their structural relation to a network of sounds and images that construct *other* signs. Signification is thus a relational process. Unlike Husserl, Saussure's consideration of the differential structure of the sign appears to challenge an idealist account of the representation of objects by consciousness. Not only has it drawn attention to the organizing principle of logocentrism which fixes and ensures the grounding of the sign, establishing a chain of binary oppositions which can enframe (and legislate against) all claims to multiple meaning, but this construction of the sign as linguistic symbol also challenges the metaphysical *logos* by identifying the formal structure of language as indispensable to the functioning of signs and the containment of meaning by the speaking subject. It was precisely this philosophical critique of subjectivity and meaning, observed above in Chapter 3, that drew Lacan to Saussurean linguistics.

Derrida's deconstruction of self-presence and its boundedness with the phoneme identifies both Husserl and Saussure as submitting to a philosophical logic which disrupts their central preoccupations with a dimension of language, its expressive and synchronic dimension, respectively. Similarly, Rousseau's account of the rise of inequality and difference reduces both to the evils of writing and thus identifies, for Derrida, 'a decisive articulation of the logocentric epoch'.[66] In all three cases, the philosophical limits and the conceptual closure of their positions can be interrogated by focusing upon the subordination of writing to the articulated presence of speech and subjectivity.

For Saussure, it is the consideration of the origin of language and speech as indistinguishable from that of writing which pushes him to reflect upon the status of writing in the constitution of the sign. Like Rousseau before him, Derrida claims that Saussure reduces writing to the status of natural reflection, a representation of speech, and understands it as a dangerous force which subverts sensibility and the alleged unity between phonic substance and sign as rational *logos*. The written word signals an impurity, a crisis of signification. In his *Discourse on the Origin of Inequality*, Rousseau points to the primitive subject's use of gesture to express wants, an act with no apparent desire for the communication of thoughts and ideas, whilst later in the essay, language and the written word are linked to the development of culture and technology. The disrupting and unsettling characteristics of writing are understood by both Rousseau and Saussure to stem from cultural, technological and political transformations.

These explanations of the relation of writing to speech, the one as natural interior, the other as external, evil manipulator, lead Saussure and Rousseau to an account of the internal structure of language which emphasize sign and sense as forming a natural unity. Saussure's reduction of the sound-image to a psychic-image produces a conception of the sign which relies upon a form of metaphysical self-presence; the presence of speech is reflective and expressive of the subject who delineates and makes present the object. Rousseau identifies an *original capacity* for speech which distinguishes man from the animal species and enables the perfectibility and self-development on the part of man. Here, speech is a natural, expressive essence of subjectivity; it is based on the equilibrium of genuine need and passion in communication and, as with other discussions of such naturalism, it secures the presence of the subject to itself. Both Rousseau and Saussure rely upon a naturalistic psychology which brings with it the unavoidable problems of sense, intuition, self-presence – all of which have also been understood to form the basis of Husserl's transcendental phenomenology. They also fail to develop, according to Derrida's reading, the concept of writing and inscription within speech itself. These traces of language, what Derrida call an *arche*-writing, are irreducible to speech and anterior to all that becomes constituted as sign. They mark the relationship with the other, the movement of temporalization, and language as writing.[67] Writing then, by its situation as excluded other of speech is here 'destined to signify the most formidable difference'.[68]

Derrida's focus upon writing as an irreducible trace produces the contestation of the phonic unity of the sign; writing 'menaces substantiality'[69] and questions the origin and the historicity of the sign in Husserl, Saussure and Rousseau. The movement of signification is considered to be a dynamic process; the production of a transcendental signified occurs only by suppressing, deferring and reducing arche-writing and difference to the narrow concern of mirroring speech rather than permitting the possible articulation of speech and writing. Here writing is not synonymous with the written word. Rather, it stands in for 'whatever eludes, subverts or opposes the discourse of logocentric reason.'[70] It is not only Husserl's phonocentrism which debilitates writing; it is the foundational concept of being as presence, and its relation to Husserl's concept of the subject as transcendental consciousness, which illustrates the primary gesture of metaphysics. This gesture attempts to fold the subject in upon a single essence or origin and involves a form of technological mastery that represses and silences the difference, the *other*, which is prior to the constitution of presence. This difference is associated with an indiscernibility at the heart of subjectivity and language. It introduces provisionality, deferral, mediation and repetition into the phonic sign such that pure self-presence is impossible to achieve. It cannot be plotted in a linear fashion as what *gives rise to* presence; neither can it be captured by dialectical synthesis. It undermines, divides, confuses the articulation of self-presence. Thus Derrida writes of it:

> In this pure difference is rooted the possibility of everything we think we can exclude from auto-affection: space, the outside, the world, the body ... Hearing oneself speak is not the inwardness of an inside that is closed in upon itself; it is the irreducible openness in the inside; it is the eye and the world within speech.[71]

Like Nietzsche's challenge to an ocularcentrism that ties subjectivity and vision to self-presence, Derrida points to inscription as a differentiating structure which 'does not depend upon any sensible plenitude, audible or visible, phonic or graphic.'[72] The exclusion of writing is symptomatic of the wider metaphysical structure that orders the concepts used. Logocentrism ignores the significance of temporality to conceptual formation and *shrinks* the space within which the structure of consciousness is delimited. There is no *un*conscious here which could introduce other temporal relations (i.e. repressed, deferred, displaced moments). It is the phoneme, tied to the subject in a natural unity of immediate presence, that intercepts the world of objects; the differentiation described as *formative* of the sign by Saussure and expressed in his rejection of the centrality of the subject as speaker, is transformed at the ontological level into a primitive intuitionism between subject and speech which 'expels its other'.[73]

Derrida calls this passing over or masking of difference and altarity the movement of différance, understood within deconstruction as the condition for the possibility and function of every sign and meaning, every subject and movement of history. However, différance is difficult to define, not least because Derrida understands it as fluid, mobile and dynamic in form but non-presentable in discourse. It is the denial of the play of différance which authorizes the plenitude and certainty of subjectivity and speech, and yet différance interrupts every self-identity and exposes the contingency of its metaphysical claims to transcendence. There is, for Derrida, no thing that *is* différance; it cannot be theorized within any type of discourse; it has no unitary conceptual form. It cannot be exposed, nor can it refer to an origin, a hidden Being. Rather, it is strategic, adventurous, without *telos* or finality.

Différance cannot be claimed by any system of thought as its founding moment because it is irrevocable. As Derrida notes, it is a reserve out-standing, incomplete and without economy. Paradoxically, it is also what gives rise to completion or presence: there is no economy without différance. It is, at best, a 'regulative concept'.[74] In Husserl's phenomenology, for example, the distinction between intuition and signification is produced by the play of différance. It organizes their constitutive differences:

> What is written as différance, then, will be the playing movement that 'produces' ... these differences, these effects of difference. This does not mean that différance ... is somehow before them. Différance is the nonfull, nonsimple, structured and differentiating origin of differences. Thus the name origin no longer suits it.[75]

If différance is that which produces the possibility of a philosophical discourse which is present to itself and thus able to differentiate itself through some means from its past, it must interweave these temporal and spatial movements of discourse. Différance can refer to a 'configuration of meanings'.[76] It must *defer* itself to the discourse within which it moves, and yet before this reduction of temporal space or *delay*, it has already produced *differences* within the order of thought. Thus the sign 'which defers presence, is conceivable only on the *basis* of the presence that it defers and *moving toward* the deferred presence that it aims to reappropriate.'[77] Derrida describes this movement of différance in discourse, the becoming-space of time or the becoming-time of space, a construction which has obvious resonances with the language of Hegelian phenomenology.[78]

However, the relation of différance to the Heideggerian ontico-ontological difference between *Dasein* and being discussed in Section I above is inescapable. This originary difference remains, for Heidegger, forever unthought by a metaphysics geared towards technological mastery. For both Heidegger and Derrida, Being is always reproduced within a field of presence and through the domination of the linguistic form. Yet there is, for Derrida, no transcendental Word of being communicable to beings. Whilst Being is not simply the ground of thought for Heidegger, it is equated with *presence* in a way that difference will always be marked on the horizon of Being, hence covering over the trace, the différance, upon which metaphysics must inevitably falter. Thus Heidegger's discourse of Being too, falls prey to logocentrism. Différance cannot be named as Being, unlike the concept of difference employed by Heidegger to account for the root or origin of authentic Being; it requires no movement of signification, no authentic phoneme, and no transcendence of the system of metaphysics. Thus, différance 'is not a present being, however excellent, unique, principal, or transcendent. It governs nothing, reigns over nothing, and nowhere exercises any authority ... The unfolding of différance is ... not solely the truth of Being, or of the epochality of Being.'[79] Given this lack of foundation, this absence of ground, can any *status* be attributed to the critical operations of différance?

Deconstruction: status, critique and method

Deconstruction operates upon the *infra-structure* of metaphysics;[80] a place within ontology, the core of philosophical existence where concepts are delineated, given substantiality, boundaries and limits. It seeks out the closures which govern and authorize discourse, signs, systems of meaning and it is, therefore, a profoundly political enterprise. On the epistemological level, deconstruction exposes the conditions of existence for the *positivity of the real* and the structure of all that is political. By opening up the fractious constitution of the ontological as *foundation* of metaphysics, deconstruction marks all discourse with an *undecidability* that destabilizes ontology and hence contests the conception of the subject as originary ground. What are the status of these critical operations? What is the *scope* of deconstruction? What, moreover, is its *relation* to the metaphysics of presence and the philosophy of the subject? These questions are identified in a discussion of the risks of deconstruction in *Of Grammatology*:

> Operating necessarily from the inside, borrowing all the strategic and economic resources of subversion from the old structure, borrowing them structurally, that is to say *without being able to*

isolate their elements and atoms, the enterprise of deconstruction always in a certain way *falls prey to its own work*.[81]

If deconstruction, as claimed by Derrida, subverts the infra-structure of metaphysics, its conceptual foundations as well as its edifice, it must necessarily operate *inside* its system; in other words, it cannot step outside the structure of language, or the conceptual apparatus of metaphysics. However, these metaphors of inside and outside betray the spatial and temporal relations that deconstruction unravels. The borders constructed by philosophical discourse – between, for example, its object and the sensible world, language and the ruse of technology, representation and the contingency of all future presentations – try to separate firmly the problematic of philosophical discourse from the conditions which give rise to it. These conditions cannot be reduced to the theoretical level of Generalities I identified in Chapter 2 by Althusser because, for deconstruction, these regions (namely, Generalities I, II and III) cannot maintain their distinctiveness. The conditions which underlie these regions are deferred, displaced, delayed and sometimes just incorporated into the problematic *without* recognition, in which case their anomalous character, their altarity, pervades the discourse and affects its constitution and coherence. For this deconstructive view, the opposition between ideology and science theorized by Althusser is itself unsustainable. The possibility of being inside or outside science leads to the reduction of the historicity of concepts to the problem of history. This opposition permits, in turn, for the entry of the concept of the subject as a *theoretical limit* in Althusser's work. Similarly, in Lacan, the concept of subject, critics of his method argued, produced the effects of a classical structure of representation which was due largely to his uncritical reception of the sign and the phonocentrism which is understood, by Derrida, to underlie it. The distinction between inside and outside must henceforth be renegotiated; it is far too narrow for deconstruction. As Derrida writes, 'the idea that we might be able to get outside of metaphysics has always struck me as naive. ... when I refer to the "closure" (*clôture*) of metaphysics, I insist that it is not a question of considering metaphysics as a circle with a limit or simple boundary.'[82] Thus, '*There is no sense* in doing without the concepts of metaphysics ... we cannot utter a single destructive proposition which has not already slipped into the form, the logic, and the implicit postulations of precisely what it seeks to contest.'[83]

The risk that deconstruction may 'fall prey to its own work' discussed above is an unavoidable risk for discourses whether they claim to be idealist, materialist or transcendental in theoretical structure. Resources from its oppositional *other* will always be present within the conceptual structure; thus *all* structures are contingent and provisional forms because the concepts inscribed within philosophical positions are themselves unstable events of thought. This is not to say that deconstruction can simply rid a discourse of its metaphysical heritage and its genealogy, rather it claims to locate the points of exclusion and forces of rupture within the discourse. *The deconstruction of the subject will always take place upon a metaphysical terrain that will continuously attempt to reincorporate it into the dominant ontological structure.* It is often argued that as a political *strategy*, this act of deconstruction has limits, it points to an aporia within thinking that cannot be surpassed, in which case, deconstruction serves best as a methodological principle for reading texts. Such a position risks jettisoning the critical import of deconstruction. The act of deconstruction, as our discussions hereon will illustrate, is not a celebration of the play of difference, but an account of the significant relation between ontological and *political* foundations and the limits of their claims to completeness. In this way, deconstruction *may* account for structures of power within political discourse, and by exposing their conceptual logic, invite us to question what may be their possible future shape and form. At the same time, such a description of deconstruction as a viable analysis of the political, that is, as a form of political *critique*, may rely upon deconstruction taking up a definable position within political discourse, and hence risks the very incorporation of which Derrida is so wary. Before turning to this matter, let us first consider Derrida's more recent reflections on the subject.

Deconstruction and the problematic of the subject

I have never said that the subject should be dispensed with. Only that it should be deconstructed. [1981][84]

It always seems to me to be more worthwhile, *once this path has been laid down*, to *forget* the word [subject] to some extent. Not to forget it, *it is unforgettable*, but to rearrange it, to subject it to *the laws of a context that it no longer dominates from the center*. In other words, no longer to speak about it, but to write it, to write 'on' it as on the 'subjectile,' for example. [1991][85]

The theorization of the concept of the subject is central to de-construction. Indeed, it has been a key component of Derrida's thinking from the 1960s to the present. We have considered the pivotal role his early writings give to self-presence in the constituting moment of philo-sophical discourse. This is a non-original moment which accompanies all philosophy and it is closely aligned with the speech and perception of the subject whilst simultaneously suppressing the spatio-temporal conditions that produce the very possibility of discourse and subjec-tivity. However, deconstruction's repositioning of the subject as an inherently unstable and contingent metaphysical form has led to claims that this theoretical enterprise reduces the subject to a textual effect which is devoid of critical import.[86] Matters are altogether more com-plex for deconstruction. Derrida does not dispense with, or liquidate, the subject, but deconstructs and resituates it in relation to language and truth. It is not enough to understand the subject as reduced to an effect of the text. These problems have already been encountered in relation to the subject as an *effect* of ideology (Althusser), or as an *effect* of the signifier (Lacan). Needless to say they will also be rehearsed in relation to Foucault's conception of the subject as an *effect* of power. We have pointed out that Derrida's use of the notion of text is general; here we must point out that his use of the concept of effect is to be developed in its productive, dynamic sense. There is no reference to cause, to determination, to an original action or entity (be it being or the text). Différance upsets the temporality that underlies all cause–effect rela-tions. The concept of effect signals an opening up, a deconstruction, of all causality to difference; it produces differential relations, multiple effects. It is misleading, therefore, to attach a reductive reading to this construction of the subject.

For deconstruction, the analysis of the subject is aligned with the focus upon language, presence, writing and différance. We have seen that in Derrida's critique of logocentrism, différance precedes all claims to presence and speech. Thus, 'the speaking or signifying subject could not be present to itself as speaking or signifying, without the play of linguistic or semiological *différance*'.[87] In other words, différance envelops the subject *before* itself, forever preventing and unsettling its attempts to *become* a subject. This ensures that the moment of constitution or closure of subjectivity, by whatever theoretical means, never quite arrives. This failure of constitution, moreover, cannot be isolated as an original fracture; it cannot simply precede the subject. Rather it co-exists with, and accompanies the subject. There is no room for chronological, or teleological reference here. Différance cannot be claimed as the origin of any philosophical activity; it cannot be the intention or the intuition of any transcendental subject. It is only by successfully answering the question 'What or who is différance?' that the constitution of différance could be attributed to the differing/deferring of a self-present subject. The structure of the question 'What is?' betrays its ontological source. It is a question which remains in the propositional mode and tied to the metaphysics of presence and it presumes that something like a substantial consciousness is actually possible without residue. These natural and necessary questions direct much of the phonic attentions of Western metaphysics. They presume the constitution of an answer, a response by an original, knowing subject. Thus Derrida surmises: 'This movement of différance is not something which happens to a transcendental subject; it produces a subject.'[88]

In the same way that Derrida viewed logocentrism as leading to the suppression of writing, we can here argue that a conception of the subject as presence, transparency, identity, amounts to the suppression and mastering of différance. The speaking subject can only become self-present to itself by passing through différance. However, this claim to mastery is always forestalled, interrupted, postponed; it cannot be guaranteed, nor can the subject be stabilized. It is only by undoing its own historicity that this relation could be secured; this is considered to be an impossible task. The deconstruction of the subject thus recognizes that the subject's condition of possibility is also the condition of its *impossibility*: to constitute itself involves opening itself to contingency, and to the play of auto-affection and self-deferral. Hence, the gesture that summons the subject to know itself is also that which establishes its ec-centric existence, its dividedness from itself. Subjectivity undergoes a perpetual play of (de)constitution or 'constitutive loss of self'.[89] In a recent discussion of this problem, Derrida uses the term *desistance* to describe the 'imprint of the ineluctable that constitutes the subject'.[90] The subject then, desists *'even before being the subject of a reflection, a decision, an action or a passion.'*[91] As Lacoue-Labarthe points out in support of this theorization, the subject 'is fictional at its very origin and only accedes to self-hood, if it ever does, through being *supplemented by a model or models which precede it.'*[92] It has been argued throughout this study that the subject is always tied to a specific problematic, a conceptual system which forms the horizon for thinking a particular concept of the subject. Different philosophical models, be they tied to a dialectic, transcendental or phenomenological in form, constitute the subject in very different ways. What they all share to varying degrees, according to Derrida, is the containment and ordering of difference. By assuming some facet of being to be ontologically given, these systems risk repressing the residual difference which then allows the subject's status to emerge as author of meaning and sense. What function does a philosophical model serve, and what may be its political significance? If there is no ontologically given subject but instead always a metaphysical gesture of containment, how can we understand the subject as a site of multiplicity *awaiting* stabilization as philosophical and political form? Deconstruction returns us to the central paradox of subjectivity, namely that every model which seeks to construct or constitute the subject also risks reifying its conditions of existence. As Derrida has shown in the case of Lacan, the displacement of the subject still requires recourse to the structure of the subject. Caught within this paradox, Lacan cannot avoid recourse to logocentric models of containment despite his efforts to resituate the subject. Let us consider further Derrida's account of this paradox.

Derrida and Lacan

If as we have argued above deconstruction focuses on the *historicity of concepts*, then the concept of the subject is constituted 'only in being divided from itself',[93] a division that was central to the Lacanian conception of the subject. Derrida is explicit in his criticisms of Lacan's philosophical system. As we shall see below these criticisms follow many common themes with the deconstruction of Lacan espoused by Lacoue-Labarthe and Nancy in Chapter 3. However, it should be clear that Derrida does nonetheless share with Lacan a preoccupation with the structuring function of language in the formulation of the subject. For both thinkers, the subject is not a meta-linguistic substance, instead it is a being dispersed and inscribed upon the field of language, a field which is *other* than the subject; it is, as Derrida writes, 'the becoming-absent and the becoming-unconscious of the subject'.[94] However, it can be argued that the *effects* of the subject are inseparable from the psychoanalytic concepts of repression and sublimation, and the reference to a deferred/displaced temporality which these concepts in turn evoke.

What may Lacan's psychoanalytic account of the subject share with deconstruction? In *Of Grammatology* Derrida writes that 'the deconstruction of logocentrism is not a psychoanalysis of philosophy', instead (and in Nietzschean style) 'logocentric repression *permits an understanding* of how an original and individual repression *became possible* within the horizon of a culture and a historical structure of belonging.'[95] If psychoanalysis explores the site of the subject and the structure of self-identity, deconstruction probes the conditions of possibility of psychoanalytic discourse itself. Is this not a strategy that psychoanalysis can perform itself? For Derrida, at least as far as Lacan is concerned, the answer must be a resounding no. Furthermore it is this failure to account reflexively for the fragility of its own claims to truth which appears to make of Lacanian discourse an uneasy companion to deconstruction. Thus, in one of his early interviews, Derrida made the case for the almost complete lack of reference in his work to the psychoanalysis of Jacques Lacan. Here he developed a number of criticisms of Lacan's project which linked his discourse with the metaphysics of presence. For example, psychoanalysis seeks a knowledge or truth of the subject's unconscious which denies the undecidability that is characteristic of deconstruction: the end of analysis, for Derrida, is an impossibility. To the extent that Lacan embraces the philosophical concepts of Hegel and Heidegger, he cannot avoid the mimetic repetition of the structure of Western metaphysics. Lacan remains uncritical of this phenomenological importation, using the notions of 'unveiling' unconscious language, revealing the *aletheia* or truth of the subject, without any explanation of why these concepts should be posed in relation to Truth/Being. Hence Lacan carries an ontological baggage that can only reduce the radicalism of his claim concerning the psychoanalytic subject constituted through the spacing and deferral of language. Furthermore, the focus of psychoanalysis is the ontological divisions, masculine and feminine, established through systematic closure and presumed to be stable universal categories. Its subject, although decentred, is defined teleologically with reference to an origin and relies on the dialectical mediation and *aufhebung* of the couplets, presence and absence, lack and desire. This illustrates, for Derrida, the phallogocentrism of Lacan's position which imposes closure upon a heterogeneous system of differences.[96] The tripartition between the symbolic, imaginary and real is viewed as performing this exclusionary moment: all that is *between* the subject and its constitution which could inscribe the *impossibility* of its identification with the social symbolic is accounted for within this 'unmodifiable transcendental or ontological structure' which reconstitutes itself indefinitely.[97] In contrast, Derrida is interested in what 'escapes it, disorganises [this structure], but without letting itself be conceived in the categories of the "imaginary" or the "real".[98]

The privilege given to speech is perhaps the central feature of Lacan's system which predisposes it towards logocentrism. Dispelled and returned through language, the unconscious speaks in analysis via metonymy and metaphor. Metaphor effectively returns the subject to him/herself. Provisionally lost, meaning is retrieved in the *full speech* of analysis. It thus assists the constitution of the subject; it *permits* self-presence. However, for Derrida, following Nietzsche, the movement of metaphor is the movement of idealization. It imitates truth; it reproduces truth as origin.[99] The figural meanings of metonymy and metaphor appear to overdetermine the arbitrary nature of un-conscious language. As Rene Major puts it, their logic still obeys 'a phonematics and the principle of identity, foundational of a philosophy of presence.'[100]

In view of the criticisms advanced above there appears to be little scope for pursuing the strategic intersections of deconstruction and psychoanalysis concerning their respective critiques of the subject. However there are three important issues which remain outstanding. First, Derrida employs *throughout* his work a number of concepts which cannot easily be severed from their psychoanalytic roots. *Of Grammatology*, for example, contains a certain kind of psychoanalytic reading of Rousseau's *Confessions*. Certainly Derrida's reading of Freud is much more complementary than that interpretation of Lacan charted above. It is perhaps to Freud that we must look for a non-linguistic account of the unconscious compatible with deconstruction.[101] Second, there is perhaps a quasi-'concept' (the word is used tentatively) within both discourses which appeals to the problems of spacing and deferral, has as its primary function the activity of disruption, and plays an intrinsic role in the (incomplete) constitution and unravelling of subjectivity: différance (or desistance) and the real.[102] It is within the conceptual structures of deconstruction and psychoanalysis that our argument can be drawn out. Third, we must point out that Derrida's more recent reflections on psychoanalysis give due regard to the proximity of Lacanian discourse to deconstruction, particular in the early works.[103] Let us look more closely at this intersection.

Derrida accords two psychoanalytic functions to différance. First, différance is an economic detour which 'always aims at coming back to the pleasure or the presence that have been deferred by (conscious or unconscious) calculation'; second, différance is the relation to 'an impossible presence, ... as the death-instinct.'[104] Both functions understand logocentrism to be governed by a desire for completeness, representation and certainty, and by a certain desire for repetition. Like Nietzsche, and Freud before him, Derrida pursues the 'heterogeneous modes of conflictuality', the general economy of forces that is prior to the subject's psychic organization. These differentiating forces are located *outside* the subject, suggesting that the subject's identity cannot be contained within the boundaries of a constituted selfhood. The subject is an effect of this matrix of forces. If it may be described as the subject's *structure* of existence, it is one that is never fully constituted but is nonetheless performed and reiterated through all cultural and political identifications. Repetition acts to confirm and stabilize identity.[105] Just as for Freud, the perceiving consciousness (ego) which gives rise to representation has already been interrupted by the heterogeneous economy of unconscious forces, so it is for Derrida that the reality-principle will constantly seek to delay/defer unconscious resonances in order to protect itself from the economy of death. At the same time, the desire of the subject to satisfy the death-instinct pushes it toward this absolute, undifferentiated origin. If différance may be understood as 'the difference between the pleasure principle and the reality principle' then it must also be the condition of possibility for the human.[106] The structure of the subject is precisely this oscillating difference, this hiatus, which signals the perpetual failure of philosophy to constitute subjectivity as a self-conscious unity.

Using the theoretical tools of psychoanalysis, Derrida links the conditions of possibility for representation with death. Representation does more than encounter the residues of the unconscious. Freud's mystic writing pad identifies the traces of the psyche as having a graphic form: 'a lithography before words: metaphonetic, nonlinguistic, alogical.'[107] The non-transcriptive trace recognizes no distinction between signifier and signified and cannot be assimilated with phonic language and the spoken word. The topography of traces that constitute the unconscious, also produce language and meaning, including what may be called the speech and writing of the subject of plenitude. We have seen in Chapter 3 that, for Lacan, the subject *disappears* and what remains is only the vocal imprint of the subject-as-signifier. For Derrida too, as soon as the subject is effectively written however, it *desists* and is simultaneously put under erasure. 'The trace is the erasure of selfhood, of one's own presence, and is constituted by the threat or anguish of irremediable disappearance.'[108] The subject's relation to this anguish, or death-drive is therefore part of a general economy of forces, a series of traces, which are able to constitute the subject, *make possible* individual repression and the repetition/ resistance of psychic life. The trace is *prior* to the formation of the subject; it is 'a root torn away from itself, necessarily impure and structurally doomed to compromise, to speculative transaction.'[109]

Now it should be clear that both deconstruction and psychoanalysis occupy what Derrida calls the *double-bind*. The double-bind articulates the permanent risk of being both inside and outside the metaphysical. Deconstruction cannot simply usurp metaphysical concepts for its own uses; it also opens itself up to the possibility of reabsorption into metaphysics. This is a position that psychoanalysis must share with deconstruction and all other radical discourses (particularly through its own attachments to *telos* and truth).[110] The double-bind is a condition of all analysis, whatever its subject matter; it is a 'transcendental sickness of the analytic.'[111] In its pursuit of the incessantly sliding signifier, does psychoanalysis encounter its own internal limit? Can the conceptual structure of the real stall this moment of incorporation? In a recent essay 'Reason from the Unconscious', Rene Major observes in Lacan 'a radicalisation of the non-correspondence or non-relation between signifier and signified to the point where the strongest insistence is given to the function of the bar which separates them, as instituting the cut in the discourse through which the subject is inscribed as discontinuity in the real.'[112] The implication of this interpretation is to link very closely the work of Derrida and Lacan as critics of traditional conceptions of subjectivity. Far from being the transcendental category envisaged by Derrida, the discussions of Chapter 3 have viewed the Lacanian real as *limiting* the very possibility of subjectivity. Can the real introduce a fissure, a truncation, a space of deferral in the subject which prevents its full constitution? Like différance, the real remains unconceptualized. It disrupts, antagonizes and haunts the subject of the symbolic, placing itself in close proximity to the corporeality of the subject, that is, the topography of drives which structure the psyche in a differentiated and heterogeneous manner.

However, this reading of the real can only be addressed with, and through, the epistemological tools of deconstruction. These include its focus upon the spatio-temporal movements of concepts which produce difference, exclusion and opposition.[113] It is the possibility of deconstructing the so-called 'tri-partite' Lacanian order, undoing the *point-de-capiton* that fixes language into a system of repetition and difference without remainder and gives rise to signification, which in turn produces this reading of the real. It may be argued that the real has a similar conceptual structure as différance. It is its disruption of signification rather than its function to usher forth the 'truth of the subject' that must be emphasized. In what ways can such a conceptualization of subjectivity, overdetermined by differentiated forces which inscribe their functions upon its structure, be utilized in political critique? It is to the question of deconstruction's mode of political critique that we will now turn.

III. DECONSTRUCTION AND POLITICAL CRITIQUE

Deconstruction cannot first be otherwise than ... a series of genealogical questions on the whole of discourse that has lent justification to politics, that has constructed political philosophy.[114]

In *Specters of Marx*, Derrida claims that deconstruction is a radicalization in a certain spirit of Marxism.[115] This recognition of a debt to Marxism is particularly interesting in light of Derrida's earlier acknowledged silence on the subject.[116] What then, is the relation of deconstruction to the politico-philosophical positions of Althusser and Lukács presented in Chapter 2? What, if anything, might deconstruction contribute to a theory of ideology and the construction of the ideological subject? To what *kind* of politics does deconstruction direct its interest?

If deconstruction explores the heterogeneous conditions governing the possibility of conceptuality and focuses upon the genealogy and historicity of meaning then both of these activities are deemed inherently political. This is not only because all concepts have a normative value, neither is it because the very distinctions between concept and world, transcendental and empirical, ideality and the real are broken down by deconstruction. Deconstruction's mode of questioning points to *the insuperability of the political horizon of philosophical questions*. There is no border between the political and the philosophical. Both share a common foundation and if philosophy has maintained a consistent disregard for its socio-political conditions of existence, deconstruction politicizes the ground of philosophy and opens up a more urgent mode of questioning concerning the possibilities of subjectivity and the political.[117]

Lukács' analysis of bourgeois philosophy as exhibiting a reified essence may be understood as illustrative of the mutuality of political and philosophical levels of analysis. Lukács develops a social ontology which unites the essence of proletarian consciousness with the possibility of knowledge and his discussion of the *antinomies* of bourgeois thought, with its entrenched dualisms that reflect the dislocated consciousness of its founders, has a certain resonance with Derrida's account of logocentrism and its attendant binarism. However, the parallel can be drawn only so far.[118] *Contra* Derrida, Lukács inscribes consciousness with an essence which is manifested in accordance with a social ontology; essence and social existence are dialectically mediated by real history, and consciousness approaches its *telos* through the unfolding or manifestation of an original relation. In short, there is an essential *complicity* between political foundation and metaphysical system in Lukács' thought. Deconstruction avoids any such complicity. The ontological containment of the concept of the subject by Lukács is viewed as an *impossibility*; its essence is always fractured, unfinished, incomplete. It can never stabilize and fill out political forms. Certainly the logic of politics is to solder social relations and identifications by forging an imaginary (ideological) wholeness, a stable social bond, a communal relation, but the deconstruction of this logic reveals its ontological interior as fragile and requiring the negotiation of constitutive differences. This account of a differentiated ontology (always undecidable, and unique in the singularity of forces which give rise to it) brings new resources to political theory. The questions of language, the form of knowledge and the possible modes of subjectivity discussed in this chapter all delineate the form of the political. Indeed, Derrida's most recent work broaches such questions directly and the analysis here will consider deconstruction's status as *political* critique.

With apparent disregard for Derrida's early deconstruction of Rousseau in *Of Grammatology*, where the logocentric assumptions surrounding the grounding of political concepts which are brought to bear on the analysis, many commentators prefer to emphasize the refusal of politics in deconstruction.[119] Often viewed as both politically irresponsible and nihilistic, deconstruction as the contestation of theoretical and conceptual foundations remains for many a largely metaphysical gesture. Peter Dews notes the *disanalogy* between texts and institutions:

Derrida cannot help but acknowledge that institutions are not simply textual or discursive structures, but rather consist of 'a powerful system of forces and multiple antagonisms' ... Given that institutions are traversed by relations of force, it is difficult to see how deconstruction could be applied to them. For deconstruction is centrally concerned with exposing the mechanisms whereby texts generate effects of meaning and truth while, at the same time undermining them .... *Political antagonisms, however, cannot be reduced to logical contradictions.*[120]

Dews' criticisms are echoed by other theorists who lament, at worst, the disappearance of the political, at best, its sheer indeterminacy when deconstruction surrenders its explanatory capacity, particularly regarding its non-reliance upon any transcendental vantage point or foundational claim to truth. Furthermore, if différance is seen to take up no ideological position or label, cast no value judgement upon the nature of political contract, order and power, it becomes inaccessible and devoid of ethical status.[121] These criticisms, however, do not consider the inter-relation of the ontological with the political, or question the *logical form* of the concept informing its normative application, and they tend therefore to dissociate concept formation from its clear political effects. This leads to a privileging of a particular form of the political, broadly associated with institutions and 'real' systems of power and gives rise to a dual theoretical manoeuvre. First, politics is understood literally as the empirical realm of positive social enquiry; any abstraction from its form always returns to the analysis of its *existence* rather than its *essence*.[122] Second, the method of abstracting from the political is always a rational or transcendental retreat undertaken to produce a deeper knowledge of the facts. Indeed, these kind of interpretations continue to maintain a series of conceptual oppositions between theory and practice, (scientific) truth and ideology, and of course, politics and the text.[123] It is perhaps the latter opposition between politics and the text which leads to the association of Derrida's alleged apoliticism with a naive pantextualism. To summarize, reading Derrida according to the *spirit* rather than the *letter* reduces the text to the literal, to the metaphysical real.

In his article 'The Deconstruction of Politics', Bill Readings argues that deconstruction cannot be translated easily into a politics. The equation of the literal and the political leads to the positing of politics as an empirical *outside* of the text. To think politics as the empirical, as the self-evident, ignores those domination effects which take place *before* the arbitrary naming of the political.[124] In such a view, essence and appearance comply with, and mirror each other: the real as the empirical is seen to be truth itself. Such a conception of the political is radically opposed to deconstruction. Deconstruction points to the limits of teleological projects that seek ideological closure (and the stability, symbiosis between subject and political form, be it that of community or nation). William Connolly notes how 'the desirability of unity actually *devalues* the political dimension of life.'[125] To seek the *telos* of politics (arguably the primary goal of all modernist projects), is to *displace that which is profoundly political*, to envision the self-presence of the political, and the eradication of difference and contradiction, the erasure of différance.

Thus far the analyses of this chapter have argued that it is at the level of ontology that the properties of self-presence are constituted. It is upon this ontico-political terrain that the fate of the political is decided. Political concepts such as justice, community, ideology and freedom are *founded* at this place, and their normative significance must be understood as arising through the initial displacements from the différance that embodies and gives them form. For Derrida, 'the space and time of this displacement [opens up] a gap, ... recalls the essential ontological fragility of the ethical, juridical, and political foundations' of these concepts. Furthermore, if 'these foundations ... remain essentially sealed within a philosophy of the subject',[126] as Derrida contends (and political theory has often rested upon an elaboration of the *nature* of the self which becomes its ground), then a critique of this subject, such as the one initiated within this particular work, produces in its wake a questioning of political foundations. Let us then consider the foundation of the concept of ideology in light of our preceding analysis.

Deconstruction, Marxism and the concept of ideology

In *Specters of Marx* Derrida emphasizes the irreducible heterogeneity of Marx's texts.[127] In his *Philosophy of Marx*, published in the same year (1993), Etienne Balibar also points to his intention in his own reading of Marx 'to project voices into the text and to interpret its silences.'[128] Both positions acknowledge the non-contemporaneity of Marx's different voices. It is this which gives Marx an enduring legacy despite the effects of the contemporary political conjuncture upon the reception of his writings.[129] Given the rather more immediate legacy represented by Althusser's (and Balibar's) influential reading of Marx, it is important to trace the ways in which Marx is read through the lens of deconstruction, which is very much *after* Althusser, if not simply *post-structuralist*.[130] Unlike Althusser whose central task is to enact an epistemological break in Marx, Derrida focuses on the openness of the oeuvre. This can be designated as that oscillating space that is at once ontotheological but at the same time opens up a space of freedom initiated by critique. From within the space of undecidability Derrida will unearth a continuity between *The German Ideology* and *Capital*. If deconstruction is a radicalization in the tradition of a certain Marxism this is only because Marxism cannot be interpreted as, or reduced to, a fixed body of ideas subject to demarcation.

Against what he views as the dogmatic and revisionist tendencies of Marxism, Derrida wishes to emphasize an indeterminate level of Marx's writings. It is this level of indeterminateness which may rescue Marx's vision of politics from eschatology and teleology (and political closure) but *without* embarking upon the Althusserian path of ahistoricism. In effect, Althusser tries too hard to rid Marx of the historical relation; against the former Derrida will reaffirm a relation to past and future, a *messianism* without teleology which he presents through the multiple figure of the spectre. For Derrida, Marxism will always be attached to the metaphysical; it traverses the spaces of anthropologism as well as the rationality of science and this renders all efforts to extricate its concepts from humanism impossible encounters that will always find their efforts forestalled. Like all other critical discourses then, Marxism occupies a double-bind that will always make its philosophical basis a precarious and risky one. It was perhaps the ambiguity and impurity of Marxism's metaphysical relation which led Althusser towards the construction of a closed, unified theory of knowledge. This could, he thought, protect Marxism from its many intruders: metaphysicians, humanists and philosophical speculators of all kinds. At the same time however, Althusser also jettisoned the *critical value* of his conception of ideology which made sense only within the context of a split between science and metaphysics. In his desire to expiate Marx and arrive at science as a kind of pure presence, Althusser, in much the same manner as the early Husserl, reduced the formation of knowledge to the level of ideality.[131] If we are now to follow Derrida in his focus on the formation of ideology then due regard must be given to the interminable aspect of critique which deprives all concepts of their closure and unity. This has already been considered in terms of the historicity of concepts and their sedimented relation to time, language and otherness. We need only recall Derrida's comment on Althusser's position here: ideology and science appear cut off from their history and from the semantics sedimented within it. There is no study of the endurance or residues of metaphysical pre-suppositions in Althusser's theoretical concepts.

Let us now consider the content of Derrida's reading of Marx and more specifically the space of ideology. How does Derrida propose to read Marx? In the first place he identifies the presence of a certain idealization of concepts in Marx's texts. This is particularly evident in the concept of ideology which is often developed with reference to religion, mysticism and theology, that which Derrida generalizes under the 'patrimony of the idol'.[132] Marx often describes ideology in terms of its production of 'ghosts, illusions, simulacra, appearances, or apparitions'.[133] From the discussions of the camera obscura in *The German Ideology* to that of commodity fetishism in *Capital Volume 1*, the religious metaphor is a central organizing principle. Whilst the apparent nominalism of the concept may appear to cover over or displace its theological enframing, the religious imagery of the concept is tied to Marx's reading of ideology as imaginary, as hallucinatory, as apparitional and phantasmatic, all of which have a *ghostly* character. Derrida observes how, for Plato, the 'phantasma' always connects the figure of the dead soul with the living-present; it lets itself appear and *give body to the idea or the concept* only against a 'background of death.'[134] It is this phantasmatic spectre which for Derrida haunts Marx's own understanding of the present and the past in the intro-ductory pages of both *The Communist Manifesto* and *The Eighteenth Brumaire* and it is the non-presence of the spectre which for Derrida gives rise to an *hauntology* (rather than an ontology) that permits the apparition, engenders the analogy, produces the concept and the mode of life.[135] Thus:

> the specter weighs, it thinks, it intensifies and condenses itself within the very inside of life ... The latter therefore no longer has and must no longer have, in so far as it is living, a pure identity to itself or any assured inside: this is what all philosophies of life, or even philosophies of the living and real individual, would have to weigh very carefully.[136]

In contrast to Hegelian idealism where spirit also appears to inhabit consciousness and inspire its journey of discovery and enlightenment,

Derrida emphasizes the (never quite) absent corporeality of the ghost, not merely as an inhabitation of a living body but also as an incarnation in another (cultural and institutional) space which is at once covered over and never wholly masked.[137]

Clearly, the spectre is not the imprint, the secret or the spirit of consciousness and for this reason Derrida objects to its derivation from a psychology of imagination or even a psychoanalysis of the imaginary. This 'ghost-effect' may live on in the subject who is haunted by the spirits of the dead. It may also produce quasi-objective incarnation effects in a technical or institutional body. Derrida writes of the relatively autonomous body of ghostly reality; the spectre cannot simply be a fiction or an illusion of the imagination.[138] The spectre is that which cannot be pinned down, accounted for, or made present, and yet, like différance, it is what may produce appearances and their absence. Thus for Marx, the mystical character of the fetish, its ghostly character, is inseparable from the production of commodities. Like a spectre, the fetish inhabits the structure of the commodity form *and* it leaves a mark on the subject's perception, its experience of the commodity and the social relations supporting it, but it cannot appear itself. Derrida's question regarding this spectral production of social illusion, what we may call the *binding* of the social relation, is rather like the question posed by Lukács and Althusser. In Derrida's words: 'how do those whom one calls "men", living men, temporal and finite existences, become subjected, in their social relations, to these specters that are relations, *equally social* relations among commodities.'[139] Is it not significant that, like Lukács and Althusser before him, Derrida also reads Marx's enigmatic formulations of the structure of the commodity form and its capacity to hide the secrets of human oppression and exploitation from the subject's 'lived-reality'? As we have observed in Chapter 2, Lukács traced the effect of the commodity form upon the subject's experience through the concept of reification but his emphasis was very much upon the disjuncture or dualism between consciousness and world, between essence and appearance. This dualism was also reflected in Lukács' rather empiricist rendering of ideology as a class-derived way of thinking about the world. Ideology becomes, for Lukács, something that may reactivate class-consciousness, but only when it has mastered and understood the world of appearances. On the other hand, Althusser's rendering of ideology as a representation of an imaginary relation unties this contract with consciousness and recognizes the transmogrifying capacity of ideology. For Althusser, it is ideology that *produces* consciousness and subjectivity which in turn become its appendages.

To some extent, we must understand Derrida as *deepening* this Althusserian insight as to the structure of ideology. Derrida's is a much closer reading, *avant la lettre*, of commodity fetishism. Whereas Althusser mapped his reading onto a Lacanian conception of the imaginary, Derrida remains critical of the category of the imaginary and its proximity to subjectivity and perception. Lacan's theory of the mirror-phase belongs to a scopic economy where it is the role of the gaze, the *imago*, to engender a perceiving subject even if it is one who doubts the existence of perception. Now given Althusser's critique in *Reading Capital* of the negative effects of a philosophy of vision, we may have expected this inexorable tie between recognition and inter-pellation, between visibility and the perceiving subject, to be unravelled a little. How can we think the production and appearance (in its effects) of *what itself cannot appear*? What is the relation between the spectre, spectrality and ideology? Perhaps these questions are too close to a phenomenology for Althusser's comfort but they remain central to Derrida's analysis for whom spectrality and phenomenology are inseparable: the former inscribes the possibility of the latter and, like différance, must remain the fragile condition of possibility for any appearance. Without the *es spukt*, the haunting, stalking and habita-tion of that place where a sense of subjectivity is born, there could be no guise of self-identity. Without spectrality, the guise of autonomy that clothes the commodity and invests the social bond would be in-explicable. This phantasmagoria, this mode of producing the appear-ance of commodity form as natural and as discontinuous with labour-power and social relations is the 'activity' of the spectre. In a manner similar to Derrida's reading of the supplement in Rousseau, the spectre seeps into Marx's social ontology of human need and it underlies his narrative of historical beginning.[140]

We can understand spectrality as that which gives (apparitional, amorphous) form to what escapes the construction of ideology. It is precisely because of the former's indeterminateness, its existence as mark, trace and inscription rather than pure presence that Derrida can claim that there can be no subject *of* ideology and no ideological subject. The logic of interpellation described by Althusser is underiv-able.[141] If the phenomenal form of the world is spectral and the subject, too, is embodied by a spectre, is *itself* a spectre, then the singular call, the 'Hey, You!' of ideology, will have to reincarnate the spectre and incorporate the alterity implicit in every subjectivity. The function and aim of ideology is to incarnate the closure of the horizon of meaning and to fix the boundaries of subjectivity as contained self-identity, but the subject can never be identical with itself, or the other. Both of these political efforts to contain subjectivity and meaning are undermined by deconstruction. As Derrida puts it, 'absolute identification is absolutely impossible'.[142]

Returning to the subject?

When discussing the place of the subject in the writings of Althusser, Lacan and Foucault (albeit very briefly), Derrida is at pains to emphasize that, despite the rather superficial tendency to declare the liquidation of the subject, mainly on the part of their commentators, each of these thinkers remain attached in some way to the ontological question of the *subjectum*. We have observed in our own analyses of Althusser and Lacan the presence of a certain paradox: the subject is at once a *requirement* of analysis and something that is radically *displaced*. Will this produce, by metaphysical default, the resurrection of the subject as *subjectum*? Moreover could this also be the case with Derrida's own reinscription of the site of subjectivity? Does not deconstruction too, draw argumentation if not philosophical sustenance from the 'metaphysics of the subject'?[143] Too much is at stake in our response to this question for us to respond readily in the affirmative. How does Derrida propose to negotiate this problem which is no less than the double-bind that ties all critical discourses to metaphysics?

Deconstruction hovers precariously around this question, and this paradox, of subjectivity. It can find no secure resting place, no ideological home, and this is precisely its significance for the discussions in this book. There is always a risk with critical thought that it may reify the past and ignore the complexities of philosophical positions, pass over its inheritance and forget its dependency on the history of philosophy. It is for this reason that a study of the genealogy of the subject remains an important project. For deconstruction, there is no subject without a passage through différance, which is at one and the same time a passage through language, otherness, history and politics. Certainly, the problematic of the subject *persists* in Derrida's writings but this is not because he wishes to resurrect the question '*What is the philosophical subject?*', a question which, for some, has been long dead and buried. If the concept of the subject endures, it is because its continuous and radical problematization *sustains* its existence. Yet deconstruction also shows us something more – *or something less* – as Geoff Bennington points out, it shows us philosophy in a reflexive mode, that is, philosophy in the process of thinking its own conditions of *existence* as well as possibility.[144] As we have observed in Section II above, deconstruction recognizes that the condition of possibility of the subject is also its condition of impossibility. In this vacillation between possibility and impossibility, the alterity that dislocates the founding gesture of subjectivity may be glimpsed. In the process of philosophy encountering its own aporias, the subject seems to unravel the very ground of its own thinking. It should be clear that Derrida's location of the question of the subject cannot simply be viewed as a resurrection of the subject.

We can illustrate this paradox more directly by considering some of Derrida's further reflections in the interview cited above.

> For me, the discussion would begin to get interesting when, beyond the vested confusion of this *doxa* [which is the death of the subject], one gets to a more serious, more essential question ... first: what becomes of those problematics that seemed to pre-suppose a classical determination of the subject (objectivity, be it science or other – ethical, legal, political), and second: who or what 'answers' to the question 'who'?[145]

Here Derrida proposes first, to return to the question of the *effects* of this rethinking of the subject on classical positions, and second, to consider the position from which the subject may speak and act. The first proposition indicates the task as one of thinking the genealogy of the subject: to show how there is no subject which, after the moment of deconstruction, can come back to the same place. This chapter has shown how much of Derrida's project has been one of thinking this uneasy relation. The second proposition opens up the paradox we have been outlining: what is still required by classical and deconstructive positions alike is a certain responsibility. This notion of responsibility is 'irreducible to and rebellious towards the traditional category of "subject" ', and it is *necessarily* 'inseparable from a whole network of connected concepts (property, intentionality, will, conscience, consciousness, self-consciousness, subject, self, person'.[146] This relation surely places deconstruction in close proximity to those classical philosophies of the subject referred to above because responsibility seems to provoke a certain intention or agency. For Peter Dews, this move to a certain ethical responsibility entails a 'pre-ontological structure of receptivity and donation' for deconstruction that in the 'later Derrida' becomes an enterprise 'which attempts to liberate concepts from their metaphysical determinations.'[147] However, we are not required to move, with Dews, to emphasize the emancipatory logic of deconstruction (which may in fact undermine its operations); the ethic of responsibility must be viewed within that aporetic context discussed above which both requires the subject even as it is undermined. The same uncomfortable status must surely be given to our notions of autonomy and power as *potentia* (taken up by Foucault in Chapter 5) as well as the network of connected concepts noted above. In this way deconstruction calls for a more *exacting* articulation of philosophical and political concepts.

Does the subject make a nostalgic return in deconstruction? Or is the structure of this question one which simplifies deconstructive operations? This chapter has developed an account of deconstruction which draws attention to an irreducible relation between philosophy, language and political theory. This focus upon language is tied to a range of ontological questions which consider the historicity of the concept of the subject, i.e. not only its conditions of (im)possibility but also its conditions of *existence*. Deconstruction opens up ontology to the problem of time; it forces spatio-temporal relations of a non-reductive kind into basic questions of essence. It this way, it undermines all ontological determinations and opens up the question of the structure of the subject. Différance cannot *determine* the subject as a philosophical concept; rather, it inhabits subjectivity and renders it fragile and unstable. It contests, in other words, its *full* constitution. For deconstruction, philosophical concepts are always rendered political in form precisely because of the displacements and repressions which ensue at the level of ontology. Hence, there can be no *subjectum* that returns in deconstruction, but only a subject sustained by a web of ontico-political relations.

Let us briefly return to the problems encountered in earlier chapters. Throughout this book, a number of different perspectives have been adopted in order to *articulate* the philosophical unease generated by the question of, and the paradox of, the subject. Our discussions of Cartesian doubt or scepticism, the unhappy consciousness (Hegel), the reification and the *Spaltung* of the subject (Lukács and Lacan, respectively) could be considered as containing the problematic of the subject and reintroducing a new figure of the subject. Each is understood by deconstruction to be a philosophical account which is always over-determined by the differential forces which inhabit its conceptual formation and will, in turn, *give rise* to these theories *of* the subject. By proposing that its own analysis be irreducible to any conception of the subject, and by deconstructing the constitutive ground of subjectivity, Derrida utilizes, as noted in the introduction to this chapter, *something other than the human subject.*

5

THE DISCURSIVE
CONSTRUCTION OF
THE SUBJECT

In one of his many responses to the question regarding the centrality of the subject in his writings, Foucault states his concern to be with the relations and forces which constitute a subject rather than with a subject whose reason and agency constitutes knowledge and endows the world with meaning. In a summary of the critical task of his work, Foucault writes that his aim is:

> to challenge again the theme of a sovereign subject which would come from the outside to animate the inertia of linguistic codes, and which would deposit in discourse the indelible trace of its freedom; to challenge again the theme of a subjectivity which would constitute meanings and then transcribe them into discourse. Against these themes . . . to pin-point the origin of the roles and the operations exercised by different 'discoursing' subjects.[1]

With these remarks, Michel Foucault's writings are placed alongside those of the other authors prefigured in this book. We must, however, be cautious. It would be a mistake to assign to Foucault the provision of a general theory of the subject. If this focus on the subject punctuates Foucault's many discursive analyses of knowledge, power and subjectification, then it is a focus engendered by a critical intervention which seeks to open up a space for thought, a thought which is always specific, diagnostic and strategic. In the modern era, a will to truth and a residual philosophy of the subject hold on tightly to the event of subjectivity and arrest the power of thought.

The subject cannot be assigned either origin or essence.[2] Instead, Foucault's writings trace the conditions which have given rise to a philosophy of the subject. However, as we have argued in the case of Derrida, these conditions do not have either a formal or a transcendental status:

> It is not a matter of defining the formal conditions of a relation to objects; it is not a matter, either, of determining the empirical conditions that at a given moment might have permitted the subject in general to be conscious of an object already given in reality. The question is one of *determining what the subject must be*, what condition is imposed on it, what status it is to have, and what position it is to occupy in reality or in the imaginary, in order to become the legitimate subject of one type of knowledge or another.[3]

Similarly, 'one has to dispense with the constituent subject, to get rid of the subject itself, ... to arrive at an analysis which can account for the constitution of the subject within a historical framework.'[4] This analysis operates at once on an ontological level and on the terrain of the political. It is an ontological project because Foucault remains interested in what engenders, modifies, shapes and opens up a mode of social being, an order of subjectivity. It is deeply political precisely because this ontological intervention resonates with, and effects, all political forms. In *The Order of Things*, Foucault will study the forms that knowledge has taken throughout the ages: the epistemological containment of possible disorder, the tabulating of identity and difference, and the spatio-temporal disruption of representation that, with the onset of modernity, gives rise to the epistemic conditions for the birth of the subject, Man.[5] In *Discipline and Punish* his interest will turn to those relations of power which produce forms of subjectivity and seek to contain and tame the subject through techniques of normalization. It is somewhat difficult to characterize this project, formulated as it is against the backdrop of post-war French thought. We will try now, at least to provide a sense of the influences upon Foucault's method, and his interest in the problem of the subject.

Between phenomenology and structuralism

Foucault's thought was deeply influenced by Nietzsche, encountered by way of his early interest in the work of Maurice Blanchot.[6] It was also influenced (but perhaps less visibly so) by the thought of Kant, Husserl and Heidegger.[7] These philosophical relations will be articulated at

various points in the chapter. It is however, difficult to compartmentalize Foucault's varied *oeuvre* and it is not my aim to do so here.
If Foucault is concerned with how particular forms of thought and
knowledge *appeared* in the world and according to what conditions,
then he must share with Husserl a concern with the first-order problems
of existence and possibility. This relation to phenomenology in its
Husserlian form is fraught with tensions, marked as it is with a concern
with the subject as a first-order philosophical problem. There is no philosophy of essences in Foucault's writings, be they of subject or truth.
However, a sense of a crisis in knowledge, as well as a concern with
the generation of appearances, imbue his thought with a phenomenological quality.[8]

Herbert Dreyfus and Paul Rabinow go as far as to claim that, with a
Husserlian gesture, Foucault practises his own novel form of phenomenological reduction and endeavours to rid discourse of the kinds of
the problem of meaning and existence that haunt the question of the
subject. Can such a exit from philosophy be engineered? Like Husserl
before him, Foucault claims that his method is one 'purged of all
anthropologism'.[9] Yet Foucault still utilizes a conception of the subject
and continues to explore the conditions governing the emergence of
subjectivity. Hence we will see a paradox of subjectivity pervading his
work: at one and the same time, Foucault rejects 'the unceasing efforts
of consciousness turned upon itself, trying to grasp itself in its deepest
conditions'[10] but he continues to concentrate his own reflections upon
the *discursive* conditions which may themselves give rise to forms of
subjectivity and consciousness. We have observed the movement of this
paradox in earlier chapters where the subject is at once a central focus
of a work and something which is to be radically displaced and
rethought. All of our discussions on the theme of the subject, particularly deconstruction, have shown the way in which the language of
philosophy is folded into ontological questions, in short, it is impossible
to break with the history of metaphysics. This history is contaminated
by conceptions of the subject which cannot be reduced, excluded or
easily elided. Rather they must be encountered anew. The paradox of
the subject may be (and we must speculate at this early stage in our
discussions) that the problems and tensions which inhere in it are themselves transferable to other ontological levels and concepts, although
not in any simple sense. In other words, the *problems surrounding
subjectivity may be reinscribed within, and imprinted upon, Foucault's
own concepts*. Will Foucault's conception of discourse, however it is

presented, itself *bear the marks* of a *displaced* problematic of the subject? This chapter will trace this paradoxical space of subjectivity (which is to be found, at one and the same time, *between* phenomenology and structuralism, and at both of their limits) at work in the thought of Michel Foucault. Let us first sketch out briefly Foucault's relation to structuralism, and to three of his contemporaries whose writings have been the focus of this study, Althusser, Lacan and Derrida.

It is often maintained that Foucault's early work on the structure of knowledge is akin to a form of structuralism. Whilst Foucault clearly shares the anti-humanist position which formally unites the thought of Althusser, Lacan and Derrida, the label of structuralism is all but a superficial one (as it is when applied to these latter three thinkers too). If Foucault explores the rules governing the emergence of specific forms of knowledge, these rules are not really law-like, ahistorical or transcendental in form. He certainly shares Althusser's critique of historicism and empiricist method that we developed in Chapter 2 and *The Archaeology of Knowledge* (discussed in Section I below) rehearses many of the problems that Althusser likewise grappled with in *Reading Capital*. Later, in *Discipline and Punish* we find Foucault pursuing a construction of subjectivity that draws upon and yet exceeds Althusser's formulations of the subject in 'Ideology and Ideological State Apparatuses' (see Section III below). However, in *The Order of Things* Foucault describes structuralism as 'the awakened and troubled consciousness of modern thought.'[11] Structuralism cannot extricate itself from the problem of the subject merely by banishing it (which is nothing less than a phenomenological bracketing) because this simply transfers the problem of the subject, through categorical inversion, to a new series of problems subordinated to the question of structure. Aware of these problems, Foucault's relation with structuralism is an uneasy one.

Foucault remained resolutely critical of Lacanian psychoanalysis in the very few references he made to it. He once noted the importance for his work of his discovery of Lacan in the 1950s, and many of Foucault's essays and books of the 1960s are marked by a preoccupation with the limits, and transgressive possibilities of, signification.[12] However, in later works, particularly *The Archaeology of Knowledge*, Foucault tended to separate his own conception of discourse from any theoretical allegiance with linguistics – especially the structuralist variety. Similarly, whilst he recognized the potentiality of psychoanalysis as a 'counter-science', as that which 'beyond man, allows one to know, with positive knowledge, what is given to and what escapes consciousness',[13] psychoanalysis remained tied, in Foucault's own analyses (see *The Order of Things*, discussed below), to the space of the human sciences. It can only answer, explain and somewhat crudely classify man's tortured dreams, thus restricting the possibility of thought to the boundaries of the subject's phenomenological experience.

Significantly, Foucault appears to share much with Derrida's deconstructive project. In common with deconstruction, the analysis of discourse seeks no origin and it is opposed to 'the search for an original foundation that would make rationality the *telos* of mankind'.[14] Instead discourse marks out the conditions of existence for the conception of rationality which imbue a tradition. Yet Foucault's archaeological method must also stand apart from deconstruction. Archaeology is not merely a surface of inscription but a site of strategic intervention in the structure of contemporary knowledge. Foucault's theoretical developments at the level of discourse identify a materiality and a sensitivity to context and event that *seem* to exceed linguistic and semiological analyses; his dialogue with Derrida over the classification of madness and the origin of reason attempts to persuade us of this.[15] However, as the discussions here on will illuminate, there does appear to be an elision in Foucault's treatment of the sign which resonates upon his own theorization of subjectivity and delimits it in significant ways. Let us then turn to this archaeological method and investigate its construction of subjectivity.

I. ARCHAEOLOGIES OF THE SUBJECT

It is in one of his major theoretical works *Les Mots et Les Choses* that some of Foucault's most interesting comments on the concept of the subject may be found. Whilst the study is orientated in the first instance towards the differing form, content and structure of knowledge throughout the ages, it does not base itself upon a contiguity between reason and progress or the unfolding of an idea towards objectivity within a transcendental space. Such a historical method gives 'absolute priority to the observing subject, ... attributes a constituent role to an act, ... places its own point of view at the origin of all historicity, which, in short, leads to a transcendental consciousness.'[16] Foucault's aim is to extricate historical analysis from such an equation with a philosophy of consciousness. His method, *per contra*, is based on a differential analysis which asks *how* order and continuity have apparently shaped the form of knowledge. The emphasis is upon rupture, discontinuity and the way in which specific transformations come about, rather than upon the surface appearances of knowledge with its apparent logic, conceptual rules and scientific laws of arrangement given by consciousness. 'We should not restrict meaning to the cognitive core that lies at the heart of a knowable object; rather, we should allow it to re-establish its flux at the limit of words and things, as what is said of a thing.'[17] Foucault's differential analysis turns to a level of knowledge that eludes consciousness and the history of ideas, one where the rules of formation of objects are not constructed with reference to the subject but rely on an 'unspoken order',[18] a level that Foucault calls, using a concept that he takes from Kant, archaeological. 'Archaeology', Foucault writes, 'is the level which makes knowledge possible.'[19] The task of archaeological analysis is to treat knowledge not as a theoretical order composed of ideas reflecting upon the real but as a discursive formation with a specific structure. To understand how this archaeological level of analysis proceeds it is necessary to embark on a study of *The Order of Things* and a consideration of Foucault's development of an archaeological method in *The Archaeology of Knowledge*.

Perhaps we can best understand *The Order of Things* as a limited semiology. Its focus is the plane of representation: the mode of constructing and naming the object of knowledge which produces in its wake, meaning, subjectivity and signification. It is limited, however, because it takes up none of the complex reverberations of language that link semiology to the speech of the subject in the work of Derrida and Lacan. An ambiguity marks Foucault's distinction between discourse and language. Discourse is not reducible to speech for Foucault, nor is it amenable to distinctions between theory and reality; discourse does not just get to work *upon* the real, it constructs the real as a discursive entity. Discourse is both the mode of constructing specific object-domains or *epistemes* and the means of containing the relations between language and the objects which constitute knowledge. Discourse varies over time and Foucault identifies a number of ruptures, epistemic points where the relationship between language as a means of representing objects (i.e. the relation between words and things) breaks down and gives way to new discursive formations. Within *The Order of Things*, the effects of this rupture are reduced to the discursive level, that of archaeology, where their conditions of existence, modalities and regularities are studied as a complex series of displacements.

Foucault's excursions into the transformation of discursive formations of knowledge pose a number of interesting questions which
resonate with those raised by Althusser and Derrida in earlier chapters:
how are systems of thought created? How can we account for systematic
changes in the form of knowledge? What modalities of order have been
recognized, posited and linked together in the positive basis of knowledge? How is it that the human subject at a particular juncture in time
and space, took itself as the object of possible knowledge? The formulation of these questions is important. They demand that Foucault
develop new conceptual resources to consider the formation and
construction of the subject. No longer the author or origin of discourse,
the subject is an object of analysis. Foucault's project in *The Order of
Things* is to isolate the conditions of possibility for the modern form of
discourse which comes to take the human subject as its epistemic centre.

As James Bernauer points out, Foucault's mode of questioning is
directed not at the nature of philosophical truth but towards the
historically true.[20] Foucault shows us how the mode and style of representation that existed in the medieval and classical ages and coincided
with discourse in an oblique but nonetheless universal relation, con-
trasts with that of the modern age, where the knot which ties discourse
to language begins to unravel, heralding the autonomy of discourse and
the birth of the subject as an epistemological category. As Foucault
comments:

> [W]hat is available to archaeological analysis is the whole of
> Classical knowledge, or rather the threshold that separates us
> from Classical thought and constitutes our modernity. It was upon
> this threshold that the strange figure of knowledge called man
> first appeared and revealed a space proper to the human sciences.
> In attempting to uncover the deepest strata of Western culture,
> I am restoring to our silent and apparently immobile soil its rifts,
> its instabilities, its flaws; and it is the same ground that is once
> more stirring under our feet.[21]

Within classical thought, representation takes on a pure form and the
meaning of the word that represents the object is largely contained. The
world corresponds to things. It is folded in upon itself, reflecting reality
and emulating the existence of objects. Discourse is a series of marks or
signatures to be deciphered as coterminous with God. The proximity
of the being of knowledge to its godly essence is expressed through

notions of resemblance and analogy. Language does not signify particular differences between objects because 'the signature and what it
denotes are of exactly the same nature'.[22] The role of language is to
articulate, reveal and seek out similitude in the order of words and
things. The mutual correspondence of *disparate* objects is epistemolo-
gically excluded. This is not to say that such differences did not exist in
the classical age but rather that they were either assimilated into the
order of discourse because of their coincidental relation to God and
the cosmos, or rendered invisible, silent within discourse. The mode
of representation in the classical epoch is seen to follow the law of
verisimilitude. Moreover, there is no subject to speak this language
of resemblance; the immanentist, analogical model which links the
world of objects to the cosmos, likewise interprets the body and mind
as mere reflections of this wider order. In so far as the self is part of this
moral space, it is likewise reflected in knowledge and has no independent value as an entity for examination. Representation thus remains
full and complete in the absence of the speaking subject. The subject
cannot enter this stage of knowledge without the whole classical scene
collapsing in upon itself.

In this analysis of the mode of representation in the classical age,
Foucault must stand apart from Derrida. In Chapter 4, writing was
viewed as the excluded other of language, its tendency to hyperbole,
invention and impure representation discredited its metaphysical (and
hence all other) use-value. Foucault endows writing with a quality of
truthfulness. Through its reflective properties, writing secures the power
of language to mirror (and mimic) order and symmetry.[23] Language
inscribes order on the world merely by following its recognized form.
Language has no complex structure in relation to the history of metaphysics, which for Derrida always hides a contract with the subject,
rather it has a unifying function, painting over the rifts and differences
that may be inscribed upon it, creating metaphysical sameness. This is
only the beginning of a significant difference between Foucault and
Derrida, a difference that will also hinge upon the distinction between
the *sign* and *discourse* and all that these may, in turn, entail.

If *The Order of Things* identifies a moment or an event in knowledge
where the system of representation begins to crack, when the being of
language is unable to contain itself within established limits, and the
analogical, often quasi-mythical, relation between words and things
bursts forth, it is the Renaissance period. Deception, disillusion, the
possibility that language – and indeed its written form might corrupt,

disrupt, the order of things (signified now in the binarism of the Port Royale School) is engendered with the birth of madness, the expressivist/romanticist turn in literature, and a distinct theory of metaphor. As Foucault writes enigmatically in a description that could serve Sade and Holderlin, as well as Nietzsche and Mallarmé, 'Words have swallowed up their own nature as signs.'[24] It is within this space of rupture between the classical age and the onset of modernity that Foucault begins many of his works. A linear historical method, which understands this transformation according to a logic of temporal succession, cannot trace the path of analysis upon which archaeology journeys. This place of rupture is also a point of transformation in the conditions of possibility of the dominant configuration of knowledge, a paradigm-shift to use Thomas Kuhn's terminology.[25] It was precisely this rupture that inaugurated the birth of man at the end of the eighteenth century.

Shadows and light: viewing the figure of man

> Before the end of the eighteenth century, *man* did not exist – any more than the potency of life, the fecundity of labour, or the historical density of language. He is quite a recent creature, which the demiurge of knowledge fabricated with its own hands less than two hundred years ago: but he has grown old so quickly that it has been only too easy to imagine that he has been waiting for thousands of years in the darkness for that moment of illumination in which he would finally be known.[26]

Foucault argues that the problem of grounding knowledge upon subjective experience did not occur within the classical age because the classical *episteme* posited a symbiotic relation between the world and its representation. Over time the objects of knowledge became too complex for the dominant *episteme* to accommodate them and the discursive construction of the objects of investigation failed to express the order of being. There arose the possibility of variation, of slippage in the internal relations of representation that introduced into discourse a questioning of the structure and form of signification itself: 'representation has lost the power to provide a foundation – with its own being, its own deployment and its power of doubling over on itself – for the links that can join its various elements together.'[27] Foucault is far too sweeping in his characterization of classical thought. Not only could the Augustinian conception of the soul be understood to anticipate the anguish experienced by the Cartesian *cogito* but so the writings of Leibniz and Spinoza could be viewed as unravelling problems of mind and body that were first articulated in Ancient thought. The claim made by Foucault here is quite specific: if a form of knowledge emerges from the reflections of these philosophers, it is not grounded upon a distinct theory of the human subject but upon a religious ontology which postulates reason only in relation to a godly substance (or in St Augustine's case, the cosmos). Certainly these thinkers often developed important theoretical schemata which *anticipated* many of the philosophical questions of modernity as we have pointed out in Chapter 1, but they were not able to think the uncertain nature of the subject's *finite* experience of time and space. They were not, in other words, able to 'know man as he is posited in modern knowledge'.[28]

The crisis in the representation of the order of being that marks the beginning of modernity is an *effect* of the impossibility of a correspondence between being and the object of representation within the empirical sciences. It can be seen most clearly in the positivities of biology, economics and philology which attempted to account for this aporetic structure of representation on an epistemological level. In the study of language, for example, the change in the level of analysis of grammar is of crucial importance. As inflection arose as an element *within* language, it related not to its general structure within the articulation of language but to the content and internal structure of language. The classical discourse which understood language as a mode of representing the world now turns in upon itself. It becomes an analytic of language itself: rule-governed, reflexive and conscious of its uncertainty as a vessel for communication.[29] As Foucault notes, 'from now on there is an interior "mechanism" in languages which determines not only each one's individuality but also its resemblances to the others: it is this mechanism ... that is now to become the basis for history.'[30]

This historical contingency of the object of knowledge was also the result of a second, related transformation, that which introduced the question of temporality, and what Gilles Deleuze has aptly called 'the dark forces of finitude',[31] into the structure of knowledge. The markings of the world which dictated the system of order in the middle and classical Ages are now seen as temporary, replaceable, tranformatory, epistemological arrangements which expose no hidden logic or primal language. Language is henceforth viewed as a limit upon what it is possible to know and the quest of philology (now more clearly presented by linguistics) and the other empirical sciences, with their focus on the historicity of being, is to search out that space within which it is *possible* to think with any certainty about knowledge.

With their opening out onto the field of historicity, the sciences move into anthropological knowledge, that is, they become *human* sciences, forever doomed to centre their analyses upon the search for a deeper understanding, a hidden origin to the subject's experience of finitude. Rather than asking what is the mode of being of the world and how the world can be understood, the human sciences ask searching questions about the form of subjectivity itself: what *is* this entity, the human subject? How can we know *of* it, of being in the world? What is it possible to think *as* subject? What, moreover, are the limits of human knowledge? It is upon these difficult, auguish ridden questions that the subject is brought onto the stage of knowledge and will be forever stamped with the imprint of these questions. From its modern inception, the subject was in tension and all too quickly became the object of philosophical disillusionment and scepticism. Simultaneously the transcendental subject of knowledge (that is, the condition of possibility *for* knowledge) and the object of knowledge (the focus of these investigations), the empirico-transcendental doublet called the subject pulled fast against its construction as epistemic centre. In effect, the empirical was redoubled into the transcendental, causing both fields of knowledge to lose their (already contested) status as a source of practical or theoretical knowledge. At the same time, the subject lost its own status as the object or knowledge, disappearing through the event of redoubling and leaving in its wake fragments of its being (unconscious, body, the unthought) for the human sciences to discover and name.[32]

From its start then, human knowledge was thrown against certain limits and questions: is a universal, objective, knowledge doomed to be impossible when the structural relation of the subject to itself is seen to be a source of disruption and insecurity in the space of knowledge? Here we find echoes of Derrida's reflections on the subject: the conditions of possibility of the human sciences also seems to dictate their *im*possibility. It was Kant who first posed this problem in relation to the possibility of knowledge: if man is finite and his claims to know reality are contingent and particular, *on what basis* can we *secure* the conditions of possibility for knowledge? How can we *close the gap* created in representation, move from concept to judgement, from object to the thought of that object, and ground the basis for knowledge within the faculty of Reason, thus returning the quality of certainty to both consciousness and knowledge? In the *Critique of Pure*

Reason Kant argues that it is only by creating *a priori* transcendental conditions or autonomous rules which can function as a criterion for the validity of judgement that the subject's relation to the objects of knowledge may be guaranteed.

Now it has been argued by a number of commentators that it is within this Kantian problematic that Foucault's archaeology must be situated.[33] We have already pointed out above that the concept of archaeology was itself taken from Kant. It should also be noted that Foucault's second thesis (the first being *Madness and Civilisation*) was a translation and introduction to Kant's *Anthropology from a Pragmatic Point of View*.[34] Whilst it may be a theoretical short-cut to highlight the significance of this text for Foucault's oeuvre as a whole, it is nonetheless important to recognize that much of Foucault's conceptual apparatus at this stage in his work appears to take its *bearing* from the structure of Kant's philosophy. This inevitably raises problems at the level of interpretation. For example, in the case of Dreyfus and Rabinow the central question becomes whether or not Foucault is able to avoid 'the transcendental/empirical doublet which haunts the discourse of anthropology?'[35] The Kantian problem cannot be avoided; Foucault cannot step outside of the antinomies engendered by metaphysics although we will see him attempting to perform this impossible manoeuvre in the *Archaeology of Knowledge*. The question is really whether Foucault's analysis can exceed and think against this logic. There is perhaps very little scope for this within *The Order of Things*. In a section entitled 'the retreat and return of origin', all of the efforts to understand the subject by appealing to something unthought, lost or hidden, are somehow accounted for: Heidegger's effort to understand the being of Man as a forgetting of *Dasein*, as well as Freud's journey away from the *cogito* to identify the source of the subject's hidden desire and its relation to the unconscious.[36] It appears that Foucault may be caught within the paradox of subjectivity already encountered in earlier chapters. What scope is there to rethink the subject when every philosophy which does so is merely executing the internal logic of the human sciences? Within what philosophical space can the question of the subject be thought?

The discursive horizon of knowledge

In *The Archaeology of Knowledge* it may seem that Foucault returns to many of the preoccupations of Althusser, particularly the latter's focus upon an autonomous level of knowledge with its own internal conditions of existence for the production of objects, together with a mode of analysis that divorces itself from all subjective relation and of any connection with brute reality. Althusser's division of knowledge identifies a level of knowledge (its problematic, Generality II) which frames the possible ways of conceiving the problems of knowledge. What Foucault calls a *discursive formation* performs a quite similar theoretical function and both formulations attempt to identify the conditions of existence of knowledge and subjectivity in a particular age. Both may also be traced back to Heidegger's discussion of *Gestell*, the enframing of knowledge according to certain philosophical presuppositions.[37] We have already noted in our analysis of *The Order of Things* how the 'rules of formation' within a particular *episteme* place constraints upon the mode of speaking and acting. What Foucault pursues in the *Archaeology of Knowledge,* perhaps ambiguously given its resonance with phenomenology, is the 'preconceptual level': 'the locus of emergence of concepts', which he understands in terms of the rules which establish a given field of discourse.[38]

It is important to labour the ambiguous status of phenomenology in Foucault's method. Deleuze points out that the kind of phenomenology with which Foucault wishes to distinguish himself is the limited, vulgar type linked solely with intentionality.[39] Unlike Husserl (whose phenomenology was, over time, far more variegated than a focus on intentionality would assume), Foucault holds no faith in the resources which may be drawn from a transcendental consciousness. Consequently, it is only by posing *anew* 'the questions of the origin, the first constitution, the teleological horizon, temporal continuity' that a possible escape from the anthropological schemas that dominant the human sciences may be generated.[40] Foucault recognizes that structuralism does not manage to complete its own escape from a concern with the transcendental, and when he writes in *The Order of Things* that structuralism is 'the awakened and troubled consciousness of modern thought' it is because structuralism, too, remains attached to problems of cause and relation, structure and history, subject and object, and continues to play out its own theoretical identity amidst these dualisms.[41] When Foucault talks about the preconceptual level then, he does not have in mind the representations of consciousness as in transcendental phenomenology, or the phenomenological *body* as in the final work of Merleau-Ponty, but a field wherein the rules that call particular concepts into existence and regulate their possible emergence, are formed and transformed. It is the preconceptual level which gives rise to the event of a particular mode of being (a subject), a possible mode of knowledge (a way of seeing and speaking) and a mode of social existence (relations between subjects).

Dreyfus and Rabinow claim Foucault as the *ultimate* phenomenologist who carries out a double bracketing not just of psychology and its metaphysical baggage (i.e. worldly subjectivity) but also of meaning and truth. Both the subject and truth are shorn of their *a priori* epistemological status as origins of knowledge. Hence the rules that Foucault thus describes do not confer upon discourse *a priori* conditions for the rational deduction of truth-claims; they have no transcendental status, neither are they external to discourse. They do not prefigure discourse; they do not establish a set of methodological principles, 'a genesis of abstractions',[42] which operate first in the consciousness of individuals and then (logically) through their own meaningful theoretical constructions, and they offer no mark of legitimacy independent of the structure of discourse. The rules of discourse are both anonymous and autonomous, emphasizing their distance from any construction of knowledge grounded by a philosophy of the subject. Foucault is not suggesting that we analyse the *systematic behaviour* of rules. We must look rather to the four regional levels of discourse (the formation of objects, enunciative modalities, concepts and strategies) in order to render significant the order of rules that alone attribute meaning to discourse. These four levels offer an indication of the limits and the possibilities of discursive practice. Let us consider briefly each in turn.

Modalities and modifications of discourse

In much the same manner as Althusser, Foucault views the object not as an empirical entity but as one that is constructed and ordered by a specific discursive arrangement. There is no pre-discursive reality that is not *always already* infected by discourse available to the archaeologist, and there is no foundational subject to reveal or discover the immanent arrangements of objects, to signify their meaning within language and knowledge. The object of mental illness for example, cannot be studied via an account of the emerging theories of psychologists and psychiatrists, but only by encountering the shifts and differences within discursive communities and non-discursive institutions and political forms, those competing discourses that, in different ways, legitimated the existence of eighteenth-century workhouses and asylums (religious texts, canons of law, utilitarianism, norms of acceptable behaviour). The objects of discourse can only be salvaged by investigating the mode through which these various discourses were able to unify – or at least *accommodate* – their internal contradictions and operate within an apparently closed structure of discourse.

In a similar way, the mode of enunciation that Foucault describes does not refer us to the unity of the subject, the subject as speaking being who is able to authenticate discourse. Certainly, Foucault is interested in the speaking subject, but speech must be inserted into the field of possible enunciations, what we may call the 'subject positions' established by a discursive formation. The function of archaeology is to analyse how particular enunciative modalities of specific discursive formations make it possible to speak *of* the subject. It is the rules of discourse that are significant, it matters not for Foucault *who* is speaking. It is discourse which speaks through subjects. The subject then, has no ontological priority over discourse. It is not the author of discourse and cannot be viewed as having any claim over the construction of discourse. It may be the case, comments Foucault, that 'the founding subject ... is given the task of directly animating the empty forms of language with his aims ... [of grasping] by intuition the meaning lying deposited within them' but this can only be an 'elision of the reality of discourse'.[43] Foucault distances the formation of concepts from the ideological pretensions of knowledge. Both subject and object can only *exist* in the dispersed field of modalities established by discourse.[44] The concept of the subject can be broached only by exploring the 'preconceptual level' described above, namely the rules which allow something called a subject to be gathered together, to take up a place for speech, thought and action.[45] Thus it is not that the subject simply disappears in Foucault's discursive analysis, 'rather its excessively determined unity is put into question.'[46] It is essential that we understand the internal mechanisms of the discursive formation which constitute the theoretical *limit* of the subject as well as its condition of *possibility*.[47]

Discourse not only disperses and animates the subject across specific planes, it actually forms the subject who becomes a questioning subject, a listening subject, a perceiving, observing subject, according to the modalities of discourse. Significantly, these modalities may also include non-discursive relations: economic, social and political effects constituted through institutional sites, codes of conduct, modes of representing information. Indeed, at this level of analysis, discursive and *non*-discursive dimensions seem to merge together. Subjectification (subject *formation* as well as *subjection*) takes place through the reduction of the subject to a range of subject-positions between the discursive and the non-discursive realms. As in Althusser's discussion of ideology's interpellation of the subject and Nietzsche's discussion of the internalization, the turning inwards, of the subject in *The Genealogy of Morality*, so discursive and non-discursive formations 'shift the subject in relation to the average or immediate perceptual level, ... make him circulate in the interior space of the body – from manifest systems to the organs, from the organs to the tissues, and finally from the tissues to the cells.'[48] In this way discourse forms, organizes, distributes and invests bodily material in order to give rise to specific forms of subjectivity. Simply put, the subject is an effect of discourse but this is not a relation of determination or causality, but rather a struggle *for* constitution. 'From the moment of its existence (and not only in its "practical applications") [discourse] poses the question of power; an asset that is, by nature, the object of a struggle, a political struggle.'[49] If at this stage in Foucault's work there is no explicit analysis of the political effects – or forms – of subjectification, his 1975 study of power in *Discipline and Punish* will correct this absence.

The discursive construction of subjectivity and knowledge then, are not governed by a principle of closure or determination but have an indeterminate moment, a threshold or opening out which signals the possibility of strategy, chance and decision. For Foucault, the notion of strategy does not refer to the founding act, project or choice of the individual subject: 'these options must be described as systematically different ways of treating objects of discourse ... of arranging forms of enunciation, ... of manipulating concepts.'[50] Likewise, whilst rules establish the *conditions* of existence of discourse, they do not *determine* the way in which the discourse may be appropriated. Discourse must function within a field of non-discursive practices, and will be characterized by a specific relation to desire. Both of these elements will play a role in the formation of the strategic possibilities of discourse and render its material formation contingent. Thus 'discourse may in fact be the place for a phantasmatic representation, an element of symbolisation, a form of the forbidden, an instrument of derived satisfaction ... [These] are not disturbing elements which ... suppress its own voice and emit in its place a travestied discourse, but, on the contrary, its formative elements.'[51] If the non-discursive and desire are precisely the *formative* elements of discourse, Foucault is content to merely identify their role as one of modification. However, whilst there is no investigation of the dynamic of these two elements, Foucault's later understanding of a non-subjective site of agency within power-relations is anticipated here.

That discourse is constituted by a group of statements is most significant for Foucault's archaeological method. Archaeology investigates the formation, structure and field of statements which is made possible by the four levels of discourse outlined above. It may be easier to first describe the statement with reference to what it is *not*. The statement is not to be reduced to a grammatical proposition nor a mode of communication. It cannot be reduced to a sentence, because the same sentence can clearly be the support of different statements.[52] Neither can it be aligned with the Lacanian concept of the symbolic which creates signification via the mediation of signifier and signified because *the statement always precedes the constitution of the sign*. Similarly, the statement cannot be equated with a speech-act, where meaning is given with reference to the way in which an intentional act is embodied by a subject.[53] Foucault does not appear to be interested in criteria of legitimacy for statements. A statement can best be described as establishing the conditions through which signs are given an existence that render them *operative* within a specific discourse. Thus for Foucault, 'The analysis of statements . . . is a historical analysis, but one that avoids all interpretation: . . . it questions them as to their mode of existence, what it means to them to have come into existence, to have left traces, and perhaps to remain there, awaiting the moment when they might be of use once more; what it means for them to have appeared when they did – they and no others.'[54]

By designating discourse autonomous of both the real as the ground which illuminates the factual content of knowledge, and the philosophy of the subject as that which authenticates this space of knowledge via the acts of speech and representation, Foucault attributes a radical primacy to statements and rules in the constitution of a discursive formation. Rules individuate and regulate the appearance of statements, the type of possible object that can be derived, and its relation to other discourses. These two concepts appear to establish the *a priori* conditions of possibility of discourse, but this is not 'a condition of validity for judgement, but a condition of reality for statements.'[55] The *a priori* is concrete not universal; it is non-subjective and contingent.[56] It takes account of statements in their dispersal, their non-coherence, their rupture, irregularity and replacement, in short their specific history – that which Foucault, in later analyses, will call (following Nietzsche) genealogy.[57]

However, the autonomy of discourse from the conceptual unfolding of the history of ideas, and from the historico-political conditions which are often seen to produce discourse, has led several commentators to question the intelligibility, the normative significance and the ultimate value of Foucault's enterprise.[58] Foucault, however, is dealing with a different order of problems, and his writings occupy a different theoretical problematic. Charges of apoliticism and relativism fail to recognize that the question of the *status* of discourse is, for an archaeological method, less important than the question of concept-formation (i.e. the specific conditions which constitute discourse) and their concrete effects. The level of discursive-formation as an object of analysis is often valorized by Foucault's critics, and instead confounded with the question of truth-conditions. These are then used as a means to measure Foucault's possible deviation from a search for the truth-content of specific discourses (hence the concern of Foucault's critics with the spectre of relativism). Consequently, for Dreyfus and Rabinow, Foucault has 'hypostatised the observed formal regularities which describe discursive formations into conditions of these formations' existence.'[59] In this way, they continue, Foucault has merely transferred the problems of *self*-grounding and subjectivity from the question of representation to that of objectification. Archaeology is seen to manifest, therefore, 'the very essence of the analytics of finitude'.[60] It remains attached resolutely to the human sciences. Instead of chasing the unrepresentable or unconscious origins and limits of discourse, archaeology seeks out the system of rules which *ground* discourse thus allowing access to those objects, subjects and actions that, *without* the analytic recourse to rules, would remain unidentified and meaningless. By the kind of categorical inversion that we alluded to in the introduction, rules are viewed as acting very much like the traditional conception of the subject: they confer meaning upon objects; they are transcendental categories.[61]

The above interpretation can be viewed as misrepresenting and undermining Foucault's project by attributing a transcendental value to the prioritization of rules to which he surely would not accede. There is a tendency in these critical readings to search for ever-deeper grounds and origins for Foucault's formulations that, paradoxically, may end up repeating the logic of the human sciences that it wishes to attach to Foucault's own position. Are Foucault and his critics caught in the double-bind of modern thought? There are two theoretical problems within the structure of Foucault's discursive analysis and they are not lost with the elision (or bracketing) of the subject. First, the boundary separating discursive and non-discursive fields of analysis is ambiguous and undertheorized. Certainly the rules of discourse have no non-discursive site, but the four modalities of discourse seem to have institutional sites as their own condition of emergence. Furthermore, if discourse is contingent, dispersed and open, as Foucault maintains, then its relation to the non-discursive is paramount and begs exploration. Second, in Foucault's analysis, the statement is freed of all linguistic subjectivity, and it is autonomous of language and the dynamics of signification. Are these the residual metaphysical problems left gaping and unanswered in the wake of the repositioned subject? Can the shift from archaeology to genealogy begun in *Discipline and Punishment* confront these problems? Before considering these latter questions, the two theoretical problems encountered in archaeology's method must be brought into closer focus.

II. FOUCAULDIAN DILEMMAS:
THINKING THE LIMITS OF DISCOURSE

[Archaeology] does not wish to rediscover the enigmatic point at which the individual and the social are inverted into one another.[62]

The conception of discourse charted above is in part an effort to overcome a number of antinomies present within epistemology. These dualisms have already been broached in earlier chapters. Theory and practice, essence and appearance, transcendental and empirical, and science and ideology, were all oppositions which threatened the autonomy of Althusserian science and were transformed by him accordingly. Nevertheless, their theoretical resolutions, namely, theoretical practice, the object-in-thought and the knowledge effect each generated a weakness in Althusser's epistemology, namely that the internal conditions for the activity of knowledge-production could always be contaminated by what lay outside science, namely, ideology. In the wake of deconstruction we can view such a theoretical malady as inevitable – perhaps an incurable sickness of that which seeks transcendence of the world in whatever form. An epistemological break will always continue to harbour that which it wishes to exclude, along, and within, its borders. Yet the conception of discourse developed by Foucault was really intended to overcome these classical antinomies. Discourse produces modes of reality; indeed even before distinctions between truth and false have become possible in relation to certain entities, discourse has already produced the conditions of possibility for a specific form of truth. However, that very little is said by Foucault about the *non-discursive* should come as no surprise because his approach to the study of discourse allows for no clear distinction, opposition or ontological split, between discursive and non-discursive spaces. As Deleuze points out, Foucault does not say whether the non-discursive can be reduced to a statement, is a residue, or perhaps merely an illusion,[63] a phantasmatic symbolization of discourse rooted in desire. However, we are able to point towards a reference for this concept of the non-discursive: as event, institutional or political site, that which is excluded, invisible to a discursive formation, but we are not able to attribute any independent role to the non-discursive in the constitution of discourse.[64] The two formations are heterogeneous not isomorphic; there can be no direct correspondence, no base–superstructure relation, between the two.[65]

Foucault clearly wants to avoid any conception of the political (as non-discursive event) which attributes to it a space *anterior* to discourse, or views it as an autonomous level of analysis. This would reduce the role of discourse to a mode of *interpreting* the political rather than a mode of *constituting* the political. Discourse could appear, in the former role, as a linguistic rather than a material construction.[66] It could also be assigned a role as cause, or as the lived experience of consciousness turned in upon itself, or the *enigmatic point* which could reveal the hidden essence of the political. If Foucault remains interested in the event, it is an interest in the *specific* event and its inter-relation with discourse rather than its significance as an autonomous realm. For example, in *Discipline and Punish*, where Foucault investigates the discursive relations between disciplinary power and knowledge, his focus is not those general power-relations which reduce power and knowledge to effects of broad historical dynamics or to the agency of the ruling class, but the way in which these external events are discursively organized. It is the epistemic rules which establish the conditions of existence for discourse – particularly the enunciative and strategic *possibilities* of discourse – that are the concern of *The Archaeology of Knowledge*. However, since there are significant, strategic interdependencies between discourse and the (non-discursive) event,[67] rules, statements and the modalities of discourse are in the difficult position of having to account for many diverse modes of existence and possibility of discourse. If the modalities of discourse effect the emergence of statements, then the non-discursive site forms the historical *a priori* of these discursive modalities. We seem to be caught within a tautology. The problems engendered by such a per-spective extend far into Foucault's conception of discourse. Indeed, by exploring some of the differences between deconstruction and archaeology these problems may be brought to the fore.

The most significant difference which emerges in the exchange between Derrida and Foucault is that between discourse and the role of the statement on the one hand, and the deconstruction of the sign on the other. As we have already noted, for Foucault, *the statement precedes the sign*. A description of the identity of a statement will reveal the subject as occupying the *position* of speaking subject. In *The Archae-ology of Knowledge* Foucault is at pains to show that language, through the enunciative function, is a property of discourse; lan-guage and its spoken form are distributed in discursive practices according to specific, regulative rules. Hence it makes no sense to entertain linguistic analysis without a consideration of the discursive dimension of language, as Foucault makes clear in the concluding chapter of *The Archaeology of Knowledge* where he responds to his imaginary critics. In his own rejoinder to Derrida's 1963 lecture on his work, Foucault distinguishes between textual and discursive prac-tices. For him, deconstruction reduces discursive practices to textual practices. In contrast, archaeology is tied to historical context; it charts and weaves the transformations and ruptures in ways of organizing and understanding modes of being in the world. Archaeology then, refers 'less to the signifying organisation of the text than to the series of events (acts, effects, qualifications) which the discursive practice of mediation carries with it.'[68]

However, Derrida argues that Foucault's reluctance to pursue the dialogical basis of the sign renders his conception of language incom-plete. This reluctance can be traced to Foucault's growing desire to distance discourse from any study of structural linguistics and the latter's analysis of modes of signification. In his 1954 essay 'Dream, Imagination and Existence', Foucault had already developed a rigorous critique of the psychoanalytic conception of the sign as symbol found in Freud and Lacan. Both thinkers, in Foucault's view, confound the symptoms of psychosis with the symbolic expression of its linguistic meaning, hence reducing the analysis of the image to that which reflects it. In short, psychoanalysis has taken the concept of the symbol as valid without trying to delimit and develop it. It cannot, for Foucault, make sense of signification. Despite Lacan's efforts (indeed his whole life was spent trying to account for this), Foucault claims that Lacanian psychoanalysis is unable to deal with *the gap* in meaning. If Lacan 'for his part has done everything possible to show in the Imago the point at which the meaningful dialogue of language seizes up or becomes spellbound by the interlocutor it constituted',[69] he did not succeed in making images 'speak'. Now although Foucault recognized the critical value of psychoanalysis, this early move away from it was not renounced, as the later reflections on the contract between psychoanalysis and power-knowledge amply illustrate (see Section III below). In *The Order of Things* Foucault had also viewed contemporary psychoanalytic theory as bound to a relation between language, subjectivity and representation which also tied it to the anthropologizing logic of the human sciences. As Cousins and Hussain point out in their study of Foucault, 'it is easy to see how ... linguistics ... could be used simply to state an algorithm of subjectivity and thus function as a philosophical theory of the subject.'[70]

Nevertheless, for Derrida, this rejection of linguistics also generates a 'disengagement from the *totality* of ... historical language.'[71] Deconstruction views language as intricately woven into philosophical concepts; it *cannot be overlooked*. It ties language and its myriad properties and relations (speech, writing, subjectivity, conceptualization, order, exclusion, historicity and otherness) to the fractured origin of philosophy. In short, deconstruction cannot be, as Foucault would have it, a mere structural analysis of texts. Much more is at stake in our understandings of structure, text, and indeed linguistics.[72]

With this unsatisfactory displacement of language (and the complex conditions of existence of speech and signification which in turn affect the constitution of the subject), Foucault also jettisons an understanding of philosophical language and the language of philosophy, both of which could certainly enrich and supplement his notion of discourse and his construction of subjectivity. In fact, the sweeping aside of the pervasive dynamics of signification and their (de)constitutive power on the history of knowledge allows Foucault to assign different discursive modes of constituting knowledge in classical and modern ages. Derrida argues that such a division between classical and modern may itself mask the exclusion of a certain différance within philosophical language.

Derrida's particular criticism is here directed towards Foucault's study *Madness and Civilisation* where the latter traces the birth of madness to the philosophical discourse of Cartesianism. Is not madness inherent in *all* language, asks Derrida? Does not Foucault inadvertently confirm the exclusionary structure of Western metaphysics when he ignores the way in which all *rational* knowledge (and not merely its distinctly modern, subject-centred forms) hides its relation to the other of reason?[73] Foucault's response to this critique emphasizes once again archaeology's appeal to the historical specificity of Cartesian discourse. Certainly Foucault's attention to the discursive context of *The Meditations*, his regard for the text as simultaneously a deductive and a demonstrative exercise which constructs in its wake a particular kind of enunciated subject as *cogito*, as well as the literary and textual effects of the work (particularly the significance of Descartes' distinction between madness and dreaming, and his account of madness as *insani* and *demens*), highlight Derrida's own tendency to generalize the exclusion of madness in Descartes' text. This discursive analysis also disperses madness in the text alluding to its presence not only in the First Meditation but also in Descartes' discussion of imagination, art and illusion.[74]

However, whether archaeological discourse can remain *autonomous* of the tensions identified by deconstruction, and distinct from their effects upon its own modality, remains unconsidered by Foucault. Rather, the latter's turn to an autonomous level of discourse distinguished from an analysis of the sign was designed precisely to evade these questions and the problems arising from them. This requirement, to disentangle and distinguish his conception of discourse from a linguistics of the sign, led Foucault to privilege a very formal account of the statement, the power of which to form and reform a discursive formation seemed unsurpassable. In so doing, archaeology appears to cover over, or at least subordinate, the non-discursive event and the transgressive potentialities of language, the latter of which was at the heart of Foucault's earlier concerns. And thus archaeology opens itself up to the problem of the status of what is *outside* of discourse (namely the non-discursive), and the status of the sign. It is these two problems that continued to haunt Foucault's work on power and seriously limit his effort 'to account for the constitution of the subject within a historical framework.'

III. GENEALOGIES OF THE SUBJECT:
POWER AND SUBJECTION

Anyone who learns to know whence he comes may marvel at being
what he is, or remembering the distortions he has undergone,
surrender to a disenchantment that will immobilize him, unless,
like Nietzsche, he resorts to the humour of genealogy and the play
of criticism.[75]

In *The Philosophical Discourse of Modernity* Jurgen Habermas writes
that 'the turn to a theory of power must be understood as an internally
motivated attack on problems with which Foucault saw himself confronted after he had carried out his unmasking of the human sciences in
The Order of Things using only the tools of discursive analysis.'[76] For
such a view, Foucault's move to a *genealogical* analysis of power in the
classical and modern ages was simultaneously a shift away from
archaeology as a mode of analysis towards the 'interpretive analytics'
of genealogy.[77] Genealogy performs a purifying role; Foucault's philosophical period is seen to be over and 'the genealogist is a diagnostician
who concentrates on the relation of power, knowledge and the body in
modern society.'[78] Now the *need* for such a shift should be apparent
from the earlier discussions of the limits pervading Foucault's archaeological method. The focus of genealogy is the more specific site of the
human body, rather than the more general site of discourse and its
conditions. It may be understood as concentrating on the *intersection*
of the discursive and non-discursive and it locates the political effects
of discursive closure upon the subject. Foucault clearly views his
genealogies as strategic interventions in the political field; they are a
form of political critique, disrupting the slow progress of the history of
ideas and cultivating 'the details and accidents that accompany every
beginning'.[79] 'Genealogy', Foucault writes, 'does not resemble the
evolution of a species and does not map the destiny of a people',[80]
rather it is situated and inscribed upon the body of the subject. It views
the body as an initally undifferentiated site which is invested, governed
and transformed by specific power relations. Genealogy seeks to expose
the process whereby history destroys the body and renders it, in a
nominalist sense, unfree.[81] As James Bernauer writes, 'genealogy is
permanent critique in the interest of an endless practice of freedom.'[82]

If genealogy promises political critique then it must be seen to take
on board the criticism identified above in Section II regarding the

determinant status of rules constructed by Foucault in the wake of his decentring of the subject. However, despite the apparent change in focus of the texts on power, (particularly *Discipline and Punish* and *A History of Sexuality, Volume 1*, both of which will be our focus from here on), it would be a mistake to establish a clear distinction between archaeology and genealogy for three significant reasons. First, the notion of genealogy, like that of archaeology, performs a *fundamental* philosophical role in Foucault's analysis by calling into question the transcendental categories of origin and essence as supports for any historical method. Genealogy reveals 'the secret that [things] have no essence or that their essence was fabricated in a piecemeal fashion from alien forms.'[83] Second, both modes of analysis have as their focus the form of discursive practices. The role of the human sciences are important in the construction of power-relations, as sciences of man they provide the knowledge which renders the body amenable to inscription. Similarly, archaeological method continues to indicate the various levels of discourse that Foucault ascribes to. Third, both archaeology and genealogy delineate the concept of the subject as it is constituted as an effect of discourse (for archaeology) and power (for genealogy). If there is a notable *shift* in Foucault's *oeuvre*, it is not one which changes once and for all his theoretical strategy, it is a shift which intensifies his project, a project which seeks to understand the ways in which something called the subject is formed, reformed, dispersed and regulated over the planes of a discursive reality. Furthermore, this emphasis on *continuity* will not permit Foucault to *displace* the theoretical problems that we have identified earlier. The problematic of the subject hovers over genealogical analysis too. As we shall see, as soon as Foucault tries to displace it the effects of this displacement resonate within his own problematic of power.

Archaeology and genealogy then, would seem to support one another through a process of reversal: the former considers how the structure of knowledge delimits the subject, the latter considers the ways in which the body of the subject becomes a site for the inscription of knowledge. Foucault's later reconceptualization of the two by the notion of 'problematization' described his project as 'genealogical in its design and archaeological in its method'.[84] If, in the context of the discussion here, we can differentiate archaeology and genealogy, it may be that the latter more adequately accommodates the institutional (non-discursive) site of power.

Discipline and Punish pursues the historical *a priori* identified in *The Archaeology of Knowledge*. This later text concentrates more explicitly upon the conditions of *emergence* of modern forms of power rather than the (largely formal) conditions of *existence* of discourse described in the earlier text. In fact, it would seem that Foucault is not only closer now to Nietzsche, whose analysis of the bond between power, knowledge and truth clearly influenced him, but also more paradoxically, to Marx and Western Marxism. Notions of force, violence, repression, consent and ideology come to take on a different sense for Foucault. Foucault's is a strategic engagement with Marxism; he derives his concepts by working against the tradition whilst maintaining a certain alliance with it.[85] Thus if Kant and Husserl were the complex precursors of Foucault's concept of discourse, it is now through Nietzsche and Marx that we must read Foucault's reflections of power.

Power: 'an impasse that we run up against'

> By power, I do not mean 'Power' as a group of institutions and mechanisms that ensure the subservience of the citizens of a given state. By power, I do not mean, either, a mode of subjugation which, in contrast to violence, has the form of a rule. Finally, I do not have in mind a general system whose effects, through successive derivations, pervade the entire social body.[86]

Certainly Foucault's reflections on power are formed against those of Marx and indeed much of twentieth-century Marxism. Power has no structural relation to a social totality neither does it presuppose an institution as the origin of its activities. Theories of state-power centralize power-relations by reducing them to abstract relations, and fail to account for the multiplicity of ways in which the subject's subjugation is achieved. Such theories rely on a conception of power as sovereignty which interprets the political field solely in terms of 'juridico-political relations', that is, relations of right and legitimacy. We need to eschew the model of Leviathan – which even pervades Marxist formulations – in order to study *technologies* of power and their specific, local effects. Power, following Foucault's archaeological analysis, is also non-subjective. It is not a capacity or a possession of a particular subject. Thus, 'it is already one of the prime effects of power that certain bodies, certain gestures, certain desires come to be identified and constituted as individuals. . . . The individual is not to be seen as a sort of elementary nucleus, a primitive atom, a multiple and inert material on which power comes to fasten or against which it happens to strike'.[87] If individuals are not holders of power they are nonetheless its vehicles and targets, since they are constituted by the force of its operations. In occupying subject-positions, both dominators and subjugators are caught within the same matrix of power-relations; hierarchy and class structure are of second-order significance here. Power is a strategic relation. Mobile, fluid and continuous, it invests institutions and individuals with possibilities for action. It is never stationary, but 'always already there', caught up in a matrix of forces which itself creates lines of division, relations of oppression and exclusion, codes of discipline and sites of subjection.

In *Discipline and Punish* we learn how power as a discursive event was historically and materially configured. If discourse is also a practice, power forms a new discursive constellation in the nineteenth century when the practice of punishment moves from a repressive matrix of relations formulated in terms of corporeal sovereign power to a disciplinary form of punishment that opens up a micro-physics of power and has as its referent the social and political body in its entirety. Like Nietzsche in *The Genealogy of Morals*, Foucault shows us how the body can be reconstructed, reformed and reconstituted by different modes of discipline. As the negative corporeal punishment associated with monarchical rule gave way to a more insistent, more pervasive form of punishment so the non-discursive siting of power changed. The birth of the prison – which had its symbolic replicas throughout society in the form of factories, schools, barracks and hospitals – opened up new possibilities for the configuration of power-relations and forms of knowledge, relations which differed from the modality of power predominating in the classical era.[88] The modern technology of power is inseparable from the regime of knowledge characterized by the practices and possibilities of discourse. Criminology, penology, psychiatry and psychoanalysis all constitute the subject in its various appearances. They construct the domain in which the subject is situated and dependent. If there is a general principle at work in this construction of power and knowledge, 'a common immanent cause which works informally',[89] it is the panopticon.

Writing in 1973, two years before the publication of *Discipline and Punish*, Jacques-Alain Miller notes that Bentham's utilitarian model of the panopticon is a machine which creates a semblance of God.[90]

Naturally imperialistic, it can systematize any social space and subjugate disorder to an outward spectacle of order and control. As both Miller and Foucault note, the panopticon is not an idea; it is a disciplinary space, a material construct which offers up its functions as a means to create economy, efficiency, effectiveness and more importantly, docility on the part of those subjects who become its investment.[91] The panopticon is a micro-physics of power which is able to explore, break down and re-arrange the human body. 'A body is docile' Foucault writes, 'that may be subjected, used, transformed and improved'.[92] How then is the panopticon able to act upon the body of the subject?

The panopticon is a mode of organizing and constructing space and time such that it exhibits maximum visibility. Deleuze calls it 'a map, a cartography that is coextensive with the whole social field'[93] and this should indicate that the panopticon is not a singular construct or model to be analysed in a single moment. Rather, it is constantly evolving, reacting and reconstituting its operative style and form according to strategic events in the political and social field. It thus recognizes no distinction between its content and outward expression, or between the discursive and non-discursive realms. If we prefer, henceforth, to consider the panopticon as it is discussed in the context of the institution of the prison, it must be stressed that the panopticon is *not* the prison and is not located *within* the prison: 'it is ... a figure of political technology that may and must be detached from any specific use.'[94]

Whilst the panopticon is polyvalent in its applications, it can nonetheless be described in terms of a number of general characteristics and functions. As a utilitarian device, it aims to match its potential as an effective disciplinary schema with the minimum requirement for supervision. Subjects (in this specific instance, criminals) are confined within separate enclosures, dispersed around an annular building. Each self-contained cell is visible from a central watch-tower; the subject can be surveyed at any time, unable to recognize the supervisor or make contact with others. As Foucault notes, 'He [the criminal] is seen, but he does not see; he is the object of information, never a subject in communication.'[95] Power individualizes, classifies, manipulates the body according to certain precepts of knowledge. It develops skills and strengths where weakness and instability previously lay. In modern society, the subject, following the law of economic utility, must be a cost-effective unit. However, the most important characteristic of the panopticon is its production of the visible. The objectifying gaze of the panopticon acts as a guise of continuous surveillance. It leads the subject to regulate behaviour automatically. Indeed, this fundamental axiom of self-surveillance appears to prevail every time: 'He who is subjected to a field of visibility and who *knows* it, assumes a responsibility for the constraints of power; he makes them play spontaneously upon himself: he inscribes in himself the power relation in which he simultaneously plays both roles: *he becomes the principle of his own subjection.*'[96]

It is with this analysis that Foucault's silent dialogue with Althusser becomes apparent. We have already pointed out that *Discipline and Punish* draws upon and yet exceeds Althusser's formulation of the subject.[97] The mode of subjection generated by disciplinary power is not akin to a theory of ideology which Foucault associates almost exclusively with its Marxist formulations. The theoretical faults of the concept of ideology are many: it stands opposed to a more truthful reality, its appearance is the mere embellishment of some prior determinant, e.g. an economic infrastructure, and it relies, somewhat dubiously, upon a relation to subjectivity, that is, to a consciousness which may uncover ideology's distortive conception of reality. Indeed, Foucault had already indicated his departure from ideology and its necessary opposition with science in *The Archaeology of Knowledge.*[98] In *Discipline and Punish*, it is clear that Foucault also wishes to blur the distinction between institutions of repression and institutions of ideology maintained by Althusser in his *Essay on Ideology and Ideological State Apparatuses*. The strength of disciplinary power is the ease of its invasion of the human; this renders the physical violence which may accompany submission unnecessary. The important question here is to what extent the subject is formed by this elusive act of submission. If the voluntary nature of such submission is no longer conceivable in Foucault's discursive analysis, how are we to understand the formation and internalization of specific forms of subjectivity? Our discussions of Althusser's concept of ideology in earlier chapters concluded that it offered no developed account of the link between the materiality of ideology and the constitution of the subject, that is, the problem of how ideology is internalized and how it produces the effects of subjectivation. This is precisely where *Discipline and Punish* may exceed Althusser's own formulations. Whereas Althusser pushes the problem of the internalization of ideology to one side, preferring to consider the mechanism of interpellation as an imaginary misrecognition inspired by little more than a verbal imperative (the 'Hey you!' that incites the subject to turn around), Foucault explores the physical processes of subjection, the ways in which the subject *inscribes within itself* the principle of subjection, and the body as a transmogrifying site of disciplinary power.

It should be apparent that the concept of ideology cannot do the work of investigating the corporeal construction of subjectivation for Foucault, despite its emphasis upon the more insidious aspects of social control and manipulation of consciousness. When Foucault writes that subjection is 'born mechanically from a fictitious relation',[99] he does not have in mind a mechanism of mystification, or even an imaginary relation, because both formulations continue to hold on to a unitary notion of consciousness, even as it is inverted with, reproduced by, or designated as an *effect* of, ideology. Foucault opposes this fictitious relation, that creates a disciplined subject according to a process of self-surveillance, with a more direct relation that renders the body submissive by the often violent inculcation of codes of conduct. Such an antinomy between a repressive power and a non-coercive, disciplinary power should not, however, obfuscate Foucault's continued focus upon the site of the *physical* body rather than the sphere of consciousness. It is certainly the case that Foucault is not interested in an exploration of some already constituted site within the subject that merely responds to power; the entire analysis of discourse and the discursive construction of the subject warns against such a prioritization of subjectivity. The philosopher of discourse does not probe some opaque interiority of the subject because the space of interiority is something which is carved out of subjectivity by power, rather than existing as a deep source of the subject's unconscious. There is, according to Foucault, no simple opposition between interior and exterior, between inside and outside, not because the interior site of the subject is merely an empty place but rather because interiority is none other than the *interiorization of the outside*.[100] In this way, Foucault politicizes the construction of the subject: all that is outside the subject forms a hinge for interiority, that which Deleuze calls, following Foucault's own discussion in 'The Thought of the Outside', a hollowing out, or a 'fold' of the outside. Moreover, this folding over, or doubling, is not some mechanical process of inversion, determination or causality. The subject is formed in a dynamic space, a space which can never be fully rationalized by power. If power is always the site of political struggle and contestation, then the subject too, is the site of continual struggle, transformation and differentiation. Furthermore, and as Deleuze observes, the process of subjectivation or 'folding' operates, clearly, in both the ontological and the social field;[101] the ontological site of the subject's constitution is one governed by dispersal and multiple possibility. The folding over of power upon form *becomes* the subject; the mode of constitution of the subject is, therefore, *immediately* politicized.

However, it is easy to see how this apparent fluidity of form and becoming (a true materialism) can become locked into particular techniques of power. There are two particular instances in *Discipline and Punish* that illustrate this reductive move. In a chapter entitled 'Docile Bodies', Foucault views the relationship between power and subjectivity in terms of signals: 'it is a question not of understanding the injunction but of perceiving the signal and reacting to it immediately, according to a more or less artificial *prearranged code*.'[102] Here, the docile body appears to be fully constituted by the process of obeying signals. By either obeying or opposing the signal, the subject develops a sense of conscience or resistance. In this way the soul, as conscience, and as sense of self, is carved out of a being who becomes a subject through the interplay of forces of power. Even resistance appears to inhere in power, to be complicit with the law. Is there a way of understanding the subject as a site of struggle that may exceed, or disrupt, the lines of power that seem to constitute it? Foucault's account of the 'homogenizing effects'[103] of the panopticon give rise to an all-pervasive 'unitary technique' of power which seems to allow little space for transgression.[104] Whilst the panopticon individualizes subjects, arranges them in hierarchies, creating a differential distribution between those who are contained or assimilated and those who are excluded, identities and differences nevertheless seem to exist in a series of systematic equivalences. 'Differences', Joan Copjec observes,'do not threaten panopticon power; they feed it.'[105]

The concentration upon the corporeal investment of power (e.g. the docile body) in *Discipline and Punish* may underestimate the extent to which this investment of the body itself requires *psychic expenditure on the part of the subject*.[106] This is not to suggest that Foucault necessarily requires a phenomenology of psychic experience to counter the sweeping effects of disciplinary techniques, although a number of theorists have claimed that it is a psychoanalytic account of the subject that he lacks. However, if the site of production (and, of course, reproduction) of subjectivity – and indeed the site of power itself – is, as *The History of Sexuality Vol. 1* claims, a 'moving substrate of force relations',[107] then it is crucial to recognize that the subject is not the *passive recipient* of power but a source of volatility, an unfinished project of social being whom power can seek to master but never contain. To locate this paradoxical form of subjectivity in Foucault's work is difficult not only because of its under-theorization, but also because the very mechanisms of power may lead the subject to reaffirm the power relations that seek to constitute it. It is this paradoxical form of the subject that we will now try to unpack.

Subjectivity and the residue of agency

Like Althusser's interpellated subjects, Foucault's disciplinary subjects *can* work 'all by themselves'. In this way, the subject seems to merge with power, renewing its own mode of subjection and reinforcing existent lines of power in the process. At the same time, however, Foucault does attach a certain significance to a force or energy which cannot be domesticated by power relations: 'there is always something in the social body ... which in some sense escapes relations of power, something which is by no means a more or less docile or reactive primal matter, but rather a centrifugal movement, an inverse energy, a discharge.'[108] We have already pointed out how the engendering of the subject is a dynamic process. This should not be obscured by what is, in many readings of Foucault, a tendency to view the production of the subject in quasi-behaviourist terms.[109] The activity whereby the subject reinforces its subjection to power and confirms its own structure (through, for example, self-surveillance) is simultaneously one that gives rise to something in the subject which resists power.

In her recent book *The Psychic Life of Power: Theories of Subjection*, Judith Butler proposes to supplement Foucault's account of subjectivation with a psychoanalytic reading of the subject whilst remaining cognizant of the ways in which the latter's own reading of the concepts of desire and the unconscious may render this an uneasy alliance to forge.[110] In *The Order of Things*, Foucault does appear to recognize the radical potentiality of psychoanalysis as a counter-science. 'Psychoanalysis', he writes, 'advances and leaps over representation, overflows it on the side of finitude';[111] it pits itself *against* man, it *exceeds* man in his positivity, by focusing on the unconscious or the unthought. Nonetheless, being deployed within the space of the human sciences, psychoanalysis is party to all the aporias uncovered by these human disciplines. It is the tireless search for the hidden origin that shapes the logic of psychoanalysis (and all other forms of modern knowledge) which Foucault chooses to emphasize in his later writings on the genealogy of the subject and sexuality.

What is the content of Foucault's reflections upon psychoanalysis? In *The History of Sexuality Vol. 1*, the discursive practice of psychoanalysis is understood primarily to reaffirm the will to truth by creating a formally unknowable, secret core within the subject: sexuality. Psychoanalysis seeks out the hidden truth of the subject's sexuality through processes of confession (i.e. the talking cure), and controls sexuality via a repressive law of prohibition.[112] According to Foucault, sexuality is itself a discursive construction, and desire merely the incitement of power's own incursions to the body. If psychoanalysis makes of the body an erotic site, it also derives a certain pleasure through its exercise: 'the specific pleasure of the true discourse on pleasure.'[113] Desire and the law are the most intimate partners, and where Nietzsche adumbrates the pleasures of the priestly conscience, Foucault depicts a form of power anchored to the pleasure it uncovers. Sexuality, moreover, is not viewed as a permanent condition of subjectivity; it is the product of a 'game of truth' called psychoanalysis, one which has, for some time, formed the historical *a priori* for possible experience.

In his 1963 essay 'A Preface to Transgression' Foucault argues that 'sexuality is only decisive for our culture to the extent that it is *spoken*.'[114] With this unequivocal remark, Foucault begins his largely cursory interpretation of psychoanalytic theory.[115] Continuing the Christian model of the penance, psychoanalysis uses the dialogical confession as a way to regulate behaviour and prohibit sexual deviance. When psychoanalysis reduces itself to such a linguistic game of truth, wherein language seeks out 'the most imperceptible movements of our self',[116] it misrecognizes its own conditions of existence. We find repeated here many of Foucault's criticisms of deconstruction because both psychoanalysis and deconstruction are understood to pursue a form of linguistic analysis (of the unconscious and of texts, respectively). This focus is to the detriment of a wider consideration of the discursive and non-discursive conditions and practices which have formed them. *The History of Sexuality Vol. 1* proposes to consider this wider angle, and psychoanalysis is duly accorded its place within the myriad of discursive events that form the horizon of the modern experience of sexuality.

For Foucault, the psychoanalytic confession does not bring a sense of atonement to the subject. If the subject is brought closer to an illusive sense of self-knowledge, it is also exposed to the anxieties of guilt and the complex effects of repression. However, the subject's desire is not simply the object of repression because the law 'is what constitutes desire and the lack on which it is predicated'.[117] Yet here Foucault forgets to add that the discursive mode of constitution is incomplete and subject to ceaseless modification. Desire and the law, resistance and power, the unconscious and techniques of regulation, are not simply causal relations where the former term is the effect of the latter. The former are the folds of power-knowledge and as such they are subject to contestation as well as regulation. Resistance, as part of the fold of prohibitory techniques which produces the subject, is brought closer to the outside, to the *real* brutalities of power which the latter tries to mask; resistance seems to exceed, therefore, any purely functional relation to power. In his reading of Foucault, Gilles Deleuze considers resistance as 'the thought of the outside'.[118] Foucault's radical idea, for Deleuze, was that of 'a dimension of subjectivity derived from power and knowledge without being dependent on them.'[119] It is this dimension that Butler appears to address in her recent reading of Foucault.

Butler's book pursues the dual moment of subjection and subjectivation. Her reflections on the construction of the subject have many resonances with the arguments and formulations developed in the current work and they are worth exploring in detail. As already noted, Butler's conception of the subject draws heavily on psychoanalytic theory. However, she remains wary of those forms of psychoanalysis which romanticize resistance, and this 'entails the reemergence of a Foucauldian perspective *within* psychoanalysis'.[120] We have pointed out that there is implicit in Foucault's construction of the subject (which is an *engendering process*) a sense of how acts of repetitive self-regulation on the part of the subject may also open up a space for resistance. Butler attaches a psychoanalytic currency to this interpretation: 'through that neurotic repetition the subject pursues its own dissolution, its own unravelling, a pursuit that marks an agency, but not the *subject's* agency – rather, the agency of a desire that aims at the dissolution of the subject, where the subject stands as a bar to that desire.'[121] To put this in other words, repetition might not consolidate the unity of normalization but instead generate effects which may challenge its operations. If the effects of power are not unitary and homogenizing, it is possible to understand the ways in which multiple points of resistance may proliferate in power's wake.

Butler rests her conception of the subject upon an inaugurating turn. This notion of turning, also described, in its more Nietzschean form, as a recoiling of power, appears to follow the Deleuzian reading of the ontological fold outlined above.[122] Deleuze describes how this folding has been 'unfolded' or flattened, and apparently captured by techniques of discipline and normalization. However, Deleuze's reading of Foucault tries to counter this interpretation, which can also lead to readings of Foucault's later writings on the self-government of the self as a nostalgic pursuit of an inner-autonomy or an intrinsic source of agency. There can be no closure of power because the fold of subjectivation 'continues to create itself.' It is this to which Deleuze refers when he talks about the aleatory nature of resistance as an encounter with chance, a reference which also echoes the concerns of the later Althusser.[123] Butler's theory of the subject also recognizes that there is no absolute subjection. However, in so far as the subject is a partially subjected social being, the subject may thwart its own desire by denying, repressing, and resisting the claims of desire. 'A subject turned against itself (its desire)', Butler notes, 'appears to be a condition of the persistence of the subject.'[124]

This 'push and pull' of the subject constitutes a vacillation at the heart of subjectivity which should be taken into account by any theory of the subject. Significantly, it does not presuppose a subject as the basis of this activity. Vacillation is not the second-order reflexive act of an already constituted consciousness contemplating its own self-relation. Of course, it may be this in a retrospective sense because, as Butler points out, the turning of the subject often has to be assumed; or, as Althusser would put it, we are always-already subjects. However, if the notion of vacillation is an attempt to account for the *inaugurating moment* of the subject, then it must indicate something more. It is clear that Foucault, Deleuze, and Butler too, understand the production of the subject in terms of this vacillating moment. Butler's formulation owes something to Hegel, where the dialectic perpetually makes and unmakes subjectivity. In contrast, both Foucault's and Deleuze's formulations owe something to Nietzsche, and perhaps Spinoza. The latter philosophers have explored this dynamic constitution of the subject, where the body is viewed as the physical–material site of ideas (about the subject and knowledge).[125]

Both sets of interpretations reconfigure the question of agency in the wake of the dislocation of an original subject of action. The vacillation between, on the one hand, the agency of desire seeking fragmentation of the subject, and, on the other hand, the continued observance of the law (viewed as a symbolic law of social power) which enables the subject to endure, marks out a (confined) space of agency. This location of agency moves discussions beyond an artificial opposition between naive voluntarism and dogmatic determinism. Hence, repetition, which, for Butler, signals this space of agency by default, 'becomes the non-place of subversion, the possibility of a re-embodying of the subjectivating norm that can redirect its normativity.'[126]

It must be pointed out, however, that Butler's discussion of subversion also relies upon a description of a performative staging of social norms and their possible *failure to constitute* the subject. Here, her reading draws upon Althusser's notion of interpellation as a hailing of individuals to take up their designated social position. Above, and in earlier discussions, we have pointed to a theoretical limit in Althusser's formulation, namely that he does not pursue the question of the internalization of ideological forms (be they norms, roles or social positions) and their concomitant effects of subjectivation. Now, Butler is willing to attribute a far greater weight to the mechanism of interpellation because she wishes to consider its possible failure. Nonetheless, she also appears to misread the centrality of misrecognition in Althusser's account. Following Lacan, *méconnaissance* is the necessary, inescapable structure of all experience, not merely because it dupes individuals as to their social status (viewing all as free individuals) but because through this movement something called a subject is produced, forever fissured and bearing the mark of this inaugurating experience. In *The Psychic Life of Power* interpellation is not viewed in this latter sense, but rather as a positively denoted form of recognition which may, in certain instances, be *mis*recognized.[127] This leads Butler to focus upon the psychoanalytic question of the unravelling of identity rather than the generalized ontological fracture which, for Lacan, constitutes and deconstitutes the subject. This observation should not detract from the saliency of Butler's conception of the subject. It is important nevertheless to underline the absent lines of debate as well as those which are explicitly elaborated in her reading.

Where may we go in Foucault's work to trace the thought of resistance? Why is there no pursuit of a psychoanalytic conception of resistance? In his recent book *The Ticklish Subject*, Slavoj Žižek has argued that a theoretical partnership between a genealogy of power and psychoanalysis is precluded by Foucault's rather narrow conception of transgression, where resistance is always coopted by the edifice of power.[128] Foucault's reluctance to consider a project of psychoanalysis which may exceed the limit of what he calls in *The Order of Things* the empirical–transcendental doublet may indicate the *obscuration* of the subject in his writings. Nonetheless, many of Foucault's early writings on the relationship between psychoanalysis and madness, specifically the latter's expression at the *limits of language* illustrate a nascent interest in the 'thought of the outside' which never fully evolved into sustained, engaged relation with the genealogy of power.[129] Hence, the struggle for a difference *outside* of repetition was never explicitly developed by Foucault. Perhaps if the reverberations of subjectivity are obscured, it is because of a more pressing problem which was never properly resolved. Might not the question of the non-discursive, that region presented, but never fully explored in *The Archaeology of Knowledge*, reintroduce itself here in the discussion of the subject? Certainly Foucault's later regard for the strategic site of discourse eschewed all epistemological concerns in favour of more diagnostic writings. Thus both the *sign of the subject* and the site of the *non-discursive*, the two problems isolated and identified in Section II of this chapter, return to haunt Foucault's work on power and resistance.

There is, however, an important caveat in this observation, in that both of the aforementioned problems have now been diluted in new relations of immanence between power and subjectivity. We have claimed above that it makes no sense to entertain a determinist or causal account of power and subjectivity. This is not only because Foucault's genealogies expose the multiple strands of any such relation, but, more significantly, because the subject is not *turned inside out* by power, that is, it is not in any simple sense an effect of power. No mechanical process of inversion, or rigid causality informs the cause–effect relation described by Foucault. Once again, it is to Nietzsche and Spinoza that we may turn for a consideration of power and subjectivity as relations of immanence; both writers contest the notion of a primary or final cause. In *Beyond Good and Evil*, Nietzsche contests the notion of *causa sui* as a 'perversion of logic' which contributes to a philosophical lapse into determinism and places artificial limits on what is possible and what can be thought. Likewise, in the case of Spinoza, we have seen that notions of attribute and mode escape the logic of cause–effect. These produce an interconnectedness between forms and ideas, between the generation of an act and its effect.[130] In Foucault's case, truth is not independent of its effect, it is not prior to its relations, rather, it is always bound up with a discursive formation, with relations of power-knowledge. There is no priority given to truth just as there is no priority given to the subject. If power engenders the subject then it also transforms itself at the same time. Relations and effects that are immanent to each other will alter, relocate and reconstitute themselves in an endless sequence. When Foucault wrote 'where there is power there is resistance' it is according to relations of immanence that he wished to view both terms. Hence the many descriptions of power as network, circuit, grid and capillary. These reflections on the rejection of cause do not obviate the above criticisms of the undeveloped regions of Foucault's work that obscure the subject, but they do shed some light upon the shape of his (implicit) ontology of the subject.

All moves to reflect upon and analyse the space of subjectivity in Foucault's work are part of a creative synthesis because such interpretations must necessarily be formed out of a fusion of different (sometimes competing) works with different modes of presentation (the fragment, the interview, the book). This chapter has tried to indicate the ways in which Foucault's *oeuvre* is governed by a continuity rather than by clear philosophical breaks. This is not to say, however, that different philosophical styles (rather than distinct methods) have not informed Foucault's writings; it is certainly between a certain phenomenology and a carefully interpreted notion of structure that Foucault's work can be situated, where due attention is given to the significance of the *between*. The concept of discourse seeded in *The Order of Things* and flowered in *The Archaeology of Knowledge* informs all of his writings and it is the latter work which points to a view of sociopolitical (discursive) formations characterized by regimes of power, knowledge and subjectivity with attendant lines of force as well as sites of contestation, struggle, transformation and possibility. Foucault's discursive construction of the subject can only be understood within this wider mesh of relations, relations which ceaselessly modify and transform it, producing (as if in power's wake) a new *potentia* of power and a new mode of subjectivity, always underdetermined and always yet to be determined.

CONCLUSION

THE PERSISTENCE OF
THE SUBJECT

persist (pə'sist), v. [ad. L. *persist-ĕre* to continue steadfastly, to persist, f. PER- 2 + *sistre* to stand. Cf. F *persister* C14th c. in Hatz.-Darm.]

  1. *intr.* To continue firmly or obstinately *in* a state, opinion, purpose, or course of action, esp. against opposition, or remonstrance. Formerly also with *infin.*

  b. To be insistent or urgent in a statement or question; to persist in saying or asserting.

  2. To remain or continue to be (something or of some quality).

  3. To remain standing (against opposing force); to stop short (at some point).

  4. To remain in existence; to last, endure.

[Oxford English Dictionary, 2nd edn. 1989]

This conclusion will return to some of the problems presented in the Introduction of this book. We are now in a position to interrogate and assess critically the claim that the subject *persists*, even in philosophical discourses which appear to announce its dissolution. Certainly, the arguments of the preceding chapters have contested the simplicity of theoretical perspectives that proclaim enigmatically the *death of the subject*. The question of the subject is an ineluctable philosophical problem; indeed it continues to orientate the thought of all the thinkers discussed in this book. Hence, the observation of the subject's persistence applies as much to the quasi-structuralist positions of Louis

Althusser and Jacques Lacan, as to the post-structuralist positions of Derrida and Foucault. Too much is subsumed under the auspices of structuralism and post-structuralism for the terms to have more value beyond that of generalization. For example, the former school of thought is often viewed as rejecting the subject *tout court*, but it is very clear from our analysis of Althusser in Chapter 2 that the subject is reconfigured and repositioned in relation to structure rather than simply annulled by it. Indeed, we have pointed to the tenuity of these labels which seem to fit the respective thinkers in name alone.

Perhaps it is more accurate to see the problems considered in this work as lying *between* phenomenology and structuralism. On a number of occasions we have drawn attention to the shadow of Husserlian phenomenology upon contemporary thought. Husserl's phenomenological reduction was designed to purge his method of anthropologism, in much the same way as structuralism sought to restrict the determining function of the subject. Husserl's return to the *constitutive conditions* of subjectivity was an exploration of the foundations for the principle of subjectivity itself, to which contemporary thought has also returned. However, the effort is no longer one of establishing the true essence and attributes of the subject, as it was for Husserl, although it is *still* a project which seeks to understand how consciousness and subjectivity are *constituted* and *determined*, if incompletely. Nonetheless, the philosophical antecedents of the positions presented in the preceding chapters are quite diverse and it is not the aim of these final remarks to try to summarize or simplify them. Each of the chapters has considered a general or common problem of the subject through quite *distinctive* interpretations. A particular conception of the subject may have appeared and, via a certain philosophical genealogy, to have orientated the thought of each, but the question of the subject always occupies a specific problematic and is always located within a particular philosophical position in each chapter.

A significant paradox has been noted to pervade the philosophical study of the concept of the subject. Not only do our references to the subject seem to assume the existence of the subject in some form or other, but the repetition of the very *question* of the subject appears to confirm its structure, a structure which announces itself in the form of the question: 'what is the subject?' This circle of referentiality is quite unavoidable. Indeed, this paradox is rendered more pressing and intractable after the series of chapters herein, because the subject has been conceived precisely as an open territory and as a site of multiple possibility. The paradox of the subject is not just whether the latter is formally displaced or repositioned in discourse (and recognized to be so); the paradox is extensive and labyrinthine in character, and it invites us to struggle with its complexities.

It is this paradox that sustains the subject, even when the subject is deemed to be absent, or ceases within a particular discourse. It attests, therefore, to the subject's enduring importance and its continuing significance for philosophy. Of course, this is not to say that the problem of the subject cannot be reorientated and rethought creatively, but this can only take place *after* an acknowledgement of the significance of philosophical inheritance, and henceforth with a *lighter*, more qualified, relation to the past. This is precisely why the style and mode of questioning noted in the Introduction to this book becomes important: the question orientates the subject and the way in which philosophical problems pertaining to it are exposed. However, the most important repercussion of the identified paradox is that its relative *neglect* opens up philosophy to the attendant risks and temptations inherent in the order of the paradox. As Derrida has shown, it is better to be vigilant about the double-bind which links a concept to its philosophical history rather than ignore the effects of its structure upon our thought. Only then are we in a position to transform this relation. Let us now rehearse these problems, and this paradox, and the extent to which they were acknowledged, in the writings of Lukács, Althusser, Lacan, Derrida and Foucault.

Given the centrality of Marxism to their reflections, the writings of both Lukács and Althusser on the problem of the subject are often assessed by the weight they give to the subject's *agency*. When placed against a concept of structure, this opposition limits and contains questions within a certain constrained form. If, in very different senses, the critics of Lukács and Althusser can label both as idealists, this criticism must be built upon, and hence reliant upon, the artificial opposition between agency and structure. Both Lukács and Althusser were aware of the ways in which philosophy, and political philosophy, could determine, contain and uphold a hegemonic conception of the subject, and use its power to effect the constitution of social reality. This renders a far more complex form to the notion of agency. However, Lukács' problem was that of the historical *genesis* of subjectivity, and whilst he explored critically the antinomies of philosophy, he maintained, nonetheless, a distinction between essence and appearance that turned his position back upon the classical conception of the subject. Ultimately, Lukács' social ontology of the subject sought an identity between subject and object which could be ascribed or posited in theory alone. It is such an ontology which inscribes the idealist moments of his thought. The paradox of the subject lay unconscious in Lukács' thought.

The paradox of the subject enters Althusser's position in several interesting ways, and it is clear that the itinerary of his thought finally caught up with the nature and weight of this paradox. We have seen that much of Althusser's writings tend to presuppose a distinction between science and ideology; this reflects his quest to construct, like Husserl before him, a rigorous science freed from the contamination of subjectivism. Of course, Althusser turns primarily not to Husserl but to Spinoza for his philosophical inspiration. For Spinoza and Althusser, the subject is tied to all that is imaginary and ideological, and the form of the 'knowledge of the third kind' (Spinoza), or science (Althusser), must be dislocated from the subject as ground of truth. However, Althusser is unwilling, throughout most of his work, to pursue the modification of the subject insisted upon by Spinoza, which enjoined body and idea, and established an interconnection between the imaginary and the true as different gradations of knowledge. Hence Althusser's epistemology remains somewhat abstract; the distinction between ideology and science remains tenuous and their borders are left unexplored. This is the case for the theory of ideology too, where the insidious power of philosophy to determine the form of the subject is not explored adequately. Ironically, it is because Althusser *recognizes* the philosophical and ideological knot of subjectivity and representation that he does not try to untie it, or does so only partially through his engagement with psychoanalysis. It is in his final writings that the paradox of the subject, and its effects, are brought to bear upon the science/ideology dualism, and upon the subject constructed by ideology. Aleatory materialism returned to the question of the subject and elicited a 'parallelism' between subjectivity and knowledge. Althusser's writings point directly to problems encountered by Derrida and Foucault, and the former's reflections on the question of the subject anticipate in important ways the positions of the latter two thinkers.

Lacanian psychoanalysis is caught forever in the paradox of subjectivity. Psychoanalysis concerns itself directly with the experience of the subject and it attempts to derive a form of knowledge based on this experience. In this way, Lacanian psychoanalysis is an exemplary case of the paradox of the subject because it is concerned with the subject both in the world (as empirical subject) and of the world (as transcendental subject). In Chapter 3, we charted the ways in which Lacanian psychoanalysis was tied to philosophical questions concerning the subject. Furthermore, Lacan's utilization of this philosophical history (specifically his use of Descartes, but also through the many Hegelian motifs scattered throughout his writings) was understood to generate a *foundational attachment* to a subject of certainty, and to the plane of representation upon which signs and signifiers could circulate and be inscribed. Of course, this philosophical foundation or structure is an *imaginary* one for Lacan, as it is, too, for Althusser and Spinoza. Nevertheless, and somewhat ironically, Lacan remains blind to the ways in which this imaginary structure is underwritten necessarily by the Cartesian subject that unwittingly supports his construction of both subjectivity and language.

Our presentation of Foucault in Chapter 5 pointed to the ways in which his archaeology of knowledge tried to maintain a conceptual distance between the discursive production of knowledge and the determining activity of the subject. At the same time, Foucault's archaeological method attributes a radical primacy to the statements and rules governing discourse, that almost seem to take the place of the subject. In other words, and like Althusser, Foucault was reluctant to consider anything other than a hegemonic conception of the subject as author of discourse. That the subject *in the process of its formation* could be implicated in discourse as a site of possibility, rather than as a mere subject position, was not considered. Consequently Foucault's critics view him as caught in the empirico-transcendental doublet which for him dictated the limits of the human sciences. This failure to observe the paradox of the subject at work within his texts generates a number of aporias which were carried through into his genealogy of power. However, in the movement from archaeology to genealogy, these aporias were reframed and confronted. According to Foucault, the construction of the subject by power can never be absolute and fully rationalized. The subject is an unfinished project of subjectivation; Foucault responds to the problem of the incomplete ideological constitution of the subject in Althusser by arguing that the repetitious acts of self-discipline do not construct a subject in passivity but mark the subject with a *potentia passiva*. It is this passion, as excess or residue that renews the concept of the subject with a new dynamism.

However, it is Derrida who remains the thinker most sensitive to the paradox of the subject and therefore, probably most likely to maintain the idea of the subject's radical persistence. The tasks and focus of deconstruction extend deep into philosophy. Deconstruction explores, locates and questions the conditions governing the possibility of conceptualization, not in order to assert new conditions, but to announce the impossibility, or the radical contingency of, all possible conditions. The implications for the concept of the subject are clear. Derrida points out the futility of hoping to break with the metaphysical underpinnings of subjectivity, without considering adequately the conditions of possibility that give rise to particular conceptions of the subject. The subject has inscribed upon its surfaces the traces of all the conceptual transformations which gave rise to it. Deconstruction endlessly traverses this paradox, which Derrida also denotes by the descriptions *aporia* and *double-bind*. If *différance* is the fluid, mobile, disruptive and contingent moment of every structure of meaning, and of every concept, then *différance* as possibility envelops the subject *before* it becomes a subject, forever preventing and unsettling its attempts to become a subject. Thus, the moment of constitution or closure of subjectivity, by whatever philosophical means, *never quite arrives*. The subject persists only through a certain ceasing to be. Derrida's attention to the paradox of the subject, elucidated above through the structural play of *différance*, together with his regard for the double-bind which ties philosophy and subjectivity, ensures that the imperative of deconstruction is one which challenges the status of the philosophical subject by locating it upon the impossible, shifting ground of its conditions, and recognizes the persistence of the subject within these interrogations. *The deconstruction of the subject will always take place upon a metaphysical terrain which will attempt continuously to incorporate it into the dominant ontological structure.*

We can conclude from this brief summary of the preceding chapters that the writings of Lukács, Althusser, Lacan, Derrida and Foucault, all traverse the paradox of subjectivity, but observe and negotiate its intervention in their constructions of the subject, in varying degrees. Certainly, all confront this paradox because each recognizes and takes up the imperative of a *critique* of the philosophical grounding of the subject in order to free the theory of knowledge from the subject's authorship. However, in most cases this means that the concept of the subject is elided and not always fully recognized for its effects upon the structure of knowledge. Althusser and Foucault are, to a certain extent, mindful of this paradox, but it is Derrida who fully acknowledges its existence and its exigency, and follows its operations most closely. Deconstruction moves within the heart of the paradox; it follows its doubts and oscillations, its enigmas and its ambiguities. Here, within its heart, *but no longer at the centre of the subject*, deconstruction reconstructs a *spectre* of the subject in the wake of its paradox.

If it is deconstruction that is most responsive to the paradox of the subject, we must make, nonetheless, a number of more general observations about the implications of the positions developed herein for the concept of the subject. First, none of the thinkers considered succumbs to the temptation presented by all forms of structuralism and post-structuralism, namely that *something else* comes to stand in for the subject, taking over the latter's function as determining origin. That structure (or power, or language) can both masquerade as subject, and can come to take up the latter's central place, through a form of categorical inversion, are two of the perpetual risks of structuralism. Althusser, Lacan, Foucault and Derrida avoid both of these problems. Second, the subject is never *simply* conceived as an effect of ideology, language, or power, because the logic of cause–effect has been deconstructed. Foucault, Derrida and Althusser (in his later work, in particular) contest the notion of a primary or final cause which determines and places limits on the subject. If ideology, power and language are understood to engender the subject, they also form part of a transformatory process which disperses the subject as much as it centres it. Cause–effect relations are productive and dynamic; causality is opened up, therefore, to difference and temporality. In this way, the subject is sustained by a network of relations, where cause and effect are immanent to each other and signify the openness of the subject's determination. Each thinker poses the question of the subject *in relation*, be it to history, to power, to the power of thought itself. In each case we have been able to point to future creations of the subject, in short, to its multiple possibilities. We have also drawn attention to the importance of the mode of questioning of the subject. What is it about *questioning* that is so significant? Let us, finally, reflect upon the nature and form of the question.

To a great extent, *the subject persists in the questions posed regarding its existence and its possibility*. As we have noted above, the repetition of some questions appear to sustain a certain structure of the subject. However, to take up the paradox of the subject within the form of the question, that is, to sustain a *reflexive* regard for the problem of the subject, is also to reframe and transform the subject of the question. For example, and with attention to the problems present in his problematic, Lacan recognizes that the subject is always constituted by the insistent demand, the unceasing exigency of the question: *Che vuoi?* (what do you *desire?*). This question is always framed within the linguistic field of the Other, and the subject can never find a satisfying, complete, response. If the question generates a certain anxiety in its bearer, as well as in the one to whom it is directed, it is because the response to the question always *stops short*, bringing only an illusive sense of fullness which immediately dissipates once again into the form of a question. The most that the response can do is interrupt the subject, opening it up (*Spaltung*) to perpetual oscillation and temporal movement. For Lacan, this structure of repetition and interruption, the 'dialectic of desire', shapes both the form and the temporality of the question, which is rendered open and without conclusion, and the structure of the subject, which becomes reliant upon the shifting ground of the signifier.

Even the apparently solid question '*what is …?*' contains this suspension of knowledge and determination. The posing of a question always opens up many possible responses. Indeed, the answer is often the *loss* of the openness and possibility with which the question always begins. It is clear that the thinkers considered in this book all recognize the ambiguous form of the question of the subject, and that a definite answer is one which closes the question of the subject. The question of the subject turns (in a reflexive sense) precisely on this ambiguity; thus, the interrogation of the subject introduces contingency into the question and hence opens up the subject to the indetermination of its form, that is, to its status *as* a question. Quite clearly, the question cannot *lose* the subject: *this is because the paradox of referentiality always pushes its way into the question of the subject.* As Blanchot writes perceptively: 'to question is to seek, and to seek is to search radically, to go to the bottom, to sound, to work at the bottom, and finally to uproot. *This uprooting which holds on to the root is the work of the question.*'[1] There can be no end to the traversing of the question of the subject, not because there is no end to the subject, but because the subject is sustained by, endures, and persists in, all the questions posed of its existence.

NOTES

INTRODUCTION

1. G.W.F. Hegel, *The Phenomenology of Spirit*, trans. A. Miller (Oxford University Press, 1977), sec. 66.
2. See A.J. Cascardi, *The Subject of Modernity* (Cambridge University Press, 1991), p. 10; Etienne Balibar 'Subjection and Subjectivisation', in Joan Copjec (ed.), *Supposing the Subject* (Verso, 1994), pp. 1–15; also of interest is D. Shanahan, *Towards a Genealogy of Individualism* (University of Massachusetts, 1992).
3. What I am broadly calling the 'historical' here might be said to offer up the 'background framework' for thinking (see Charles Taylor's discussion in *Sources of the Self* (Cambridge University Press, 1989), ch. 1). However, the historical is only one of a multiplicity of 'scenes' which frame thought's relation to, and folding in upon, existence. Here I emphasize the historico-political level because this particular overdetermination of thought is not always recognized.
4. V. Descombes, *Modern French Philosophy* (Cambridge University Press, 1980), p. 23.
5. Paul Ricoeur, 'The Question of the Subject: The Challenge of Semiology', in his *Conflict of Interpretations: Essays in Hermeneutics* (Northwestern University Press, 1974), p. 236.
6. See the recent collection edited by Eduardo Cadava, Peter Connor and Jean-Luc Nancy, *Who Comes After the Subject?* (Routledge, 1991).
7. Indeed, as Derrida argues in *Of Spirit*, trans. G. Bennington and R. Bowlby (Chicago University Press, 1991), it is not just a particular mode of questioning but the very status and privilege of the question.
8. See J. Derrida ' "Eating Well" or the Calculation of the Subject: an Interview with Jacques Derrida', in Cadava *et al.* op. cit. and S. Bordo and M. Moussa, 'Rehabilitating the "I" ', in H.J. Silverman (ed.), *Questioning Foundations: Truth/Subjectivity/Culture* (Routledge, 1993). More recently, Slavoj Žižek has defended the centrality of the Cartesian *cogito* to contemporary reflections on the subject. It is important, he writes, 'to bring to light its forgotten obverse, the excessive, unacknowledged kernel of the *cogito*, which is far from the pacifying image of the transparent Self' (*The Ticklish Subject: The Absent Centre of Political Ontology* (Verso, 1999), p. 2). For Derrida and others, it is not so much the hyperbolic experience of the *cogito*, which *is* certainly acknowledged, but the more troubling question of metaphysical residues of Cartesianism in certain constructions of the subject. We will have occasion to explore this issue later in the book (particularly in relation to Lacan).

9. This distinction between structuralism and post-structuralism is itself rather tenuous and perhaps only retrospectively imposed upon a very diverse body of theoretical enquiry. Derrida even claims that phenomenology in its first phase is structuralist. See 'Genesis and Structure in Husserl's Phenomenology', in *Writing and Difference*, trans. A. Bass (Routledge and Kegan Paul, 1978).

10. Derrida, 'Eating Well', op. cit., pp. 104–5.

11. It is this distinction which forms the heart of Kant's critical system and passes by way of Husserl's 'paradox of human subjectivity' in *The Crisis of the European Sciences*, trans. D. Carr (Northwestern University Press, 1970), p. 178. This paradoxical existence also marks the status of the empirical–transcendental doublet discussed by Foucault in *The Order of Things* (see Chapter 5 of the present study).

12. Kierkegaard also observes that the paradox 'wills its own downfall' and will consequently lack understanding if it loses its passion for engagement with the ineluctable question. This observation may itself help to account for the rather spurious death of the subject in postmodernism noted earlier in this introduction. Its terms of reference cannot ignore this paradox. For Kierkegaard's discussion of the paradox of thought see his *Philosophical Fragments*, ed. and trans. H.V. Hong and E.H. Hong (Princeton University Press, 1985), pp. 37–48, quoted here at pp. 37, 39. An excellent book by David Carr, *The Paradox of Subjectivity: the Self in the Transcendental Tradition* (Oxford University Press, 1999) was also published as the present work was completed.

13. For example, both Etienne Balibar and Giorgio Agamben take issue with the Hegelianism implicit in methods which may claim the abolition of the subject-of-consciousness but nonetheless retain the essential structure of the dialectic, or return to the contemplation of the structure and logic of subjectivity. This is the theoretical risk of all philosophical work on the subject, the present one included. See Balibar, *The Philosophy of Marx*, trans. C. Turner (Verso, 1994) and Agamben, *Infancy and History: Essays on the Destruction of Experience*, trans. L. Heron (Verso, 1993).

14. In his essay 'Prolegomena to Any Post-Deconstructive Subjectivity', Simon Critchley appears to make such a claim. See S. Critchley and P. Dews (eds), *Deconstructive Subjectivities* (State University of New York Press, 1996), p. 26. One of the aims of this study is to point out that the constitution of the subject is more complex than the 'logic of effect' would appear to allow. Indeed the different ways in which notions of constitution are used (as opposed to those deriving from construction) in relation to the subject have very significant implications.

CHAPTER 1

1. G. Deleuze and F. Guattari, *What is Philosophy?*, trans. H. Tomlinson and G. Burchill (Verso, 1994), pp. 16, 18, emphasis added.

2. V. Descombes, *Modern French Philosophy*, trans. L. Scott-Fox and J.M. Harding (Cambridge University Press, 1980), p. 76.

3. Arguably it is the case that the conception of a determinant subjectivity is one that can only be *retrospectively* attributed to the philosophical past. See also

Critchley 'Prolegomena to Any Post-Deconstructive Subjectivity', in S. Critchley and P. Dews (eds), *Deconstructive Subjectivities* (SUNY Press, 1996).

4. One recent collection which aims to present a more differentiated picture of contemporary philosophy's historical presuppositions is K. Ameriks and D. Sturma (eds), *The Modern Subject: Conceptions of the Self in Classical German Philosophy* (State University of New York Press, 1995).

5. See, however, A. Schrift, *Nietzsche's French Legacy* (Routledge, 1995) for one such attempt.

6. Some philosophers nonetheless contest this Cartesian primacy. In 'Citizen Subject', Etienne Balibar claims that Descartes does not name the thinking thing, *cogito*, as subject. His philosophy is still wedded to substance. It is to Kant that we must turn for the first formulation of subject as a sovereign being. It is at this point, too, that the political subject, i.e. the citizen, emerges. See 'Citizen Subject', in *Who Comes After the Subject?*, E. Cadava, P. Connor and J.L. Nancy (eds) (Routledge, 1991), pp. 33–57.

7. The term is S. Bordo's. See *The Flight to Objectivity: Essays on Cartesianism and Culture* (SUNY Press, 1987).

8. H. Arendt, *The Human Condition* (Chicago University Press, 1958), p. 275.

9. Rene Descartes, *Discourse on Method and the Meditations*, trans. F.E. Sutcliffe (Penguin 1987), p. 98.

10. *Ibid.*, p. 98.

11. G. Lloyd, *Part of Nature: Self-Knowledge in Spinoza's Ethics* (Cornell University Press, 1994), p. 61.

12. Giorgio Agamben also draws attention to the linguistic underpinnings of the Cartesian *subjectum*: 'The impalpability and insubstantiality of this ego is betrayed by the difficulty Descartes experiences in naming it and identifying it outside the realm of the pure utterance *I think, therefore I am . . .*'. See his *Infancy and History*, trans. L. Heron (Verso, 1993), p. 22. See also P. Ricoeur, *Oneself as Another* (Chicago University Press, 1992), Introduction: the Question of Selfhood.

13. H. Arendt, *The Life of the Mind Volume One: Thinking* (Harcourt Brace, 1977), p. 48.

14. For Hume's views relating to this point see particularly *A Treatise on Human Nature Book One* (Fontana Press, 1987), Part IV, Sec. VI.

15. I. Kant, *Critique of Pure Reason* (2nd Impression), trans. N. Kemp Smith (Macmillan Press, 1992), A 158, B 197, p. 194.

16. M. Heidegger, 'The Age of the World Picture' (Appendix No. 9), in *The Question Concerning Technology and Other Essays*, trans. W. Lovitt (Harper Torch Books, 1977), p. 148.

17. See for example Spinoza's discussion in his *Ethics*, trans. S. Shirley (Hackett Publishing, 1992), Part III, Prop. 2.

18. Thus Genevieve Lloyd writes, 'The divine attributes cease to be properties of a transcendent God and become instead ways in which reality is construed, articulated or expressed.' See her *Spinoza and the Ethics* (Routledge, 1996), p. 31.

19. For Pierre Macherey, this criticism has its basis in a faulty reading of Spinoza's conception of thought as an attribute of substance. The concept of attribute does not reside in thought and hence Spinoza does not present thought as outside of substance without connection to it. Attribute expresses the relation that thought

(as well as other forms of being) may have to substance as modifications of the latter. For Macherey's brilliant philosophical comparison see *Hegel ou Spinoza* (Librairie Francois Maspero, 1979); chapter 3 of his study has been translated in W. Montag and T. Stolze (eds), *The New Spinoza* (Minnesota University Press, 1999). Also of interest are the essays on Spinoza and contemporary thought in Part IV of *In A Materialist Way*, trans. W. Montag and T. Stolze (Verso, 1998).

20. Spinoza, *Ethics*, op. cit., Part I, Appendix, p. 61. There is considerable debate concerning the atheistic/theistic resonances in Spinoza's text which I will not develop herein.

21. *Ibid.*, Part II, Prop. 10, Corollary, p. 69.

22. *Ibid.*, Part II, Prop. 48, p. 95.

23. G. Deleuze, *Spinoza: Practical Philosophy*, trans. R. Hurley (City Lights Books, 1988), pp. 123–4.

24. G. Lloyd, *Part of Nature*, op. cit., p. 56.

25. Y. Yovel, *Spinoza and Other Heretics: The Adventures of Immanence* (Princeton University Press, 1989), p. 29ff.

26. *Ethics*, op. cit., p. 69.

27. Genevieve Lloyd also points out that the 'notion of transition between levels of ideas . . . is crucial to understanding Spinoza's treatment of consciousness and self-knowledge.' See *Part of Nature*, op. cit., p. 45.

28. *Ethics*, Part II, Prop. 40, Sch. 2, p. 90.

29. Deleuze, op. cit., p. 82.

30. *Ethics*, op. cit., p. 90, emphasis added.

31. *Ibid.*, p. 61.

32. C. Norris, *Spinoza and the Origins of Modern Critical Theory* (Blackwell, 1991), p. 68.

33. *Ethics*, op. cit., p. 90.

34. Antonio Negri has argued convincingly that at this point in the *Ethics* one cannot discount the interruption to its writing announced by the draft of the *Theological–Political Treatise*. The latter text, concerned as it is with the power of the imagination in the constitution of social reality (through theological mystification particularly), is recuperated into the metaphysical discourse of the *Ethics*, giving the later parts of this text a clear political foundation. See *The Savage Anomaly: The Power of Spinoza's Politics*, trans. M. Hardt (Minnesota University Press, 1991), ch. 5.

35. *Ethics*, op. cit., Part III, Prop. 31, p. 122.

36. For Balibar's penetrating analysis see chapter 4 of *Spinoza and Politics*, trans. P. Snowdon (Verso, 1998). Also of interest here is Warren Montag, *Bodies, Masses, Power: Spinoza and his Contemporaries* (Verso, 1999). We will return to Balibar's text in our analysis of the construction of the subject by ideological practices in the following chapter of this study.

37. *Ibid.*, Part II, Prop. 5, p. 65–6.

38. Spinoza utilizes a geometrical analogy to explain this important distinction. In his *Treatise on the Emendation of the Intellect* he writes: 'A true idea is something different from its object (ideatum). *A circle is one thing, the idea of a circle another.* For the idea of a circle is not something having a circumference and a centre, as is a circle, nor is the idea of a body itself a body. And since it is

something *different from its object*, it will also be something *intelligible through itself*' (in *Ethics*, Emendation, Sec. 33, p. 240; my emphasis).

39. Yovel, op. cit., p. 147. Antonio Negri holds a similar view in *The Savage Anomaly*, op. cit., p. 12.

40. Lloyd, for example, notes that 'Spinozistic bodies are socialised bodies, and our minds reflect that socialization of bodies.' *Part of Nature*, op. cit., p. 164.

41. *Ibid.*, p. 6.

42. See M. Poster, *Existential Marxism in Postwar France* (Princeton University Press, 1975).

43. A full account of Hegel's influence is outside the scope of this inquiry and will not be pursued herein. For interesting studies of Hegel's influence on French Philosophy, see J. Butler, *Subjects of Desire: Hegelian Reflections in Twentieth Century France* (Columbia University Press, 1987); M.S. Roth, *Knowing and History: Appropriations of Hegel in Twentieth Century France* (Cornell University Press, 1988), and V. Descombes, *Contemporary French Philosophy*, op. cit.

44. More generally, the term 'phenomenology' signifies the study of phenomena, of that which appears to consciousness, a return to the things themselves asking how experience may constitute the world of things, and a reflection upon the historical temporality of being. To some extent all three views may embrace the Hegelian project. However, phenomenology stands as a description of the philosophies of Husserl and Heidegger as well as Hegel. The discussion in this book will point to the ways in which different phenomenological accounts of subjectivity inform post-structuralist accounts of the subject. Particularly useful on the various influences of phenomenology in the human sciences is J.F. Lyotard, *Phenomenology*, trans. B. Beaklek, Foreword by G.L. Ormiston (SUNY Press, 1991).

45. Clearly, Hegel's *Logic* is of crucial importance here. The central formulations of Concept and Substance are also present in the *Phenomenology* and I take this text as my main focus. The first text may be said to deal with the essence of knowledge, the latter with its existence in actuality, but both are subject to the speculative dialectic present in the *Phenomenology*.

46. G.W.F. Hegel, *Phenomenology of Spirit*, trans. A.V. Miller (Oxford University Press, 1977), Sec. 20, p. 11.

47. Cited in Descombes, *Contemporary French Philosophy*, op. cit., p. 13.

48. *Phenomenology of Spirit*, op. cit., Sec. 33.

49. *Ibid.*, Sec. 18.

50. For example, 'everything turns on grasping and expressing the true, not only as Substance but also as Subject.' *Ibid.*, Sec. 17.

51. K. Marx and F. Engels, *The German Ideology: Part One* (Lawrence and Wishart, 1985), p. 51.

52. Marx, 'Economic and Philosophic Manuscripts of 1844', in *The Marx–Engels Reader, 2nd edn*, ed. R. Tucker (W.W. Norton, 1978), p. 115.

53. *Early Works*, D. McLennan (ed.) (Blackwell, 1972), p. 148.

54. See for example, *ibid.*, p. 150.

55. Tucker, op. cit., pp. 112, 121.

56. This position is most clear in the epistemological primacy Marx gives to labour in the early understanding of private property: 'How, we now ask, does *man* come to *alienate*, to estrange, *his labour*? How is this estrangement rooted in the nature

of human development? We have already gone a long way to the solution of this problem by *transforming* the question as to the *origin of private property* into the question as to the relation of *alienated labour* to the course of humanity's development. For when one speaks of *private property*, one thinks of being concerned with something external to man. When one speaks of labour, one is directly concerned with man himself. This new formulation of the question already contains its solution.' Tucker, *ibid.*, p. 80 (emphasis in the original).

57. Not least because there was no French translation of Hegel's *Phenomenology* before Hyppolite's work in 1946. Until this point students relied upon notes, lectures and impressions, all of which carried the weight of philosophical interpretation. See J. Hekman, 'Hyppolite and the Hegel Revival in France', *Telos* Vol. 16, 1973, pp. 128–45 (reprinted as introduction to Hyppolite's *Genesis and Structure in Hegel's Phenomenology* (Northwestern University Press, 1974), hereafter referred to as GS).

58. B. Baugh, 'Subjectivity and the *Begriff* in Modern French Philosophy', *The Owl of Minerva*, Vol. 23, No. 1, 1991, pp. 63–75, quoted at p. 64.

59. 'Given-being' is the term Kojève uses to describe the subject in the simple world of immediate satisfaction where it is submerged in animal life.

60. A. Kojève, *Introduction to the Reading of Hegel* (Basic Books, 1969), p. 38.

61. This is the view of Shadia Drury in *Alexandre Kojève: The Roots of Postmodern Politics* (MacMillan Press, 1994).

62. Roth, op. cit., p. 110.

63. Kojève, op. cit., p. 53.

64. *Ibid.*, pp. 178, 212.

65. *Ibid.*, p. 212 and fn. 15. Kojève states that it is Kant and Heidegger who explore the dualist ontology in the most developed form. Some of the problems generated by Kojève's ontological dualism are discussed in V. Descombes, *Modern French Philosophy*, op. cit., ch. 2.

66. *Ibid.*, pp. 229–230.

67. It must be noted that Kojève significantly revised this interpretation of dialectical synthesis. In an added comment to the 2nd edition of his lectures, Kojève offers a more pessimistic reflection on the nature of the end of History. He argues for the perpetual opposition of subject and object, 'To remain human, Man must remain a "Subject *opposed* to the Object," even if "Action negating the given and Error disappears".' (*ibid.*, fn. 5, pp. 158–62).

68. GS, pp. 170, p. 160.

69. GS, pp. 145, and see Hyppolite's *Studies on Marx and Hegel* (Harper Torchbooks, 1973), p. 159, hereafter SMH.

70. GS, p. 21, and SMH, p. 154.

71. SMH, p. ix.

72. SMH, p. 156.

73. GS, p. 149.

74. GS, p. 150

75. GS, p. 191.

76. SMH, p. 14.

77. SMH, p. 160.

78. SMH, pp. 165–6.

79. See Hyppolite's essay 'Hegel's Phenomenology and Psychoanalysis', trans. A. Richer, in W.E. Steinkraus (ed.), *New Studies in Hegel's Philosophy* (Holt, Reinhart and Winston, 1976). We will explore this relation further in Chapter 3.
80. Butler, op. cit., p. 82.
81. SMH, p. 9; my emphasis.
82. Hegel, *Phenomenology*, op. cit., Sec. 801, p. 487.
83. Hyppolite's later essay 'The Structure of Philosophical Language According to the 'Preface' to Hegel's Phenomenology of the Mind', in R. Macksey and E. Donato (eds), *The Structuralist Controversy: The Languages of Criticism and the Science of Man* (Johns Hopkins University Press, 1972), pp. 157–85 also draws parallels between the formal structure of language and the project of psychoanalysis.

CHAPTER 2

1. P. Anderson, *Considerations on Western Marxism* (Verso, 1979), p. 49.
2. Martin Jay, *Marxism and Totality: The Adventures of a Concept from Lukács to Habermas* (Polity, 1984) and Lucien Goldmann, *Lukács and Heidegger: Towards a New Philosophy* (Routledge and Kegan Paul, 1977).
3. Mihály Vajda, for example, claims that it is difficult to distinguish the two standpoints. As we shall see below, both blame the false rationalism of science for producing the crisis of man (Husserl's thesis) and that of capitalism (Lukács' thesis). Ultimately, of course, Lukács' position is class-based and therefore exceeds what is, for Vajda, the philosophical 'impartiality' of Husserl's position. See Vajda's 'Lukács and Husserl', in Agnes Heller (ed.), *Lukács Revalued* (Blackwell, 1983).
4. See E. Husserl 'Philosophy as a Rigorous Science', in *Phenomenology and the Crisis of Philosophy*, trans. and intro. by Q. Lauer (Harper Torchbooks, 1965).
5. For an illuminating discussion of this period see Andrew Arato, 'The Neo-idealist Defence of Subjectivity', *Telos*, Vol. 21, 1974.
6. G. Lukács, *History and Class Consciousness*, trans. R. Livingstone (Merlin Press, 1971), p. 164. Hereafter referred to as HCC.
7. G. Lukács, *The Theory of the Novel*, trans. A. Bostock (Merlin Press, 1971), p. 114.
8. *Ibid.*, p. 53.
9. Lukács uses this term on a number of occasions in this text. See for example, *ibid.*, p. 120.
10. *Ibid.*, p. 122.
11. L. Goldmann, 'The Early Writings of Georg Lukács', *Triquarterly*, Vol. 9, 1967. In his 1967 Preface to HCC Lukács himself notes the influence of Kierkegaard on his early development (p. ix). In the earlier *Soul and Form* (Merlin Press, 1974) Lukács had also written a largely biographical essay on Kierkegaard.
12. See L. Colletti, 'From Bergson to Lukács', in his *Marxism and Hegel* (New Left Books, 1973), p. 170.
13. See *The Theory of the Novel*, pp. 114–15. In HCC, Lukács would later make similar criticisms in relation to the role of art in Fichte. For a more productive

reading of the role of culture in politics and philosophy see 'The Old Culture and the New Culture' [1920], *Telos*, 5, Spring 1970.

14. *Soul and Form*, op. cit., p. 167.

15. For a discussion of the crisis besetting Lukács' writings and his journey into Marxism see Gyorgy Márkus 'The Soul and Life: The Young Lukács and the Problem of Culture', *Telos*, Vol. 23, 1977.

16. HCC, p. 134.

17. Thus Lucien Goldmann writes that 'the Lukácsian thesis is precisely that there [can] be no ontological basis outside the knowledge of society and history.' See Goldmann, op. cit., p. 13.

18. HCC, p. 143.

19. It would be interesting to pursue a genealogy of this concept given its relation to Marx, Hegel, to the neo-Kantian writings of Dilthey, as well as to Simmel and Weber but we don't pursue this in the present work.

20. HCC abounds with references to and quotations from Marx's discussion of commodity fetishism, but Lukács' more humanist analysis also seems to share affinity with the views on alienation of the early Marx. However, the publication of HCC, preceded by ten years the unearthing of Marx's *Paris Manuscripts*. As Arato points out in his article cited above in note 5, Simmel was also making these connections and it is likely that Lukács was also influenced by his formulations.

21. Given the wide ranging scope of this concept, it may seem to become a catch-all term for the mystification of commodities and forms of knowledge as abstract and 'thing-like'. In an effort to systematize these different formulations, Andrew Arato views the concept of reification as a 'genuinely dialectical' concept yielding a whole series of historical levels. See his 'Lukács' Theory of reification', *Telos*, Vol. 11, 1972, p. 25.

22. HCC, p. 89.

23. *Ibid.*, p. 91.

24. *Ibid.*, p. 89.

25. *Ibid.*, pp. 110–49.

26. *Ibid.*, p. 110.

27. *Ibid.*, p. 111.

28. *Ibid.*, pp. 112, 114.

29. It is worth pointing out that in his 'Philosophy as a Rigorous Science' Husserl also writes that 'To follow the model of the natural sciences almost inevitably means to reify consciousness.' See *Phenomenology and the Crisis of Philosophy*, op. cit., p. 103.

30. HCC, p. 128.

31. *Ibid.*, p. 128

32. Jay, op. cit., p. 111.

33. *Ibid.*, p. 118.

34. This Bergsonian connection is an interesting one, particularly in view of the revival of Bergson by scholars of Deleuze. Lack of space prevents a detailed study of Lukács' relevance to these discussions. In some of his correspondence of this period Lukács often writes critically of Bergson but it is clear that he, along with many of his contemporaries, engaged with the French philosopher's work. In this context see *Georg Lukács: Selected Correspondence 1902–1920, Dialogues with*

Weber, Simmel, Buber, Mannheim and Others, selected and trans. Judith Marcus and Zoltan Tar (Columbia University Press, 1986). For further discussion of this relation see Colletti op. cit. For a short, clear account of Bergson's theory of matter, see his *Introduction to Metaphysics* trans. T.E. Hulme, Introduction by T.A. Goudge (The Liberal Arts Press, 1955); also L. Kolakowski, *Bergson* (Oxford University Press, 1985).

35. See Lukács' discussion in HCC, pp. 135–7.
36. *Ibid.*, p. 144.
37. *Ibid.*, p. 147. In his essay on Hegel's ontology written at a much later date, Lukács notes the disparity between the Hegelian *system*, which remains rationalist (as identified in HCC), and his *method* which holds the concepts of immediacy and mediation, to which Lukács attaches great theoretical importance. See *The Ontology of Social Being: Hegel*, trans. D. Fernbach (Merlin Press, 1978).
38. *Ibid.*, pp. 40–52.
39. M. Merleau-Ponty, 'Western Marxism', in *Adventures of the Dialectic* (North Western University Press, 1973), p. 41.
40. See Lukács' discussion in HCC, pp. 189–91.
41. See the essay 'Class Consciousness', in HCC, pp. 46–82.
42. See Lukács' comparison, *ibid.*, p. 166.
43. *Ibid.*, p. 169.
44. *Ibid.*, p. 179.
45. *Ibid.*, p. 127. Clearly, it would be possible to identify a parallel between Lukács and Heidegger here, as Goldmann has done. This extends for Goldmann, to an analogy between the concept of Being in Heidegger and totality in Lukács.
46. See Lukács' discussion of this doubt, HCC, p. 170.
47. In Weber's analysis, the category of objective possibility is linked to the methodological construction of ideal types which allows discrete empirical events to be understood according to a general model. If class consciousness is viewed as an ideal type against which empirical consciousness may be distinguished, then the 'objectively possible' position of class consciousness may be understood as the horizon of ascribed consciousness. For a discussion of this category in both Weber and Lukács see A. Feenberg, *Lukács, Marx and the Sources of Critical Theory* (Oxford University Press, 1981), pp. 145–51. Again, however, it must also be noted that the formulation owes something to Husserl's own critique of philosophical method. On the distinction between empirical and pure consciousness see 'Philosophy as a Rigorous Science', op. cit., p. 92.
48. HCC, p. 52.
49. Jay, op. cit., p. 112. For a contrasting reading of Lukács as a neo-Kantian, see G. Rose, *Hegel Contra Sociology* (Athlone Press, 1978), particularly pp. 27–31.
50. HCC, p. 150.
51. HCC, p. 124.
52. See, for example, the editors introduction in R. Macksey and E. Donato (eds), *The Structuralist Controversy: The Languages of Criticism and the Sciences of Man* (Johns Hopkins University Press, 1972).
53. P. Ricouer, 'The Question of the Subject: The Challenge of Semiology', in *The Conflict of Interpretations* (Northwestern University Press, 1974), p. 250.

54. V. Descombes, *Modern French Philosophy* (Cambridge University Press, 1980), p. 95.
55. 'Marxism and Humanism', in *For Marx*, trans. B. Brewster (Verso, 1990), p. 229.
56. See Althusser's preface, 'To My English Readers', *ibid.*, p. 12.
57. See F. Navarro's discussion of her interview with Althusser, in 'An Encounter with Althusser', *Rethinking Marxism*, Vol. 10, no. 3, Fall 1998.
58. Althusser's thesis, namely that there is an epistemological break between the early and later Marx, will not be discussed here. For an account of Althusser's debt to the French philosopher of science, Gaston Bachelard and his formulation of this critical position, see T. Benton *The Rise and Fall of Structuralist Marxism* (Macmillan, 1984).
59. L. Althusser, *Essays in Self-Criticism* (New Left Books, 1973), p. 133.
60. L. Althusser, 'Marx's relation to Hegel' in *Montesquieu, Rousseau, Marx: Politics and History* (Verso, 1972), p. 174.
61. L. Althusser, *The Spectre of Hegel: Early Writings*, trans. G.M. Goshgarian, ed. and introduction by F. Matheron (Verso, 1997), p. 151.
62. *Ibid.*, p. 152.
63. *Ibid.*, p. 85.
64. See 'Man, That Night', in *The Spectre of Hegel*, op. cit., pp. 170–72.
65. 'Marx's Relation to Hegel', op. cit., p. 173.
66. P. Ricouer, 'Althusser (1)', *Lectures on Ideology and Utopia* (Columbia University Press, 1986), p. 113.
67. *Reading Capital*, trans. B. Brewster (Verso, 1979), p. 94.
68. *Ibid.*
69. *Ibid.*
70. A parallel argument can be found in 'On Content in the Thought of G.W.F. Hegel', in *Spectres of Hegel*, op. cit.
71. *Reading Capital*, op. cit., p. 141.
72. *Ibid.*, p. 132.
73. *Ibid.*, p. 134.
74. For example, Gregory Elliott writes that Althusser's anti-Hegelianism leads him to '[carry] out an adroit philosophical alliance' with the anti-humanism of structuralism. See his *Althusser: The Detour of Theory* (Verso, 1987), p. 62.
75. Among the essays to focus on the Spinoza-Althusser relation are C. Norris, 'Spinoza *versus* Hegel: the Althusserian Moment', in *Spinoza and the Origins of Modern Critical Theory* (Blackwell, 1991); P. Patton, 'Althusser's Epistemology: the limits of the theory of theoretical practice', *Radical Philosophy*, no. 19, 1978; W. Montag, 'Spinoza and Althusser Against Hermeneutics: Interpretation or Intervention?', in A. Kaplan and M. Sprinkler (eds), *The Althusserian Legacy* (Verso, 1992).
76. *Reading Capital*, op. cit., p. 17.
77. L. Althusser, 'On Spinoza', in *Essays in Self-Criticism*, op. cit., p. 136.
78. *Reading Capital*, op. cit., p. 37.
79. *Ibid.*, p. 19. Significantly for Althusser's argument, Marx too, in his early work embraced this philosophy of vision and 'read the human essence at sight, immediately, in the transparency of its alienation', p. 17.

80. The term is Paul Hirst's. See his 'Althusser and Philosophy', *Theoretical Practice*, Vol. 2, 1971, p. 19.

81. It is worth pointing out that Althusser does acknowledge Descartes' concerted effort to separate the order of knowledge and the order of being, but recognizes the ultimate dualism of the Cartesian method which forces it to take up a form of rationalist empiricism in order to generate reliable, certain knowledge. See the discussion in *Reading Capital*, op. cit., pp. 35, 49, n. 26.

82. *Ibid.*, p. 36.

83. *Ibid.*, p. 40.

84. 'On the Materialist Dialectic', in *For Marx*, op. cit., p. 184, n. 21.

85. As Althusser puts it: 'the formulation of a *problem* is merely the theoretical expression of the conditions which allow a *solution* already produced outside the process of knowledge because imposed by extra-theoretical instances and exigencies (by religious, ethical, political or other 'interests') *to recognise itself* in an artificial problem manufactured to serve it both as a theoretical mirror and a practical justification', *Reading Capital*, op. cit., p. 52.

86. *Reading Capital*, op. cit., p. 58.

87. Quoted in *ibid.*, p. 46.

88. See for example, Elliott, *The Detour of Theory*, op. cit., p. 111.

89. Deleuze *Spinoza: Practical Philosophy* (City Lights Books, 1988), p. 88. Althusser has no similar understanding of parallelism, except, as Paul Patten also notes ('Althusser's Epistemology', *Radical Philosophy*, Vol. 19, Spring 1978, p. 17), that between an adequate concept and its object.

90. See for example Freud's discussion in 'The Work of Displacement', in *The Interpretation of Dreams*, Vol. 4 of the Penguin Freud Library (Penguin Books, 1991), pp. 414–19.

91. 'Contradiction and Overdetermination', in *For Marx*, op. cit., p. 101.

92. See 'Politics and Friendship: An Interview with Jacques Derrida' (conducted by M. Sprinkler), in Kaplan and Sprinkler (eds), *The Althusserian Legacy*, op. cit., p. 203.

93. The challenge of this logic to forms of economic determinism is significant. It gives the element of ideology a relative autonomy and a structural effect upon the constitution of the materiality of capitalist forms, as well as of the subject, which make considerable in-roads into an understanding of the structural logic of advanced capitalism. Hence when Alex Callinicos contends that Althusser's position reduces the structure of capitalism to a structure of representation and subordinates an analysis of the laws of motion of capitalism to an account of the formation of concepts and their relation to things, he ignores 'the existence of different times and rhythms ... the type of articulation, displacement and torsion' which for Althusser underlie any 'law of capitalism' (*Reading Capital*, *ibid.*, p. 100). For examples of Callinicos' view, see *Is There a Future for Marxism?* (Macmillan, 1982), pp. 26, 122.

94. As Althusser writes 'From the first moment to the last, the lonely hour of the "last instance" never arrives', *For Marx*, op. cit., p. 113.

95. Althusser's distinction here owes much to the Gramscian conceptualization of consent (as a form of ideological hegemony) and coercion (as a form of state directed repression).

96. See Althusser's autobiography, *The Future Lasts a Long Time*, trans. R. Veasey (Chatto and Windus, 1993). Sections on Spinoza, and Machiavelli, were not included in this edition of the autobiography. They have recently been published in English as 'The Only Materialist Tradition, Part I: Spinoza', in W. Montag and T. Stolze (eds) *The New Spinoza* (Minnesota University Press, 1998), pp. 1–19.
97. Althusser, 'Ideology and Ideological State Apparatuses (Notes towards an Investigation)', in *Essay on Ideology* (Verso, 1984), p. 45.
98. Althusser, 'Ideology', *ibid.*, p. 36.
99. See *Louis Althusser: Writings on Psychoanalysis*, O. Corpet and F. Matheron (eds), Introduction by J. Mehlman (Columbia University Press, 1996). This volume omits one important essay: 'Three notes on the theory of discourse' which can be found in *Louis Althusser: Écrits sur la psychanalyse*, STOCK/IMEC 1993 pp. 143–173.
100. *Louis Althusser: Writings on Psychoanalysis*, op. cit., pp. 120–21.
101. This correspondence was, however, very one-sided. It is noteworthy that it was Althusser who instigated the invitation of a lectureship to Lacan at the Ecole pratique des hautes études. See O. Corpet and F. Matheron (eds), *Louis Althusser: Writings on Psychoanalysis*, introduction by J. Mehlman (Columbia University Press, 1996), pp. 143–73. For further discussion of Althusser's relation to Lacan and his interest in psychoanalytic theory see E. Roudinesco, *Jacques Lacan*, trans. B. Bray (Polity Press, 1997), ch. 23.
102. 'Freud and Lacan', in *Essays on Ideology*, op. cit., pp. 164–5; emphasis added. This essay can also be found in the French edition (and English translation) of *Writings on Psychoanalysis*.
103. See the essay 'In the Name of the Analysands', *ibid*. In his 1980 essay 'The Discovery of Dr. Freud', Althusser also claimed that Lacan's scientific theory had become subordinated to a mere philosophy of psychoanalysis. *Ibid.*, p. 91.
104. Paul Hirst argues convincingly that Althusser fails to problematize the concept of the subject by presupposing a concrete individual prior to the process of interpellation, and then explaining what Hirst reads as the *genesis* of the subject, according to a *single* spectacle and an individual act of cognition which transforms that individual into a subject with a coherent identity. 'This is to retain,' Hirst argues, 'the classical conception [of the knowing subject] whilst bracketing certain of its ontological implications' (p. 400). See his 'Althusser and the Theory of Ideology', *Economy and Society*, Vol. 5, no. 4, 1976. For a more recent effort to investigate these ontological assumptions see 'Conscience Doth Make Subjects of Us All', in J. Butler, *The Psychic Life of Power: Theories in Subject* (Stanford University Press, 1997).
105. It is Etienne Balibar in his recent work *Spinoza and Politics*, trans. P. Snowdon (Verso, 1995) who has articulated this politico-philosophical affinity between discipline and the body, ideology and imaginary. See chapter 5 of his book for a fine analysis.
106. For a very perceptive argument see W. Montag, 'The Soul is the prison of the Body: Althusser and Foucault 1970–75', in J. Lezra (ed.), *Depositions: Althusser, Balibar, Macherey and the Labour of Reading* (Yale University Press, 1995).

107.   For a more thoroughgoing effort to marry linguistic analysis with an Althus-serian reading of ideology, see M. Pêcheux, *Language, Semantics and Ideology* (Macmillan, 1982).

108.   See Mehlman's introduction to *Louis Althusser: Writings on Psychoanalysis*, op. cit., pp. 4–5. The letter was probably written in 1977.

109.   'Freud and Lacan', *Essays on Ideology*, op. cit., p. 160. Yet neither does the posthumous collection of essays on psychoanalysis do much to develop them. For Althusser's changing theoretical stance to psychoanalysis, see W. Montag, 'The Emptiness of a Distance Taken: Freud, Althusser, Lacan', *Rethinking Marxism*, Vol. 4, no. 1, Spring 1991, pp. 31–38.

110.   Paul Hirst has also noted the dependence of these two realms as a source of contradiction in Althusser's work. He nevertheless points out that we may consider what Althusser has achieved with the concept of ideology as 'relatively independent of his theory of knowledge' (p. 123). However, I would argue that as soon as we pose the question of the subject, the simultaneous considera-tion of these two realms becomes essential. For Hirst's comments see 'Prob-lems and Advances in the Theory of Ideology', in T. Eagleton (ed.), *Ideology* (Longman, 1994).

111.   Ricouer 'Althusser (1)', *Essays on ideology and Utopia*, op. cit., p. 117; Derrida 'Politics and Friendship', in Kaplan and Sprinkler (eds), op. cit., pp. 187–8, 197.

112.   Derrida, *ibid.*, p. 202. There is certainly no philosophical genealogy of the com-plex inheritance of concepts of subject and object, or ideology and science, to be found anywhere in the oeuvre of Althusser.

113.   On this point see the fascinating discussion between Fernando Navarro and Althusser in F. Navarro, *Filosofia y Marxismo: Entrevista a Louis Althusser* (Siglo Veintiuno Editores, 1988). This interview has been translated into French in *Sur La Philosophie* (Gallimard, 1994). References to quotations in the argument that follows are to the French edition. Navarro recounts this point in her reflections on Althusser: 'An Encounter with Althusser', *Rethinking Marxism*, Vol. 10, no. 3, Fall 1998, p. 96. On the significance of the theme of the void in Althusser's writ-ings see Francois Matheron 'The Recurrence of the Void in Louis Althusser', in the same volume of *Rethinking Marxism* devoted to rereading Althusser.

114.   See A. Negri, 'The Later Althusser', in A. Callari and D.F. Ruccio (eds), *Post-modern Materialism and the Future of Marxist Theory: Essays in the Althus-serian Tradition* (Weslyan University Press, 1996), p. 58. I am indebted to Negri's analysis of Althusser in what follows.

115.   See *Sur La Philosophie*, op. cit.

116.   *Ibid.*, pp. 42, 43, 59.

117.   *Ibid.*, p. 43.

118.   Negri, op. cit., p. 62.

119.   Althusser, 'The Only Materialist Tradition, Part I: Spinoza', in Montag and Stolze (eds), *The New Spinoza*, op. cit., p. 13.

120.   Negri, op. cit., p. 54.

121.   *Ibid.*, pp. 12–13.

122.   There is clearly a problem in drawing a connection between interpellation in the ideological realm and its epistemological formulation. Interpellation involves a speculatory event, built as it is upon Lacan's account of the 'mirror-phase'.

It thus appears, at least in the way it is used, wholly consistent with Althusser's own reading and critique of the philosophy of *vision* discussed in *Reading Capital*.

123. *Sur La Philosophie*, op. cit., p. 63.
124. *Reading Capital*, op. cit., p. 68. See also Vincent Descombes' discussion of Althusser in his *Modern French Philosophy*, op. cit., p. 122–6.
125. Negri, 'The Later Althusser', op. cit., p. 59.
126. Althusser, 'The Only Materialist Tradition: Part 1: Spinoza', op. cit., p. 12.

CHAPTER 3

1. See Paul Ricouer 'Consciousness and the Unconscious', in *The Conflict of Interpretations: Essays in Hermeneutics* (Northwestern University Press, 1974), p. 99.
2. It is worth noting at this early stage that almost all of Lacan's writings are based on notes and transcriptions (often recorded by students) of his weekly seminars to trainee analysts, philosophers and other interested intellectuals. This together with his often elliptical style, and a tendency towards allusion rather than direct reference, often makes the seminars difficult reading. It also places the question of interpretation at the centre of Lacan's work. As Elisabeth Roudinesco points out in her excellent biography *Jacques Lacan*, trans. B. Bray (Polity, 1997), Jacques-Alain Miller, the psychoanalyst entrusted by Lacan to publish and edit his *oeuvre*, has often stripped Lacan of his diverse development, glossed over the multifarious intellectual antecedents which marked his development, and emphasized a strictly structuralist, a logical Lacan by privileging the post-1964 seminars. The reading offered in this chapter will focus on diversity above unification, seeking its support in Roudinesco's view that 'Lacanianism, born of subversion and a wish to transgress, is essentially doomed to fragility and dispersion' (p. 433).
3. Roudinesco's biographical study (*ibid.*) illustrates how time and time again Lacan borrowed without due recognition from numerous theoreticians and philosophers.
4. Roudinesco, *ibid.*, p. 254.
5. Lacan, 'The Symbolic Order', in J. Alain-Miller (ed.), *The Seminar of Jacques Lacan Book I: Freud's Papers on Technique 1953–54*, trans. J. Forrester (Cambridge University Press, 1988), p. 232.
6. Freud, 'The Ego and the Id', in *On metapyschology*, Vol. 11 (Penguin Freud Library, 1991), p. 356.
7. *Ibid.*, p. 364; emphasis added.
8. Lacan, 'The Freudian Thing', in *Écrits: A Selection*, trans. A. Sheridan (Routledge and Kegan Paul, 1977), p. 143.
9. *Ibid.*, p. 118.
10. Freud, 'The Interpretation of Dreams VII: The Psychology of Dream-Processes', in *The Interpretation of Dreams*, Vol. 4 (Penguin Freud Library, 1991), p. 762.
11. I have explored Lacan's concepts of subject, language and structure in an essay contained in *The Edinburgh Encyclopedia of Continental Philosophy*, General ed. Simon Glendinning (Edinburgh University Press, 1999), pp. 548–57. Parts of this section draws upon the reading put forward in this essay.

12. Lacan, 'The mirror stage as formative of the function of the I as revealed in psychoanalytic experience', *Écrits*, op. cit., p. 1.
13. L. Laplanche and J.B. Pontalis, *The Language of Psychoanalysis*, trans. D. Nicholson-Smith (The Hogarth Press, 1973), p. 251.
14. See 'Mirror-Stage', op. cit., p. 6.
15. The term is taken from Malcolm Bowie *Lacan* (Fontana Press, 1991), p. 23.
16. *Ibid.*, p. 23.
17. 'Mirror-Stage', op. cit., p. 4.
18. Lacan, 'Aggressivity in Psychoanalysis', in *Écrits*, op. cit., p. 22.
19. *Ibid.*, p. 8.
20. Lacan, 'The subversion of the subject and the dialectic of desire in the Freudian unconscious', in *Écrits*, p. 311.
21. J. Lacan, 'Desire, Life and Death', in J. Alain-Miller (ed.), *The Seminar of Jacques Lacan Book II: The Ego in Freud's Theory and in the Technique of Psychoanalysis 1954–55*, trans. S. Tomaselli and J. Forrester (Cambridge University Press, 1988), p. 224.
22. Cited in 'some questions for the teacher', *ibid.*, p. 218.
23. S. Freud, *Jokes and Their Relation to the Unconscious* (Penguin Freud Library, 1991).
24. Roudinesco points out that Lacan was first introduced to Saussure by Henri Delacroix in the 1930s. Delacroix taught philosophy to Sartre and drew on Saussure's lectures of 1915 in his own work on language and thought, op. cit., p. 26.
25. J. Culler, *Saussure* (Fontana, 1985), p. 120.
26. F. de Saussure, *Course in General Linguistics*, trans. W. Baskin (Fontana, 1974), p. 112.
27. Lacan 'The agency of the letter in the unconscious or reason since Freud', in *Écrits*, op cit. p. 150.
28. *Ibid.*, p. 154.
29. J. Nancy and P. Lacoue-Labarthe, *The Title of the Letter: A reading of Lacan*, trans. F. Raffoul (SUNY Press, 1992), p. 37.
30. Bowie, op. cit., p. 66.
31. Lacan, 'Subversion of the subject and the dialectic of desire', *Écrits*, op. cit., p. 316.
32. See 'The function of language in psychoanalysis', in *Speech and Language in Psychoanalysis*, trans. and ed. A. Wilden (Johns Hopkins University Press, 1968), pp. 19, 37.
33. *Ibid.*, p. 61.
34. Lacan cited in A. Lemaire, *Jacques Lacan*, trans. D. Macey (Routledge and Kegan Paul, 1977), p. 71.
35. *Ibid.*, p. 6.
36. S. Freud, 'Moses and Monotheism', in *The Origins of Religion* (Penguin Freud Library, 1990).
37. See Lacan's *Four Fundamental Concepts of Psychoanalysis*, trans. A. Sheridan, ed. J. Alain-Miller (Peregrine Press, 1986), ch. 16.
38. This is Fredric Jameson's understanding of the real. See his 'Imaginary and Symbolic in Lacan', *Yale French Studies*, Vol. 55/56, 1977.
39. Translator's note, *Écrits*, op. cit., p. x.

40. *Seminar Book II*, op. cit., p. 27. There are three readings of the real in Lacan's work. For a discussion see E. Ragland-Sullivan, 'The Real', in E. Wright (ed.), *Feminism and Psychoanalysis: A Critical Dictionary* (Blackwell, 1992), pp. 374–7.

41. See, for example, Bowie, op. cit., pp. 58, 71–2.

42. R. Boothby, *Death and Desire: Psychoanalytic Theory in Lacan's Return to Freud* (Routledge, 1991), p. 134.

43. Lacan, 'Agency of the Letter', *Écrits*, op. cit., p. 170.

44. Nancy and Lacoue-Labarthe, op. cit., p. 29.

45. For further discussion on the relation between subjectivity, speech and alienation, see B. Fink, *The Lacanian Subject* (Princeton University Press, 1995), particularly chs. 4 and 5.

46. 'Subversion of the Subject and the Dialectic of Desire', in *Écrits*, op. cit., p. 297.

47. This chapter will not consider the relationship between feminism and psycho-analysis; the question of gendered subjectivity. I refer the reader to Teresa Brennan (ed.), *Feminism and Psychoanalysis* (Routledge, 1989); Jane Gallop *Thinking Through the Body* (Columbia University Press, 1988); Luce Irigarary, *Speculum of the Other Woman*, trans. G.C. Gill (Cornell University Press, 1985); Julia Kristeva, *Desire in Language: A Semiotic Approach to Literature and Art*, trans. L.S. Roudiez, (Columbia University Press, 1980). I have considered the rela-tion between Lacan and a feminist epistemology in 'Feminism, Subjectivity and Psychoanalysis', in M. Whitford and K. Lennon (eds), *Knowing the Difference: Feminist Perspectives on Epistemology* (Routledge, 1994).

48. Lacan, 'Agency of the Letter', *Écrits*, op. cit., p. 167.

49. Lacan, 'Subversion of the Subject', *ibid.*, p. 298.

50. 'Agency of the Letter', op. cit., p. 175. Lacan's analysis of metaphor and metonymy here, draws upon the work of Roman Jakobsen. See his 'Two Aspects of Language and Two Types of Aphasic Disturbances', in R. Jakobsen and H. Morris, *Fundamentals of Language* (Mouton Press, 1956).

51. Lacan, 'Truth Emerges from the Mistake', in *Seminar Book II*, op. cit., p. 262.

52. Noted by W.J. Richardson in 'Psychoanalysis and the Being-question', in W. Ker-rigan and J.H. Smith, *Interpreting Lacan* (Yale University Press, 1983) p. 156.

53. Nancy and Lacoue-Labarthe emphasize an ambiguity in the diverse conceptual resources imported into Lacan's discourse (Saussurean, Freudian, Cartesian, Hegelian, Heideggerian) which enter the constitution of the subject-as-signifier in conflicting and irreconcilable ways. Attention has already been drawn to the linguistic and the existential dimensions of Lacan's construction of desire, which was understood as creating contradictions in his treatment of the concept of desire in language. This philosophical inconsistency must be viewed, in Nancy and Lacoue-Labarthe's interpretation, as extending to the concept of the subject itself.

54. J. Lacan, *Four Fundamental Concepts*, op. cit., p. 35.

55. Lacan, 'Agency of the Letter in the Unconscious', op. cit., pp. 165, 166.

56. I have pursued the theme of Lacan's relation to Hegelianism in 'Philosophy and Psychoanalysis: Lacan, Kojève and Hyppolite on the concept of the subject', *Parallax*, Vol. 4, 1997, pp. 41–54.

57. E.S. Casey and and J.M. Woody, 'Hegel, Heidegger, Lacan: The Dialectic of Desire', in Kerrigan and Smith (eds), *Interpreting Lacan*, op. cit., p. 77.

In *Consciousness and the Unconscious* (Hutchinson, 1984), p. 80, David Archard goes as far as to say that there is a 'grafting of Hegel onto Freud'.

58. G.W.F. Hegel, *The Phenomenology of Spirit* (Oxford University Press, 1977), p. 111; emphasis added.

59. D. Macey, *Lacan in Contexts* (Verso, 1988), p. 98.

60. See A. Wilden's interpretative essay 'Lacan and the Discourse of the Other', in *Speech and Language in Psychoanalysis*, op. cit., pp. 192–3. It is also worth noting here that in 1936 Lacan and Kojève agreed to join forces to write a study on Hegel and Freud. Lacan's section of the text never materialized although Kojève himself gave Lacan a draft of his part on Hegel of which the former, according to Elizabeth Roudinesco, was later to make use. See Roudinesco, *Jacques Lacan*, op. cit., pp. 105–6.

61. Mikkel Borch-Jacobsen's reading of Lacan's philosophical debts in *Lacan: The Absolute Master* trans. D. Brick (Stanford University Press, 1991) also outlines the theoretical itinerary which takes Lacan from Hegel and Heidegger to Kojève. However, whilst Borch-Jacobsen aligns Lacan's conceptual system very closely with that of Kojève, he raises a number of important comments regarding the consistency of Lacan's philosophical arguments, comments which will be considered below. The argument presented here, in part recognizes the problems identified in Lacan's work but argues nonetheless that a particular reading of the concept of the real may offer a way out of these problems. This move however, involves distancing Lacan from Kojève in certain significant respects.

62. 'Subversion of the Subject', op. cit., p. 296.

63. As Casey and Woody note 'there is no redemption or reconciliation to be had through history because the subject of desire can never be absorbed in history, but only subverted or repressed there.' See 'Hegel, Heidegger and Lacan: The Dialectic of Desire', op. cit., p. 105.

64. See Lemaire, *Jacques Lacan*, op. cit., p. 72.

65. 'Subversion of the Subject', op. cit., p. 296. In a later seminar entitled 'Encore', Lacan writes of the Hegelian *Aufhebung* as 'one of those sweet dreams of philosophy'. See 'A Love Letter', in J. Mitchell and J. Rose (eds), *Jacques Lacan: Feminine Sexuality and the école freudienne*, trans. J. Rose (W.W. Norton and Pantheon Books, 1985), p. 156.

66. Jean Hyppolite attended many of Lacan's *Séminaires* and his views are often noted in the discussions which ended the sessions. His essay 'Hegel's Phenomenology and Psychoanalysis' (trans. A. Richer) in W.E. Steinkraus (ed.), *New Studies in Hegel's Philosophy* (Holt, Reinhart and Winston, 1976) also proposes an interpretation of self-consciousness as a mirror play (p. 61). The discussion here will draw parallels between Hyppolite and Lacan at the level of their conceptions of subjectivity, drawing upon earlier developments in Chapter 1.

67. J. Hyppolite, *Genesis and Structure in Hegel's Phenomenology* (Northwestern University Press, 1974), p. 250.

68. *Ibid.*, p. 191.

69. M. Bowie, *Psychoanalysis and the Future of Theory* (Blackwell, 1993), p. 24.

70. Lacan, 'The Function of Language in Psychoanalysis', op. cit., p. 85.

71. See Juliet Flower MacCannell's comments in *Figuring Lacan: Criticism and the Cultural Unconscious* (Croom Helm, 1986), p. 21.

72. Nancy and Lacoue-Labarthe, op. cit., p. 98.
73. Lacan, 'Truth Emerges from the Mistake', in *The Seminar of Jacques Lacan Book I*, op. cit., p. 264.
74. Lacan, 'Agency of the Letter', op. cit., p. 165.
75. Nancy and Lacoue-Labarthe, op. cit., p. 98.
76. *Ibid.*, pp. 27–8.
77. *Ibid.*, p. 82. Borch-Jacobsen similarly notes that Lacan's subject is tied to the subject of consciousness and 'divides itself only because it represents itself; therefore, it is nothing but the Cartesian subject'. See his essay 'The Alibis of the Subject: Lacan and Philosophy' (trans. D. Brick) in S. Shamdasni and M. Münchow (eds), *Speculations after Freud: Psychoanalysis, Philosophy and Culture* (Routledge, 1994), p. 80.
78. Nancy and Lacoue-Labarthe, op. cit., p. 136.
79. M. Heidegger 'Logos (Heraclitus, Fragment B 50)', in *Early Greek Thinking: The Dawn of Western Philosophy*, trans. D. Farrell Krell and F.A. Capuzzi (Harper and Row, 1984). This is noted by the major commentaries on Lacan's relation to Heidegger considered here (W. Richardson, Borch-Jacobsen and Nancy and Lacoue-Labarthe). All note the significance of Lacan's translation of Heidegger's essay in *La Psychoanalyse*, Vol. 1, 1956. Roudinesco also draws attention to the 'very free and high-handed' translation of this text; again, Lacan appears to mould an idea to his own purposes. See *Jacques Lacan*, op. cit., pp. 226–30.
80. Heidegger, 'Logos (Heraclitus Fragment B 50)', op. cit., p. 77.
81. *Ibid.*, p. 64.
82. See Nancy and Lacoue-Labarthe, op. cit., pp. 82–3; p. 134. Metaphor and metonymy reinscribe the truth of the subject upon the signifying chain, and bring *aleithia* within a presence/absence dichotomy which loses much of the Heideggerian nuance attached to it.
83. We may assume for the purposes of this argument that Nancy and Lacoue-Labarthe's understanding of the real is likely to parallel the reading by Jacques Derrida. For Derrida, the real is the 'third term', the mediating principle of the dialectic relation between symbolic and imaginary. The real is therefore fully containable in Lacan's tri-partite system. For an elaboration of this perspective see Derrida's *Positions*, trans. A. Bass (Athlone Press, 1981), pp. 107–11.
84. In his argument concerning the limits of Lacanian theory, an account which parallels on several points that offered by Lacoue-Labarthe and Nancy discussed in the text, Borch-Jacobsen notes that in a very early article on family complexes (1938) Lacan writes of an *affective* identification with an object which precedes any specular image of that identification, the contents of which cannot be represented in/by consciousness. This affective–corporeal dimension of the subject recedes in importance as Lacan's 'system' develops. Borch-Jacobsen attributes this dichotomization of affect and language to Lacan's inheritance of Kojève's dualist ontology discussed more fully in Chapter 1 of this study. For Borch-Jacobsen's account see his *Lacan: The Absolute Master*, op. cit., ch. 2, pp. 66–71 and 'Basta Cosi!' (interview conducted by Chris Oakley), in Todd Dufresne (ed.), *Returns to the French Freud: Freud, Lacan and beyond* (Routledge, 1997), pp. 209–27.
85. Lacan, 'Psychoanalysis and Cybernetics, or on the Nature of Language', in *The Seminar of Jacques Lacan Book II*, op. cit., p. 297.

86. In an interesting essay entitled 'The Echo of the Subject' Philippe Lacoue-Labarthe considers the 'reverberations' of the subject through music, drawing attention to an acoustic dimension distinct from that of the specular structure of experience. See *Typographies: Mimesis, Philosophy, Politics* (Harvard University Press, 1989).

87. See M. Henry *The Genealogy of Psychoanalysis*, trans. D. Brick (Stanford University Press, 1993), ch. 1. It is this relation which has been explored within much contemporary feminist philosophy.

88. In his study of the concept in *The Lacanian Delusion*, trans. G. Sims (Oxford University Press, 1990), François Roustang notes how Lacan moved to a scientific rendering of the real in his later work. This effort to systematize relinquished any focus on the affective content of the real.

89. Thus Lacan writes, 'You can only know what can happen to a reality once you have definitively reduced it to being inscribed in a language.' See 'Introduction to the big Other', *The Seminar of Jacques Lacan Book II*, op. cit., p. 239.

90. Lacan, *Écrits*, op. cit., p. 174.

91. *Ibid.*, p. 144.

92. For Castoriadis's critique of Lacan, see the first part of *Crossroads in the Labyrinth*, trans. K. Soper and M. Ryle (The Harvester Press, 1984).

93. For a conservative reading of Lacan see L. Lemoine-Luccioni, *The Dividing of Women, or Woman's Lot* (Free Association, 1987).

94. See C. Castoriadis *The Imaginary Institution of Society*, trans. K. Blamey (Polity, 1987).

95. G. Agamben, *Infancy and History: Essays on the Destruction of Experience,* trans. L. Heron (Verso, 1993), op. cit., pp. 6–7.

96. I have pursued this theme in 'Community, selfhood and subjectivity', in A. Brier and B. Lovelock (eds), *Community and Communication* (Avebury Press, 1997).

97. See also the comment by V. Descombes in *Modern French Philosophy* (Cambridge University Press, 1980), p. 106.

98. Agamben, op. cit., p. 9.

99. F. Jameson, op. cit., p. 338.

100. M. Dolar, 'Beyond Interpellation', in *Qui Parle*, Vol. 6, no. 2, 1993, pp. 77, 90.

101. S. Žižek, *The Sublime Object of Ideology* (Verso, 1989), pp. 174–5.

102. M. Dolar 'The Legacy of the Enlightenment: Foucault and Lacan', *New Formations*, no. 14, 1991, p. 54.

103. For a fascinating discussion of the dynamics of ideology in the light of this comment, see E. Laclau, 'The Death and Ressurrection of the Theory of Ideology', *The Journal of Political Ideologies*, Vol. 1, no. 3, 1996, pp. 201–20.

104. See Ernesto Laclau's discussion of the relation between power and objectivity in *New Reflections on the Revolution of Our Time* (Verso, 1990), p. 61.

105. It must be borne in mind, of course, that Althusser himself did initiate a dialogue with Lacan over some aspects of their work.

106. See Lacan, *Four Fundamental Concepts of Psychoanalysis*, op. cit., p. 53.

107. See W. Richardson, 'Psychoanalysis and the Being Question', in Kerrigan and Smith (eds), *Interpreting Lacan*, op. cit.

108. See most recently Žižek's *The Ticklish Subject: The Absent Centre of Political Ontology* (Verso, 1999).

NOTES **217**

CHAPTER 4

1. We should make clear from the outset however, that Derrida's use of language is not a form of linguistic idealism, as, for example, Jurgen Habermas maintains. See *The Philosophical Discourse of Modernity* (Polity, 1989), particularly ch. 7.
2. Derrida is aware that this misreading is responsible for a number of superficial criticisms: 'Deconstruction is always deeply concerned with the "other" of language. I never cease to be surprised at critics who see my work as a declaration that there is nothing beyond language, that we are imprisoned in language; it is, in fact, saying the exact opposite. The critique of logocentrism is above all else the search for the "other of language"'. See the interview in Richard Kearney (ed.), *Dialogues with Contemporary Thinkers* (Manchester University Press, 1984), p. 123.
3. According to Bill Martin, 'the search for this mirror defines Derrida's whole reading of the history of philosophy.' See his *Matrix and Line: Derrida and the Possibilities of a Postmodern Social Theory* (SUNY Press, 1992), p. 75. It is not the mirror but its mode of presenting perception and subjectivity that Derrida explores.
4. The question concerning the status of the conditions of possibility opened up by deconstruction is an important one; it will be broached at various points in this chapter. It will be argued that deconstruction cannot pose the question of conditions from a transcendental vantage point. Indeed, this vantage point is deeply historical. It is bound up with the production of space, time, concept and, most significantly, language. The transcendental is *named* by philosophy. It is a linguistic event which cuts up, differentiates and creates value. Deconstruction traces the construction of this boundary and, in so doing, it shows how all positions of transcendence, be they Kantian or Husserlian, are marked by a residue which pushes them to breakdown. For readings that pursue the transcendental vis-à-vis language see G. Agamben *Infancy and History*, trans. L. Heron (Verso, 1988) and D. Wood '*Différance* and the Problem of Strategy', in David Wood and Robert Bernasconi (eds), *Derrida and Différance* (Parousia Press, 1985) and Wood's *Philosophy of the Limit* (Unwin Hyman, 1990).
5. J. Derrida, 'Implications' interview with Henri Ronse [6 December 1967] in *Positions*, trans. A. Bass (University of Chicago Press, 1981), p. 6.
6. Derrida, 'Sending: On Representation', trans. P. Caws, in G.L. Ormiston and A.D. Schrift (eds), *Transforming the Hermeneutic Context: From Nietzsche to Nancy* (SUNY Press, 1990), p. 114. Heidegger's discussion of representational thinking may be found in 'The Age of The World Picture' in *The Question Concerning Technology and Other Essays*, trans. and Introduction by W. Lovitt, (Harper Torchbooks, 1977).
7. *Ibid.*, p. 114. If the *subjectum* can be equated with the function of the *cogito*, it is worth noting that in other works, Derrida notes the hyperbolic experience of the cogito: 'nothing is less reassuring than the *cogito* at its proper and inaugural moment.' See 'Cogito and the History of Madness' in *Writing and Difference*, trans. and Introduction by A. Bass (Routledge and Kegan Paul, 1978), p. 56.
8. On the critique of self-reflection by deconstruction, see Rudolphe Gasché, *The Tain of the Mirror* (Harvard University Press, 1986).

9.   Translated as *Speech and Phenemona* and *Of Grammatology*, respectively.
10. 'Force of Law: The 'Mystical Foundation of Authority', in D. Carlson, D. Cornell and M. Rosenfeld (eds), *Deconstruction and the Possibility of Justice* (Routledge, 1993). Here Derrida makes this claim with regard to justice.
11. However, deconstruction does identify and attribute a certain power to the role of metaphor in philosophical discourse. For Derrida, it is often the play of *metaphor* which links the spatial and temporal dimensions between metaphysical and conceptual formulations. Metaphor comes to fill the temporal and spatial gap in meaning, and produces an ideal objectivity assumed by the subject to be of its own making. Yet metaphor itself has no certain boundaries or points of reference: it cannot be deciphered or fully understood, but, like a concept, metaphor, too, 'has a history, yields knowledge, demands from the epistemologist construction, rectification, critical rules of importation and exportation.' Metaphors inhabit philosophical texts, they are used to render meaning and coherence where no such clarity is due. See 'White Mythology: Metaphor in the Text of Philosophy', in *Margins of Philosophy* (Harvester Wheatsheaf, 1982); quote taken from p. 264. The function of metaphor is discussed at appropriate points in this chapter.
12. Rodolphe Gasché, op. cit., pp. 279–80.
13. J. Derrida, *Of Grammatology*, trans. G. Spivak (Johns Hopkins University Press, 1974), p. 70.
14. J. Derrida, 'Politics and Friendship' (an interview conducted with M. Sprinkler), in A. Kaplan and M. Sprinkler (eds), *The Althusserian Legacy* (Verso, 1992).
15. *Positions*, op. cit., p. 24.
16. *Ibid.*, p. 12.
17. See Derrida's interview with Christopher Norris, in A. Papadakis, C. Cooke and A. Benjamin (eds), *Deconstruction: Omnibus Volume* (Academy Editions, 1989), pp. 71–5.
18. Derrida, 'Letter to a Japanese Friend', in Bernasconi and Wood (eds), op. cit., p. 2.
19. See Derrida's discussion in 'Politics and Friendship', op. cit., pp. 187–91. Thus Marian Hobson points out that Derrida considers a plurality of ethically loaded, locatable structures. See her *Jacques Derrida: Opening Lines* (Routledge, 1999), p. 136.
20. Post-modernism in no way escapes this appeal to historical form and logic, implying a uni-linear progression from the premodern to the modern. See for example Derrida's discussion with Christopher Norris, op. cit., p. 73 and Drucilla Cornell, *The Philosophy of the Limit* (Routledge, 1992), Introduction.
21. *Positions*, op. cit., pp. 57–8.
22. In 'Structure, Sign and Play in the Discourse of the Human Sciences' Derrida writes that structure 'has always been neutralised or reduced, and this by a process of giving it a centre or referring it to a point of presence, a fixed origin. The function of this centre was not to orient, balance, and organise the structure … but above all to make sure that the organising principle of the structure would limit what we might call the *freeplay* of the structure … even today the notion of a structure lacking any centre represents the unthinkable itself.' See *Writing and Difference* (Routledge and Kegan Paul, 1978), pp. 278–9.
23. Derrida, 'Letter to a Japanese Friend', in Wood and Bernasconi (eds), op. cit., p. 2.
24. 'Structure, Sign and Play', op. cit., pp. 264, 249.

25. *Ibid.*, p. 260.
26. The concept of the knowledge-effect was interposed between these dualisms but arguably could not transcend them. Ultimately these dualisms limit the radical nature of Althusser's epistemology, although Althusser's last speculative writings upon an aleatory materialism went some way towards overcoming these problems. See Chapter 2 of this work for a discussion of Althusser's epistemology.
27. 'Structure, Sign and Play', op. cit., p. 264.
28. *Ibid.*, p. 265.
29. This was the concept offered by Kojève, and later Henri Corbin, as a translation of Heidegger's *Dasein*. For a discussion of this anthropological translation of Heidegger see Tom Rockmore's *Heidegger and French Philosophy: Humanism, Anti-humanism and Being* (Routledge, 1995).
30. Jacques Derrida, 'The Ends of Man', *Philosophy and Phenomenological Research*, Vol. 30, no. 1, 1969, p. 41 (reprinted in *Margins of Philosophy* (Harvester, 1982), pp. 109–36).
31. *Ibid.*, p. 44.
32. *Ibid.*, p. 35. This perspective echoes Heidegger's concern with metaphysical humanism: 'the *humanitas of homo humanus* is determined with regard to an already established interpretation of nature, history, world, and the ground of the world, that is, of beings as a whole.' See his 'Letter on Humanism', in David Farrell Krell (ed.), *Heidegger's Basic Writings* (Harper, 1977), p. 202.
33. M. Heidegger, *Identity and Difference*, trans. J. Stambaugh (Harper and Row, 1974), p. 30.
34. Heidegger, 'The Principle of Identity', *ibid.*, p. 32.
35. Heidegger, 'Letter on Humanism', op. cit., p. 224.
36. *Ibid.*, p. 196.
37. *Ibid.*, p. 213.
38. *Ibid.*, p. 203.
39. *Ibid.*, p. 229.
40. In 'The Principle of Identity', for example, Heidegger writes 'it is man, open toward Being, who alone lets Being arrive as presence', op. cit., p. 31.
41. For this argument see 'The Ends of Man', op. cit., pp. 47–8.
42. *Of Grammatology*, op. cit., p. 19.
43. F. Nietzsche, extract from 'On Truth and Lie in an Extra-Moral Sense', in *The Portable Nietzsche*, trans. W. Kaufmann (Penguin Books, 1976), p. 46–7.
44. The term is Martin Jay's, taken from *Of Downcast Eyes: The Denigration of Vision in Twentieth Century French Thought* (University of California Press, 1993).
45. F. Nietzsche, *On the Genealogy of Morals*, trans. C. Diethe, (ed.) K. Ansell-Pearson (Cambridge University Press, 1994), Part 3, Sect. 12.
46. See *The Will to Power*, trans. W. Kaufmann and R.J. Hollingdale (Vintage Books, 1967), Sect. 490, p. 270.
47. See *Beyond Good and Evil: Prelude to a Philosophy of the Future*, trans. W. Kaufmann (Vintage Books, 1966), Sect. 16, 17.
48. *Ibid.*, Part 1, Sect. 9.
49. *Genealogy of Morals*, op. cit., pp. 26–7.
50. *Ibid.*, p. 29.
51. *Ibid.*, p. 37.

52. Thus Derrida writes 'The system of "hearing (understanding)-oneself-speak" through the phonic substance – which *presents itself* as the nonexterior, nonmundane, therefore nonempirical or non-contingent signifier – has necessarily dominated the history of the world during an entire epoch, and has even produced the idea of the world, of world-origin, that arises from the difference between the worldly and the non-worldly, the outside and the inside, ideality and non-ideality, universal and non-universal, transcendental and empirical etc.' *Of Grammatology*, op. cit., pp. 7–8.

53. Each of these philosophical methods contribute to the method of phenomenological reduction but is not easily attributed to any of them.

54. For a very clear, introductory exposition of Husserl see David Wood 'An Introduction to Derrida', *Radical Philosophy*, Vol. 21, 1979, p. 20.

55. See Derrida's discussion in *Speech and Phenomena*, trans. D.B. Allison (Northwestern University Press, 1967) and in *Positions*, op. cit., pp. 30–32.

56. See Husserl's discussions in his 1907 lecture, *The Idea of Phenomenology* (Martinus Nijhoff, 1964).

57. See Derrida's 'Genesis and Structure in Husserl's Phenomenology', in *Writing and Difference*, op. cit.

58. *Speech and Phenomena*, op. cit., p. 22.

59. *Ibid.*, pp. 52–4.

60. *Ibid.*, p. 14.

61. *Ibid.*, p. 15.

62. See 'Genesis and Structure', op. cit., p. 324.

63. *Positions*, op. cit., p. 5.

64. As Derrida points out, 'transforming a traditional concept into an indicative or metaphorical concept does not eliminate its heritage', *Speech and Phenomena*, op. cit., p. 8.

65. It should be pointed out that Adorno's earlier critique of Husserl's phenomenology is similarly directed towards a questioning of beginnings. He writes that 'ostensibly originary concepts ... are totally and necessarily mediated in themselves, ... "laden with presuppositions" (p. 12), and of the subject promoting itself 'by furnishing the principle from which all being proceeds'(p. 14). However, significant theoretical differences of method separate Derrida and Adorno: (i) the latter's conception of the antinomic structure of philosophy owes more to Hegel and Lukács than the former's; (ii) as Sabine Wilke points out ('Adorno and Derrida on Husserl', *Telos*, no. 84, 1990), in Adorno's reading, the tendency is to reduce Husserl's work to bourgeois thought; social relations are sublimated into ontology (p. 172). As with Lukács (see Chapter 2 of this book), subject–object relations are a product of reification. Derrida, on the other hand, uses his analysis of Husserl to develop a mode of deconstruction which is not inflected with the language of Marxism which for Derrida remains on several counts logocentric in its conceptual formulations. For Adorno's study see his *Against Epistemology: Studies in Husserl and the Phenomenological Antinomies* (Blackwell, 1982). For Derrida's more recent discussion of Marx see Section III of this chapter.

66. *Of Grammatology*, op. cit., p. 162.

67. *Ibid.*, p. 47. In *The Origin of Geometry*, Husserl also talks of the value of inscription, indeed the constitution of scientific (absolutely ideal) objects requires inscription to ensure both repetition and transmission. However, the possibility of writing is intrinsically related to speech; writing records, recapitulates, reconstitutes the founding act of speech. 'If writing brings the constitution of ideal objects to completion, it does so through phonetic writing: it proceeds to fix ... *an already inscribed utterance.*' Hence, whilst Husserl recognizes the significance of material inscription, it is incorporated into the experience of transcendental consciousness; it is not experienced as an impurity *other* to the subject, prior to expression and the constitution of self-presence.
68. *Ibid.*, p. 56.
69. *Ibid.*, p. 26.
70. C. Norris, *Derrida* (Fontana Press, 1987), p. 87.
71. *Speech and Phenomena*, op. cit., pp. 82, 86.
72. *Of Grammatology*, op. cit., p. 62.
73. *Ibid.*, p. 39.
74. See Derrida, 'In Conversation with Christopher Norris', op. cit., p. 73.
75. 'Différance', in *Margins*, op. cit., p. 11.
76. *Ibid.*, p. 8.
77. *Ibid.*, p. 9.
78. A detailed consideration of Derrida's relation to Hegelian phenomenology is outside the scope of the present analysis. In an early interview however, Derrida notes that différance 'blocks every relation to theology' but when challenged by Walter Kaufmann in a discussion preceding the lecture on 'Différance'(1968) to develop the constitution of the problem of difference within metaphysics, Derrida notes Hegel as the philosopher most sensitive to difference within metaphysics, going as far as to note 'a certain irreducibility of différance in his text'. See 'The Original Discussion of "Différance"(1968)', in Bernasconi and Wood (eds), op. cit., pp. 93–95. Derrida plays on the meaning of *relève/aufhebung* in Hegel's work, which means both to elevate and replace/relieve. See the discussion in 'The Ends of Man', pp. 40–41 and Différance, p. 19, n. 23.
79. 'Différance', op. cit., p. 22.
80. I take this term from Rudolphe Gasché, 'Deconstruction as Criticism', *Gylph*, Vol. 6, 1979.
81. *Of Grammatology*, op. cit., p. 24; emphasis added.
82. 'Interview with Richard Kearney', op. cit., p. 111.
83. 'Structure, Sign and Play', op. cit., p. 250.
84. 'Interview with Richard Kearney', op. cit., p. 125.
85. ' "Eating Well", or the Calculation of the Subject: An Interview with Jacques Derrida' (conducted by Jean-Luc Nancy) in E. Cadava, P. Connor and J.L. Nancy (eds), *Who Comes After the Subject?* (Routledge, 1991), p. 105.
86. In *Logics of Disintegration* Peter Dews argues that Derrida's project generates a difficulty in conceiving of *any* concept of subjectivity, instead offering us a stark choice between 'a view of the subject as an immobile centre, a core of self-certainty, or the acceptance that there is no subject at all, except as an "effect" of the play of the text', p. 32.

87. 'Différance', op. cit., p. 16.
88. *Speech and Phenomena*, op. cit., p. 92.
89. I take this phrase from Lacoue-Labarthe's discussion in 'Obliteration' (trans. T. Trezise) in his *The Subject of Philosophy* (Minnesota University Press, 1993), p. 82.
90. J. Derrida, 'Desistance', Introduction to P. Lacoue-Labarthe, *Typographies: Mimesis, Philosophy, Politics*, ed. C. Fynsk (Harvard University Press, 1989), p. 4. The French verb *se désister* has a reflexive construction in French, which is always obligatory: to renounce a suit or legal action, a responsibility. It can also designate a temporal interruption, to cease, to stop, to leave.
91. *Ibid.*, p. 5. The problem, as formulated in the discussion here, is clearly illustrated by Lacoue-Labarthe's own perspective, quoted by Derrida: 'What interests us here ... is neither the subject nor the author. Nor is it the "other," whatever one places under the term, of the subject or the author. It would be rather (to limit ourselves provisionally to the sole question of the subject) what is *also* at play in the subject, while being absolutely irreducible to some subjectivity (that is to say, to any objectivity whatsoever); what, in the subject, "deserts" [a term which announces *désister* for Derrida] ... the subject *itself*, and which, prior to any self-possession ... is the dissolution, the defeat of the subject in the subject or *as* the subject: the (de)constitution of the subject, or the "loss" of the subject' (p. 16, n. 9). The source of this quotation is Lacoue-Labarthe's 'Obliteration' *The Subject of Philosophy*, op. cit., pp. 81–2.
92. P. Lacoue-Labarthe, *Heidegger, Art and Politics* (Blackwell, 1990), p. 83.
93. *Positions*, op. cit., p. 29.
94. *Of Grammatology*, op. cit., p. 69.
95. 'Freud and the Scene of Writing', in *Writing and Difference*, op. cit., pp. 196–7; emphasis added.
96. On this point see Barbara Johnson's introduction to Derrida's *Dissemination* (University of Chicago Press, 1981).
97. *Positions*, op. cit., p. 113, n. 46. Also 'For the Love of Lacan', *Cardozo Law Review*, Vol. 16, 1995, p. 713.
98. *Positions*, p. 84.
99. See 'White Mythology', in *Margins*, op. cit.
100. Rene Major, 'Reason from the Unconscious', *Oxford Literary Review*, Vol. 12, 1990, p. 22.
101. This relation will not be pursued here.
102. The similarity in the conceptual usage and theoretical activity of these two terms has been noted by other authors, but not explicitly developed. See Mark Taylor, *Altarity* (University of Chicago Press, 1987), p. 276. Richard Boothby's analysis of Derrida also alludes to this relation. See his *Death and Desire* (Routledge, 1991), p. 154.
103. See 'For the Love of Lacan', op. cit., cited at p. 714. There is also a very helpful discussion in C. Howells, *Derrida: Deconstruction from Phenomenology to Ethics* (Polity, 1999).
104. 'Différance', op. cit., p. 19.
105. See also J. Butler, *The Psychic Life of Power* (Stanford University Press, 1997).

106. *Ibid.*, p. 19. Mark Taylor also recognizes the relation between différance and Thanatos: 'Death ... is not merely an absence and is not simply non-being, but is the non-absent absence that disrupts all presence and interrupts every present', op. cit., p. 291.

107. 'Freud and the Scene of Writing', p. 210.

108. *Ibid.*, p. 230.

109. J. Derrida, 'Speculations – On Freud', *Oxford Literary Review*, vol. 3, no. 2, 1980, p. 93.

110. In a seminar discussing the contribution of his work in the field of law (QMW College, University of London, 18 July 1995) Derrida pointed to deconstruction, Marxism and psychoanalysis as the critical discourses of our time, the value and intersections of which should be re-articulated. For Derrida's thoughts on Marxism, see below.

111. See Christina Howells, *Derrida*, op. cit., p. 121. The description is from Derrida's *Resistances of Psychoanalysis*, trans. P. Kamuf, P. Brault and M. Naas (Stanford University Press, 1998), p. 37.

112. R. Major, op. cit., p. 17.

113. Other writers have emphasized the equation of the real and the scientific in Lacan's work. See, for example, Francois Roustang, *The Lacanian Delusion* (Oxford University Press, 1990). My reading contests Roustang's position.

114. 'Politics and Friendship', op. cit., p. 212.

115. Derrida, *Specters of Marx: The State of the Debt and the Work of Mourning*, trans. P. Kamuf (Routledge, 1994), p. 92.

116. 'Politics and Friendship', op. cit., pp. 197–8.

117. As Phillipe Lacoue-Labarthe writes, 'There is no philosophical foundation that is not philosophical, because the philosophical is itself foundational.' *Typographies*, op. cit., p. 289.

118. In the discussion following Derrida's presentation 'Différance', Lucien Goldmann observes a 'close kinship' between the Lukácsian distinction between theory and praxis and the Derridean distinction between difference and différance, and further emphasizes (in a position that is shared with a number of other theorists considered in this section), that Derrida is unable to explicate social conditions. For Goldmann, Derrida thus 'retains praxis while at the same time he eliminates the subject.' See the discussion in *Derrida and Différance*, op. cit.

119. See for example Nancy Fraser 'The French Derridians: Politicizing Deconstruction or Deconstructing the Political?', *New German Critique*, Vol. 33, 1984, and Simon Critchley, *The Ethics of Deconstruction* (Blackwell, 1992), ch. 5.

120. Dews, op. cit., p. 35; emphasis added. Dews continues by observing that when Derrida begins to make more explicit statements of political criticism, 'he tends to revert to a conventionally Heideggerian account of technology and bureaucracy, and their possible dangers' (p. 35). In a more recent essay, Dews distinguishes between early deconstruction and the more recent *political* interventions: 'Whereas formerly Derrida denied that there could be any meaning, truth or history outside of metaphysics, his whole enterprise is now in effect an attempt to *liberate* these concepts from their metaphysical determinations.' See 'The Limits of Disenchantment', *New Left Review*, no. 213, 1995, p. 67.

121. This is the argument put forward by Luc Ferry and Alain Renaut in *French Philosophy of the Sixties: An Essay on Anti-humanism* (University of Massachusetts Press, 1990), pp. 143–5.

122. This opposition between the 'existence' and the 'essence' of politics can be seen to correspond to the distinction between *la politique* and *le politique* proposed by Phillipe Lacoue-Labarthe and Jean-Luc Nancy, discussed by both Fraser, and Critchley, op. cit.

123. We are familiar with the first two sets of oppositions in relation to Althusser's epistemology although his use of the concept of the imaginary, and later, the theory of aleatory materialism, sought to weave a path within and between these antinomies.

124. Bill Readings, 'The Deconstruction of Politics', in Lindsay Waters and Wlad Godzich (eds), *Reading De Man Reading* (University of Minnesota Press, 1989), pp. 223–43.

125. W. Connolly, *Political Theory and Modernity* (Blackwell, 1989), p. 65.

126. This and the preceding quotation are taken from 'Eating Well: Or the Calculation of the Subject', op. cit., p. 104.

127. *Specters*, op. cit., p. 33.

128. *The Philosophy of Marx*, trans. C. Turner (Verso, 1995), p. 113.

129. Both texts clearly owe something to Blanchot's '*Les Trois Paroles de Marx*' [1968] to be found in the collection titled *Friendship*, trans. E. Rottenberg (Stanford University Press, 1997).

130. Just as Althusser cannot be described simply as a structuralist so Derrida cannot easily be compartmentalized as a *post*-structuralist.

131. The major differences between Althusser and Derrida may be glimpsed in their markedly different readings of Husserl. Whereas Althusser in his 'surreptitious borrowings' from Husserl (for Derrida) constructed a notion of the object *in thought*, a space immune from the exigencies of empirical subjectivity, Derrida maintains a sense of the *indeterminacy* of objectivity and subjectivity preferring to trace their multiple conditions of existence. We have drawn attention to Althusser's use of Spinoza in this area. It may be the case that Derrida underplays this particular debt in his discussion of Althusser's borrowings (see Politics and Friendship, particularly p. 189). On the other hand, the phenomenology of Husserl casts a certain shadow over the conjuncture under consideration in this book. Husserl's relevance to structuralism has already been noted.

132. *Specters*, op. cit., p. 147.

133. *Ibid.*, p. 45.

134. *Ibid.*, p. 147.

135. As Derrida points out much of this use of the ghost metaphor is generated by Marx's critical reading in *The German Ideology* of Stirner's notion of usage of the Hegelian *spirit*, but Derrida also unravels a supplementary logic of the spectre that makes it an inescapable relation. There is no paradox in Marx's own appeal to the ghostly and the spectral in his rendering of ideology.

136. *Specters*, op. cit., p. 109.

137. *Ibid.*, pp. 126–7.

138. *Ibid.*, p. 148. No reference is made by Derrida in this context to Althusser's own account of relative autonomy or to the latter's theorization of the imaginary.

Surely Althusser's essay on ideology, which led so many developments within the theory of ideology was worthy of analysis here?

139. *Ibid.*, p. 154.

140. For Derrida's reading of Rousseau, see *Of Grammatology*.

141. 'Eating Well', op. cit., p. 103.

142. See Derrida's discussion in 'Desistance', op. cit., p. 30, n. 22. For a discussion of the incarnation of meaning in ideology, see E. Laclau 'The Death and Resurrection of the Concept of Ideology', *Journal of Political Ideologies*, Vol. 1, no. 3, 1996, pp. 201–20.

143. Christina Howells claims that Derrida's conception of the subject seems caught within the logic of a reversal in that it appears closer to the non-subject of structuralist discourse. See *Derrida*, op. cit., ch. 6.

144. See generally, Bennington's essay on Derrida, in S. Critchley and W. Schroeder (eds), *A Companion to Continental Philosophy*, (Blackwell, 1998).

145. 'Eating Well', op. cit., p. 98.

146. *Ibid.*, p. 109; 'Force of Law', op. cit., p. 20.

147. Dews, *The Limits of Disenchantment* (Verso, 1997), pp. 72 and 67, respectively.

CHAPTER 5

1. See Foucault, 'Politics and the Study of Discourse', *Ideology and Consciousness*, no. 3, Spring 1977.

2. See *The Order of Things: An Archaeology of the Human Sciences* (Tavistock, 1973), p. 332. Hereafter referred to as OT.

3. 'Maurice Florence' (trans. Catherine Porter) in G. Gutting (ed.), *The Cambridge Companion to Foucault* (Cambridge University Press, 1994), pp. 314–15. This entry in an encyclopedia of French philosophy was written by Foucault just before his death.

4. 'Truth and Power', in C. Gordon (ed.), *Power/Knowledge: Selected Interviews and Other Writings 1972–77* (Harvester Wheatsheaf, 1980), p. 117.

5. Throughout *The Order of Things* Foucault uses the notion of Man generically to refer to the object and subject of knowledge. I follow this categorization for consistency.

6. There are a number of references to Blanchot in Foucault's early work, as well as an important essay devoted to the former's *récits*, 'The Thought of the Outside', referenced below.

7. In what is reported to be the last interview given before his death, Foucault notes that his whole philosophical development was determined by his reading of Heidegger whom he read between 1951 and 1952, before his reading of Nietzsche. See 'The return of Morality', in *Foucault Live* (Scmiotext(e), 1989), p. 326.

8. Given the many interests and indeed, the multiple possibilities of phenomenological thought, it is clear that we can offer this reading of Foucault without having to embrace either a rigorous, scientific style of phenomenological thinking or an egological one. For a perceptive reflection on this theme see Maurice Blanchot, 'Atheism and Writing, Humanism and the Cry', in *The Infinite*

Conversation trans. S. Hanson (Minnesota University Press, 1993), particularly pp. 250–52. Also Gilles Deleuze, *Michel Foucault*, trans. S. Hand (Athlone Press, 1988), particularly pp. 107–9, and Gérard Lebrun, 'Notes on Phenomenology in Les Mots et les Choses', in *Michel Foucault Philosopher*, trans. T. Armstrong (Harvester Wheatsheaf, 1992).

9. *The Archaeology of Knowledge*, trans. A. Sheridan (Tavistock, 1972), p. 16. Hereafter referred to as AK.

10. AK, p. 13.

11. OT, p. 208. See in addition Foucault's comments on structuralism and subjectivity in 'The Archaeology of Knowledge', *Foucault Live* (Semiotext(e), 1989).

12. In this regard, see particularly 'On Transgression' [1963], 'Language to Infinity' [1963] and 'The Father's "No"' [1992], all translated in D. Bouchard (ed.), *Language, Counter-Memory, Practice* (Cornell University Press, 1977); *Death and the Labyrinth: The World of Raymond Roussel* [1963], trans. C. Ruas (Doubleday, 1986); 'The Thought of the Outside' [1966], in *Foucault/Blanchot*, trans. J. Mehlman and B. Massumi (Zone Books, 1987), as well as, more obviously, *Madness and Civilisation: A History of Insanity in the Age of Reason* [1961], trans. R. Howard (Routledge, 1971).

13. OT, p. 378.

14. AK, p. 13.

15. The relevant essays here are Derrida's 1963 lecture 'Cogito and the History of Madness', in *Writing and Difference* (Routledge and Kegan Paul, 1978) and Foucault's reply 'My Body, This Paper, This Fire', *Oxford Literary Review*, Vol. 4, no. 1, 1979.

16. OT, p. xiv. For an account of this phenomenological method which gives primacy to the subject of history, see the analysis of Lukács in Chapter 2.

17. 'Theatrum Philosophicum', in D. Bouchard (ed.), *Language, Counter-Memory, Practice* (Ithaca, 1977), p. 174.

18. OT, p. xx.

19. *Ibid.*, p. 31.

20. James Bernauer, *Foucault's Force of Flight: Towards an Ethics for Thought* (Humanities Press, 1990), p. 4.

21. OT, p. xxiv.

22. *Ibid.*, p. 29.

23. See OT, pp. 38, 39. Foucault also notes that the priority of writing gives rise to two other levels of language, that of commentary and below it, the hidden text. This framework was to be disrupted with the fragmentation of language and the birth of the empirical sciences. See the discussion in OT, p. 43.

24. *Ibid.*, p. 49. For Foucault's comments on these thinkers see, for example, 'The Thought of the Outside', op. cit., p. 18, p. 54

25. Both Dreyfus and Rabinow, *Michel Foucault: Beyond Structuralism and Hermeneutics* (Harvester Wheatsheaf, 1982) and Dominique Lecourt, *Marxism and Epistemology: Bachelard, Canguilhem, Foucault* (New Left Books, 1973) refer to the similarity of method between Foucault and Kuhn. The former tend to view the normative dimension of Kuhn's scientific revolution in knowledge to be more persuasive than Foucault's autonomous and non-normative analysis (see p. 60); the latter is more critical of posing any such contrast. Kuhn's philosophy is idealist,

offering up no possibility of a Marxist historical analysis (unlike Bachelard). For
Lecourt, Foucault's method is, however, unable to apply itself to a Marxist analysis
of materialist transformations in knowledge because it remains abstracted from
an analysis of ideology. See *Marxism and Epistemology*, Part 3, and Chapter 2 of
this study for a further discussion of Marxist epistemology.

26. OT, p. 308.
27. *Ibid.*, pp. 238–9.
28. *Ibid.*, p. 318.
29. Dreyfus and Rabinow, op. cit.; note this changing mode from analysis to analytic:
     'An analytic is an attempt to show on what grounds representation and analysis of
     representation are possible and to what extent they are legitimate', p. 28.
30. OT, p. 236.
31. G. Deleuze, op. cit., p. 88.
32. The whole of chapter 9 of *The Order of Things* forms the horizon for this
     discussion.
33. See for example Drefus and Rabinow, op. cit.; K. Hutchings *Kant, Critique and
     Politics* (Routledge, 1996), ch. 5; S. Parsons 'Foucault and the Problem of Kant',
     Praxis International, Vol. 8, 1988–9, pp. 317–28.
34. Didier Eribon, *Michel Foucault* (Faber and Faber, 1992), pp. 110–13.
35. Dreyfus and Rabinow, op. cit., p. 34.
36. A consideration of Foucault's relation to Heidegger is outside the scope of this
     present work. See, however, Dreyfus and Rabinow, op. cit., especially pp. 38–9,
     42–4, 11, 57; H.L. Dreyfus 'On the Ordering of Things: Being and Power in
     Heidegger and Foucault', in T.J. Armstrong (ed.), *Michel Foucault Philosopher*
     (Harvester Wheatsheaf, 1992), pp. 80–95. On Foucault and Merleau-Ponty, see
     R.A. Cohen, 'Merleau-Ponty, the Flesh and Foucault', *Philosophy Today*, Vol. 28,
     1984, pp. 329–38.
37. See M. Heidegger, 'The Age of the World Picture', in W. Lovitt (ed.),
     The Question Concerning Technology and Other Essays (Harper Torchbooks,
     1977).
38. AK, ch. 5 particularly p. 62.
39. Deleuze, op. cit., p. 108.
40. AK, p. 202.
41. See Foucault's conclusion to AK. Unsurprisingly, both Althusser and Foucault
     reject the label 'structuralist'; Althusser because the form of his thought owes more
     to Spinozist formulations of subject and object and Foucault because his account of
     history is far more nuanced than any structuralist formulation could be. Foucault's
     self-critique at the close of *The Archaeology of Knowledge* intimates many further
     disagreements with structuralism. For an interesting discussion on this theme,
     see 'Structuralism and Post-Structuralism: An Interview with Michel Foucault'
     (Conducted by G. Raulet), *Telos*, Vol. 55, 1983.
42. AK, p. 62.
43. 'The Order of Discourse' in R. Young (ed.), *Untying the Text* (Cambridge
     University Press, 1987), pp. 124–5.
44. A number of writers have noted the relation between the idea of pre-constituting
     discourse or discursive practices and Heidegger's notion of a 'clearing' for
     thought. For both thinkers, systems of possibility, and the modes according to

which Man is represented as both subject and object, are opened up – and often delimited – by the episteme of a given Age.

45.   OT, pp. 253–63.

46.   M. Blanchot 'Michel Foucault as I Imagine Him', in *Foucault/Blanchot*, trans. J. Mehlman and B. Massumi (Zone Books, 1987), p. 76.

47.   Foucault had already broached this question of the dispersal (rather than simply the disappearance) of the subject in a number of previous essays. There, however, his concern was with writing under the *absence* of authorship, writing as a 'spreading forth of language in its raw state, an unfolding of pure exteriority' where the subject that speaks is 'less the responsible agent of a discourse (what holds it, what uses it to assert and judge, what sometimes represents itself in it by means of a grammatical form *designed to have that effect*) than a non-existence in whose emptiness the unending outpourings of language uninterruptedly continues.' ('Thought of the Outside', op. cit., p. 11; emphasis added). Many of Foucault's contemporaries, Blanchot, Bataille, Barthes, as well as Lacan, were concerned with this space of writing where something other than the subject may speak. Foucault's *The Archaeology of Knowledge* gives this regard a more formal quality and the non-discursive siting and transgressive possibilities of language appear to be covered over by, or at least subordinated to, this formal system of discourse. For other essays where Foucault develops this theme see the pieces mentioned in note 12 as well as, more obviously, 'What is an Author', in P. Rabinow (ed.), *The Foucault Reader* (Penguin, 1984).

48.   AK, p. 52.

49.   *Ibid.*, p. 120

50.   *Ibid.*, pp. 69–70.

51.   *Ibid.*, p. 68.

52.   B. Brown and M. Cousins, 'The Linguistic Fault: the case of Foucault's archaeology', *Economy and Society*, Vol. 9, no. 3, 1980 p. 261.

53.   See AK, pp. 82–8.

54.   *Ibid.*, p. 109.

55.   *Ibid.*, p. 127.

56.   J. Rajchman, *Michel Foucault: the Freedom of Philosophy* (Columbia University Press, 1985), p. 103.

57.   AK, p. 127.

58.   A number of theorists broach the question of relativism. See, particularly, N. Fraser, *Unruly Practices* (Polity Press, 1991), ch. 1 and 2. Also Dreyfus and Rabinow, op. cit.; J. Habermas, *The Philosophical Discourse on Modernity* (MIT Press, 1987).

59.   Dreyfus and Rabinow, op. cit., p. 83.

60.   *Ibid.*, p. 93. The authors do not extend their argument to take into account this effect on Foucault's other studies. Genealogy is seen to take precedence over archaeology, Foucault's analysis becomes more diagnostic: 'an interpretive analytics', and less philosophical. Foucault's later works, it seems, transcend the problems of the former. See, particularly, chapter 5 of *Michel Foucault: Beyond Structuralism and Hermeneutics*.

61.   In 'Foucault and the problem of Kant', S. Parsons argues that the theoretical difficulties Foucault encounters in his archaeological investigations result from the uncritical adoption of the Kantian problematic. It is claimed that firstly

Foucauldian rules, like Searle's constitutive rules, draw out the boundaries for the formation of objects, and constitute and regulate the appearance of objects in discourse. Secondly, the responsibility attached to rules and statements gives the archaeologist no autonomy from discourse. Hence, it becomes difficult to foresee the origin of historical change. And yet, Parsons concludes, if Foucault also wishes to identify statements as a source of rupture and discontinuity, then 'the whole legitimacy of an archaeological analysis is predicated upon the idea that the statements of the archaeologist can *consciously determine* the ending of "The Age of Man".' (p. 322; my emphasis). 'In introducing rules as constitutive, Foucault, in effect, defines rules in terms of Kant's definition of God: rules are constitutive, they create existence' (p. 324). In common with the argument developed by Dreyfus and Rabinow, Parsons claims that rules function very much like a meaning conferring subject. See 'Foucault and the Problem of Kant', *Praxis International*, Vol. 8, 1988–9, pp. 317–28. Also C. Norris, 'What is Enlightenment? Kant according to Foucault', in G. Guttings (ed.), *The Cambridge Companion to Foucault* (Cambridge University Press, 1994).

62. AK, p. 139.
63. G. Deleuze *Foucault*, op. cit., p. 49. Deleuze and Guattari's last work together *What is Philosophy?* (Verso Books, 1994) discusses the concept in a way that exceeds all oppositions between discursive and non-discursive formations. In many ways the first part of this book is a critical departure from Foucault's analysis in *The Archaeology of Knowledge*.
64. Thus Brown and Cousins note that 'there is no *general* form of the connection between a discourse (and indeed its transformation) and a general class of "external" events which could function as a totality, either in the form of the "real" or as a cause', op. cit., p. 254.
65. Deleuze, op. cit., p. 31.
66. In this context see the analysis of E. Laclau and C. Mouffe in *Hegemony and Socialist Strategy* (Verso, 1985), pp. 105–10.
67. Foucault writes of intra-, inter-, and extra-discursive dependencies. See 'Politics and Method', *Ideology and Consciousness*, Vol. 8, 1981, p. 13.
68. See, particularly, Foucault's essay 'My Body, This Paper, This Fire', op. cit., pp. 18–19.
69. 'Dream, Imagination and Existence' [1954], in K. Hoeller (ed.), 'Dream and Existence', Special issue of *Review of Existential Psychology and Psychiatry*, 1986, p. 37.
70. M. Cousins and A. Hussain, *Michel Foucault* (Macmillan, 1984), pp. 74–5.
71. See Derrida's 'Cogito and the History of Madness', op. cit., p. 35.
72. See in this context the recent collection edited by A.I. Davidson, *Foucault and his Interlocutors* (Chicago University Press, 1998), who notes in his introduction that Foucault's analyses of discourse amounts to a 'philosophy of language' and also points to the latter's interest in structural linguistics. However, Davidson gains credence for his arguments from a number of essays that *precede* Foucault's 1972 text, *The Archaeology of Knowledge*, where his contrived distance (by no means a real one) from linguistics is emphasized. Here I want merely to draw attention to the variety of interpretations of what surely is an ambiguous relation between discourse and language in Foucault's work.

73. The extent to which this view may condemn Foucault's account of madness is debatable. At times Foucault seems aware of these problems, as evidenced in his later critique of psychoanalysis. See also Blanchot's comments in 'Michel Foucault as I Imagine Him', op. cit., pp. 67–8.

74. See 'My Body, This Paper, This Fire', op. cit., particularly pp. 15–19. A full discussion of the exchange between Derrida and Foucault is outside the scope of this chapter. I refer the reader to the following studies: R. Boyne, *Foucault and Derrida: The Other Side of Reason* (Unwin Hyman, 1990); Edward Said 'The Problem of Textuality: Two Exemplary Positions', *Critical Inquiry*, Vol. 4, no. 4, 1978; S. Felmam, 'Madness and Philosophy *or* Literature's Reason', *Yale French Studies*, Vol. 52, 1975; A. Wordsworth, 'Derrida and Foucault: Writing the History of Madness', in D. Attridge, G. Bennington and R. Young (eds), *Untying the Text* (Cambridge University Press, 1987). Derrida rearticulated his views on Foucault's writing in ' "To Do Justice to Freud": The History of Madness in the Age of Psychoanalysis', *Critical Inquiry*, Vol. 20, 1994.

75. *Ibid.*, p. 84.

76. J. Habermas, op. cit., p. 247.

77. See the general argument put forward by Dreyfus and Rabinow, op. cit.

78. *Ibid.*, p. 105.

79. 'Nietzsche, Genealogy, History', in D. Bouchard (ed.), op. cit., p. 143.

80. *Ibid.*, p. 146.

81. Rajchman, op. cit. ch. 2.

82. Bernauer, op. cit. p. 19.

83. 'Nietzsche, Genealogy, History', in D. Bouchard (ed.), op. cit., p. 142.

84. For this important reformulation see: 'What is Enlightenment', p. 46 and the interview 'Polemics, Politics and Problematisations', both in *The Foucault Reader*, op. cit., and more generally the Introduction to *The Use of Pleasure: The History of Sexuality*, Vol. 2, trans. R. Hurley (Penguin, 1987).

85. This observation should appear less paradoxical if we recall that Foucault was once the student of Althusser and would have read Marx (although not exclusively) through a distinctly Althusserian lens. For a very perceptive discussion of Foucault's continuing affinity with Marx, see 'Foucault and Marx: the Question of Nominalism' in *Michel Foucault Philosopher*, op. cit., pp. 38–57.

86. M. Foucault, *The History of Sexuality Volume One: An Introduction* (Penguin, 1990), p. 92.

87. *Ibid.*, p. 98.

88. A number of liberal political philosophers have engaged with Foucault's characterization of modernity. All contend that Foucault wishes to undermine the emancipatory ideals of liberalism. It is Foucault's alleged neutrality towards different modes of punishment together with his epistemological relativism which allows him no way of criticizing a given regime of power. Certainly *Discipline and Punish* wishes to show the dark underside of liberalism: 'The Enlightenment which discovered the liberties also invented the disciplines' (p. 222). Yet, as we have argued above, charges of neutrality and relativism often fail to engage with the substance of Foucault's position. See R. Rorty, *Contingency, Irony and Solidarity* (Cambridge University Press, 1989), pp. 61–7; C. Taylor, 'Foucault on Freedom and Truth', *Political Theory*, Vol. 12, 1984, pp. 152–83.

89. Deleuze, op. cit., p. 38.
90. Jacques-Alain Miller, 'Jeremy Bentham's Panoptic Device' [1973], trans. Richard Miller, *October*, Vol. 41, Summer 1987, pp. 3–29. Miller's essay recognizes many of the functions of 'panopticon power' noted by Foucault two years later. It is interesting however that Foucault makes no reference to Miller's text in the bibliography of *Discipline and Punish*.
91. On the construction of docility, see *Discipline and Punish*, Part 3, pp. 135–69.
92. *Ibid.*, p. 136.
93. Deleuze, op. cit., p. 36
94. *Discipline and Punish*, op.cit., p. 205.
95. *Ibid.*, p. 200.
96. *Ibid.*, p. 203–4.
97. For a more detailed discussion of the relation between these two thinkers, see W. Montag 'The Soul is the Prison of the Body: Althusser and Foucault, 1970–1975', *Yale French Studies*, no. 88, 1997, pp. 53–77.
98. On the theoretical problems pervading the conception of ideology, see 'Truth and Power', in C. Gordon (ed.), *Michel Foucault: Power/Knowledge* (Harvester, 1980). For Foucault's rejection of ideology–science dualism see *The Archaeology of Knowledge*, op. cit., pp. 183–4.
99. Discipline and Punish, p. 202.
100. See Deleuze's analysis in *Foucault*, ch. 5.
101. *Ibid*, p. 116.
102. *Discipline and Punish*, op. cit., p. 166.
103. *Ibid.*, p. 221.
104. It is this formulation of power that leads Habermas to argue that the concept of power is the *a priori* condition for the constitution of both subjectivity and knowledge. Thus, 'no one can escape the strategic conceptual constraints of the philosophy of the subject merely by performing operations of reversal upon its basic concepts. Foucault cannot do away with all the aporias he attributes to the philosophy of the subject by means of a concept of power borrowed from the philosophy of the subject itself.' See Habermas, op. cit., p. 274. A similar interpretation can be found in Vincent Descombes: 'in the inversed idiom of the critique of the subject ... we find the human subject diagnosed as impersonal and anonymous power, no longer masked by human traits.' See his 'Apropos of the Critique of the Subject', in Cadava *et al.*, *Who Comes After the Subject*, op. cit., p. 127.
105. J. Copjec, 'The Orthopyschic Subject', *October*, Vol. 49, 1989, p. 55.
106. In 'Power and Subjectivity in Foucault', *New Left Review*, no. 198, 1984, Peter Dews claims that 'the notion of the body remains little more than a cipher in Foucault's work of this period' (p. 89).
107. *History of Sexuality*, op. cit., Vol. 1, p. 93.
108. *Power/Knowledge*, op. cit., p. 138.
109. See for example the otherwise exemplary reading of Foucault by Cousins and Hussain, op. cit., particularly p. 256.
110. J. Butler, *The Psychic Life of Power* (Stanford University Press, 1998), pp. 3, 87. In his essay 'Power and Subjectivity in Foucault', op. cit., Peter Dews notes that the theory of *libidi*nal and psychic containment offered by psychoanalysis

requires a theory of power which enforces this containment. Another study which pursues the psychoanalytic in both Lacan and Foucault is John Rajchman *Truth and Eros: Foucault, Lacan and the Question of Ethics* (Routledge, 1991). However, Rajchman attends centrally to Foucault's later writings which are not the focus of the present argument.

111. OT, p. 374.
112. For an account of the relation between psychoanalysis and the Confessional see *The History of Sexuality*, Part 5. In the second edition of *Mental Illness and Psychology*, Foucault views psychoanalysis as situating man along two axes: (1) an external dimension of exclusion and punishment; and (2) an internal dimension of moral assignation and guilt (cited in J. Bernauer, op. cit., p. 43).
113. *History of Sexuality*, op. cit., p. 71.
114. 'A Preface to Transgression' in Bouchard (ed.), op. cit., p. 48; emphasis added.
115. For an antagonistic dialogue between the Lacanian school and Foucault see 'The Confession of the Flesh', in *Power/Knowledge*, op. cit., particularly pp. 209–22.
116. Foucault, 'About the Beginnings of the Hermeneutics of the Self: Two Lectures at Dartmouth', *Political Theory*, Vol. 21, no. 2, 1993, p. 222.
117. *History of Sexuality*, op. cit., p. 81.
118. See Deleuze, 'What is a *Dispositif*?', in Armstrong (ed.), op. cit., p. 90.
119. *Ibid.*, p. 101.
120. *The Psychic Life of Power*, op. cit., p. 87.
121. *Ibid.*, p. 9.
122. There is no reference to Deleuze in this context. Sometimes it does seem that Butler considers this turning as an act of the self, although in her introduction she is acutely aware of the paradox of referentiality that inform such positions. This is obviously one of the risks of a psychoanalysis that does not recognize its socio-political embodiment.
123. Deleuze, *Foucault*, op. cit., pp. 104, 114.
124. Butler, op. cit., p. 9.
125. See particularly Fredrich Nietzsche, *Beyond Good and Evil: Prelude to a Philosophy of the Future*, trans. W. Kaufmann (Vintage Books, 1966), especially Part 1, Sect. 15, Part 2, Sect. 36, and Baruch Spinoza, *Ethics*, trans. S. Shirley (Hackett Publishers, 1992), especially Part 2, Prop. 39, 40. Interestingly, Butler concludes a recent essay on Foucault, with a reflection on the importance of Spinoza. See 'Revisiting Bodies and Pleasures', in *Theory, Culture and Society*, Vol. 16, no. 2, 1999, pp. 21–40.
126. *Psychic Life of Power*, op. cit., p. 99.
127. Here I direct the reader to Butler's discussion, *ibid.*, pp. 95–6. The problem, so far as the present discussion goes, is that resistance *and the conception of the subject* might not be discussed in terms of its material effects, namely the ways in which the effects of subjectivation are also part of the subject who *does* misrecognize the staging of the norm. The salience of this problem is present in Foucault's claim that 'power is tolerable only in so far as it masks a substantial part of itself' (*History of Sexuality*, p. 86), in other words, only to the extent that it is misrecognized. This view is very close (and yet theoretically distanced from) Althusser's own formulation.

128. Žižek continues, 'In short, Foucault does not consider the possibility of an effect outstripping its cause, so that although it emerges as a form of resistance to power and is as such absolutely inherent to it, it can outgrow and explode it.' *The Ticklish Subject: The Absent Centre of Political Ontology* (Verso, 1999), p. 256. I have some difficulty with this criticism. Of course, Žižek's Lacanian position may very well be incompatible with Foucault in ontological terms, but we have argued, assisted by Deleuze's and Butler's readings, that there is an element of excess in Foucault's conception of the subject. What is missing, for Žižek, is the obscene supplement at power's heart which helps sustain its operations. Unlike Foucault, Lacan attempts to theorize this supplement, and it may act to undermine symbolic power (pp. 256–7). Here, in terms of the political effects of their ontological positions, I don't consider there to be that much difference between Foucault and Lacan. Both *seem* to delimit socio-political forms, allowing the general critic to accuse them of an inert structuralism. Yet both, on deeper readings, develop accounts of subjectivity which act to dispel these claims of structural or discursive closure. As this work was completed, an interesting book co-authored by Butler, Žižek and Laclau was published which tackles some of these questions and themes: *Contingency, Hegemony, Universality: Cotemporary Dialogues on the Left* (Verso, 2000).
129. See for example, 'Maurice Blanchot: The Thought of the Outside', in *Foucault/ Blanchot*, op. cit.
130. *Beyond Good and Evil: Prelude to a Philosophy of the Future*, trans. and commentary by W. Kaufmann (Vintage Books, 1966), Book One, particularly Sect. 21. In *The Will to Power*, Book Three, Sect. 551 Nietsche writes that 'an event is neither effected nor does it effect', op. cit., p. 296. For Spinoza's critique of cause see the appendix of Part One of the *Ethics*, trans. S. Shirley (Hackett, 1992).

CONCLUSION

1. Maurice Blanchot, 'The Most Profound Question', in *The Infinite Conversation* trans. S. Hanson (Minnesota University Press, 1993), p. 11; emphasis added.

BIBLIOGRAPHY

Agamben, G., *Infancy and History: Essays on the Destruction of Experience*, trans. L. Heron (London: Verso, 1983).

Althusser, L., 'Philosophy as a Political Weapon', trans. B. Brewster, in *Lenin and Philosophy and Other Essays* (London: New Left Books, 1971).

Althusser, L., 'Marx's relation to Hegel', in *Montesquieu, Rousseau, Marx: Politics and History*, trans. B. Brewster (London: New Left Books, 1972).

Althusser, L., *Essays in Self-Criticism*, trans. G. Lock (London: New Left Books, 1973).

Althusser, L., *Essays in Ideology*, trans. B. Brewster (London: Verso, 1984).

Althusser, L., 'Theory, Theoretical Practice and Theoretical Formation: Ideology and Ideological Struggle', trans. J. Kavanagh, in G. Elliott (ed.), *Philosophy and the Spontaneous Philosophy of the Scientists* (London: Verso, 1990).

Althusser, L., *For Marx*, trans. B. Brewster (London: Verso, 1990).

Althusser, L., *The Future Lasts a Long Time*, trans. R. Veasey (London: Chatto and Windus, 1993).

Althusser, L., 'Trois notes sur la théorie des discours', in *Louis Althusser: Écrits sur la psychanalyse* (Paris: Editions STOCK/IMEC, 1993).

Althusser, L., *Sur La Philosophie* (Paris: Gallimard, 1994).

Althusser, L., *Louis Althusser: Writings on Psychoanalysis*, ed. O. Corpet and F. Matheron, Introduction by J. Mehlman (New York: Columbia University Press, 1996).

Althusser, L., *The Spectre of Hegel: Early Writings*, trans. G. M. Goshgarian, ed. and Introduction by F. Matheron (London: Verso, 1997).

Althusser, L., 'The Only Materialist Tradition, Part I: Spinoza', in *The New Spinoza*, ed. W. Montag and T. Stolze (Minneapolis: Minnesota University Press, 1998).

Althusser, L. and Balibar, E., *Reading Capital*, trans. B. Brewster (London: Verso, 1979).

Ameriks, K. and Sturma, D. (eds), *The Modern Subject: Conceptions of the Self in Classical German Philosophy* (New York: SUNY Press, 1995).

Anderson, P., *Considerations on Western Marxism* (London: Verso, 1979).

Arato, A., 'Lukács' Theory of Reification', *Telos*, Vol. 11, 1972.

Arato, A., 'The Neo-idealist Defence of Subjectivity', *Telos*, Vol. 21, 1974.

Archard, D., *Consciousness and the Unconscious* (London: Hutchinson, 1984).

Arendt, H., *Between Past and Future: Eight Exercises in Political Thought* (New York: Faber Books, 1954).

Arendt, H., *The Human Condition* (Chicago: Chicago University Press, 1958).

Arendt, H., *The Life of the Mind Volume One: Thinking* (New York: Harcourt Brace, 1977).

Balibar, E., 'Subjection and Subjectivisation', in Joan Copjec (ed.), *Supposing the Subject* (London: Verso, 1994).

Balibar, E., 'Foucault and Marx: the Question of Nominalism', in T. J. Armstrong (ed. and trans.), *Michel Foucault: Philosopher* (London: Harvester Wheatsheaf, 1992).

Balibar, E., *The Philosophy of Marx*, trans. C. Turner (London: Verso, 1995).

Balibar, E., *Spinoza and Politics*, trans. P. Snowdon (London: Verso, 1998).

Barrett, M., *The Politics of Truth* (Cambridge: Polity Press, 1991).

Baudrillard, J., *Forget Foucault* (New York: Semiotext(e), 1987).

Baugh, B., 'Subjectivity and the *Begriff* in Modern French Philosophy', *The Owl of Minerva*, Vol. 23, no. 1, 1991, pp. 63–75.

Bergson, H., *Introduction to Metaphysics*, trans. T. E. Hulme, Introduction by T. A. Goudge (London: The Liberal Arts Press, 1955).

Bellamy, E., 'Discourses of Impossibility: Can Psychoanalysis be Political?', *Diacritics*, Vol. 23, no. 1, 1993, pp. 24–38.

Bennington, G., 'Derrida', in S. Critchley and W. Schroeder (eds) *A Companion to Continental Philosophy* (Oxford: Blackwell, 1998).

Benton, T., *The Rise and Fall of Structuralist Marxism* (London: Macmillan, 1984).

Berman, M., *All That is Solid Melts into Air* (London: Verso, 1983).

Bernauer, J., *Michel Foucault's Force of Flight: Towards an Ethics for Thought* (Atlantic Highlands, NJ: Humanities Press, 1990).

Blanchot, M., 'Michel Foucault as I Imagine Him', in *Foucault/Blanchot*, trans. J. Mehlman and B. Massumi (New York: Zone Books, 1987).

Blanchot, M., *The Infinite Conversation*, trans. S. Hanson (Minneapolis: Minnesota University Press, 1993).

Blanchot, M., *Friendship*, trans. E. Rottenberg (Stanford: Stanford University Press, 1997).

Boothby, R., *Death and Desire: Psychoanalytic Theory in Lacan's Return to Freud* (New York: Routledge, 1991).

Borch-Jacobsen, M., *Lacan: The Absolute Master*, trans. D. Brick (Stanford: Stanford University Press, 1991).

Borch-Jacobsen, M., 'The Alibis of the Subject: Lacan and Philosophy', trans. D. Brick, in S. Shamdasni and M. Münchow (eds), *Speculations After Freud: Psychoanalysis, Philosophy and Culture* (London: Routledge, 1994).

Borch-Jacobsen, M., 'Basta Cosi!' (interview conducted by Chris Oakley), in Todd Dufresne (ed.), *Returns to the French Freud: Freud, Lacan and Beyond* (London: Routledge, 1997).

Bordo, S., *The Flight from Objectivity: Essays on Cartesianism and Culture* (New York: SUNY Press, 1987).

Bordo, S. and Moussa, M., 'Rehabilitating the "I"', in H. J. Silverman (ed.), *Questioning Foundations: Truth/Subjectivity/Culture* (London: Routledge, 1993).

Bowie, M., *Lacan* (London: Fontana Press, 1991).

Bowie, M., *Psychoanalysis and the Future of Theory* (Oxford: Blackwell, 1993).

Brennan, T., *History After Lacan* (London: Routledge, 1993).

Brown, B. and Cousins, M., 'The Linguistic Fault: the Case of Foucault's Archaeology', *Economy and Society*, Vol. 9, no. 3, 1980.

Butler, J., *Subjects of Desire: Hegelian Reflections in Twentieth Century France* (New York: Columbia University Press, 1987).

Butler, J., *The Psychic Life of Power* (Stanford: Stanford University Press, 1998).

Cadava, E., Connor, P. and Nancy, J. L. *Who Comes After the Subject?* (London: Routledge, 1991).

Callinicos, A., *Is There a Future for Marxism?* (London: Macmillan, 1982).

Callinicos, A., 'Foucault's Third Theoretical Displacement: Technology of the Self', *Theory, Culture and Society*, Vol. 3, no. 3, 1986, pp. 171–7.

Carr, D., *The Paradox of Subjectivity: the Self in the Transcendental Tradition* (Oxford: Oxford University Press, 1999).

Cascardi, A., *The Subject of Modernity* (Cambridge: Cambridge University Press, 1991).

Castoriadis, C., *Crossroads in the Labyrinth*, trans. K. Soper and M. Ryle (Brighton: Harvester, 1984).

Castoriadis, C., *The Imaginary Institution of Society*, trans. K. Blamey (Cambridge: Polity, 1987).

Cohen, R. A., 'Merleau-Ponty, the Flesh and Foucault', *Philosophy Today*, Vol. 28, 1984.

Colletti, L., *Marxism and Hegel* (London: New Left Books, 1973).

Connolly, W., 'Taylor, Foucault and Otherness', *Political Theory*, Vol. 13, no. 3, 1985.

Connolly, W., *Political Theory and Modernity* (Oxford: Blackwell, 1989).

Copjec, J., 'The Orthopsychic Subject', *October*, Vol. 49, 1989.

Cornell, D., *The Philosophy of the Limit* (New York: Routledge, 1992).

Cousins, M. and Hussain, A., *Michel Foucault* (London: Macmillan, 1984).

Critchley, S., *The Ethics of Deconstruction* (Oxford: Blackwell, 1992).

Critchley, S., and Dews, P. (eds), *Deconstructive Subjectivities* (New York: SUNY Press, 1996).

Cutler, A., 'The Concept of Epistemological Break', *Theoretical Practice*, Vols 3 + 4, 1971.

Dallery, A. B. and Scott, C. E. (eds), *The Question of the Other* (New York: SUNY Press, 1989).

Davidson, A. I. (ed. and Introduction), *Foucault and his Interlocutors* (Chicago: Chicago University Press, 1998).

Deleuze, G., *Foucault*, trans. Sean Hand (Minneapolis: University of Minnesota Press, 1987).

Deleuze, G., *Spinoza: Practical Philosophy*, trans. R. Hurley (San Francisco: City Lights Books, 1988).

Deleuze, G., 'What is a *Dispositif*?', in T. J. Armstrong (ed./trans.), *Michel Foucault: Philosopher* (London: Harvester Wheatsheaf, 1992).

Deleuze, G., *Expressionism in Philosophy: Spinoza*, trans. M. Joughin (New York: Zone Books, 1992).

Deleuze, G. and Guattari, F., *What Is Philosophy?*, trans. H. Tomlinson and G. Burchill (London: Verso, 1994).

Derrida, J., *Speech and Phenomena*, trans. B. Allison (Evanston: Northwestern University Press, 1967).

Derrida, J., *Of Grammatology*, trans. G. Spivak (Baltimore: Johns Hopkins University Press, 1974).

Derrida, J., *Writing and Difference*, trans. A. Bass (London: Routledge and Kegan Paul, 1978).

Derrida, J., 'Speculations – On Freud', trans. I. McLoed, *Oxford Literary Review*, Vol. 3, no. 2, 1980.

Derrida, J., *Dissemination*, trans. B. Johnson (London: Athlone Press, 1981).

Derrida, J., *Positions*, trans. A. Bass (London: Athlone Press, 1981).

Derrida, J., *Margins of Philosophy*, trans. A. Bass (Brighton: The Harvester Press, 1982).

Derrida, J., 'Interview with Richard Kearney', in Richard Kearney (ed.), *Dialogues with Contemporary Thinkers* (Manchester: Manchester University Press, 1984).

Derrida, J., 'The Original Discussion of *Différance* (1968)', in R. Bernasconi and D. Wood (eds), *Derrida and Différance* (Coventry: Parousia Press, 1985).

Derrida, J., 'In Conversation with Christopher Norris', in A. Papadakis, C. Cooke and A. Benjamin (eds), *Deconstruction: Omnibus Edition* (London: Academy Editions, 1989), pp. 71–5.

Derrida, J., 'Sending: On Representation', trans. P. Caws, in G. L. Ormiston and A. D. Schrift (eds), *Transforming the Hermeneutic Context: From Nietzsche to Nancy* (New York: SUNY Press, 1990).

Derrida, J., *Of Spirit*, trans. G. Bennington and R. Bowlby (Chicago: Chicago University Press, 1991).

Derrida, J., ' "Eating Well", or the Calculation of the Subject: An Interview with Jacques Derrida" (conducted by Jean-Luc Nancy), in E. Cadava, P. Connor and J. L. Nancy (eds), *Who Comes After the Subject?* (New York: Routledge, 1991).

Derrida, J., 'Politics and Friendship' (an interview conducted with M. Sprinkler), in A. Kaplan and M. Sprinkler (eds), *The Althusserian Legacy* (London: Verso, 1992).

Derrida, J., 'Force of Law: The Mystical Foundation of Authority', trans. M. Quaintance, in D. Carlson, D. Cornell and M. Rosenfeld (eds), *Deconstruction and the Possibility of Justice* (New York: Routledge, 1993).

Derrida, J., ' "To Do Justice to Freud": The History of Madness in the Age of Psychoanalysis', trans. P. Brault and M. Naas, *Critical Inquiry*, Vol. 20, 1994.

Derrida, J., *Specters of Marx: The State of the Debt and the Work of Mourning*, trans. P. Kamuf (London: Routledge, 1994).

Derrida, J., 'For the Love of Lacan', *Cardozo Law Review*, Vol. 16, 1995.

Derrida, J., *Resistances of Psychoanalysis*, trans. P. Kamuf, P. Brault, M. Naas (California: Stanford University Press, 1998).

Descartes, R., *Discourse on Method and the Meditations*, trans. F. E. Sutcliffe (Harmondsworth: Penguin, 1987).

Descombes, V., *Modern French Philosophy* (Cambridge: Cambridge University Press, 1980).

Descombes, V., 'Apropos of the Critique of the Subject', in Cadava *et al.* *Who Comes After the Subject* (New York: Routledge, 1991).

Dews, P., 'Power and Subjectivity in Foucault', *New Left Review*, no. 198, 1984.

Dews, P., 'The Return of the Subject in late Foucault', *Radical Philosophy*, no. 51, 1986, pp. 136–41.

Dews, P., *Logics of Disintegration: Poststructuralism and the Claims of Critical Theory* (London: Verso, 1987).

Dews, P., 'The Limits of Disenchantment', *New Left Review*, no. 213, 1995.

Dews, P., 'Foucault and the French Tradition of Historical Epistemology', in *The Limits of Disenchantment* (London: Verso, 1995).

Dolar, M., 'The Legacy of the Enlightenment: Foucault and Lacan', *New Formations*, no. 14, 1991.

Dolar, M., 'Beyond Interpellation', *Qui Parle?*, Vol. 6, no. 2, 1993.

Dreyfus, H. L., 'On the Ordering of Things: Being and Power in Heidegger and Foucault', in T. J. Armstrong (ed.), *Michel Foucault Philosopher* (Hemel Hempstead: Harvester Wheatsheaf, 1992).

Dreyfus, H. L. and Rabinow, P., *Michel Foucault: beyond Structuralism and Hermeneutics* (Hemel Hempstead: Harvester Wheatsheaf, 1982).

Drury, S., *Alexandre Kojève: The Roots of Postmodern Politics* (London: Macmillan, 1994).

Elliott, G., *Althusser: The Detour of Theory* (London: Verso, 1987).

Eribon, D., *Michel Foucault* (London: Faber and Faber, 1992).

Feenberg, A., 'Culture and Practice in the Early Marxist Work of Lukács', *Berkley Journal of Sociology*, Vol. 26, 1981.

Felmam, S., 'Madness and Philosophy *or* Literature's Reason', *Yale French Studies*, Vol. 52, 1975.

Ferry, L. and Renaut, A., *French Philosophy of the Sixties: An Essay on Antihumanism*, trans. M. Schnackenberg Cattani (Amherst: University of Massachusetts, 1990).

Fink, B., *The Lacanian Subject* (Princeton: Princeton University Press, 1995).

Flynn, B., *Political Philosophy at the Closure of Metaphysics* (Atlantic Highlands: Humanities Press, 1992).

Flynn, T. R., 'Foucault and the Eclipse of Vision', in D. M. Levin (ed.), *Modernity and the Hegemony of Vision* (Berkeley: California University Press, 1993).

Foucault, M., *The Order of Things: An Archaeology of the Human Sciences*, trans. unidentified (London: Tavistock, 1970).

Foucault, M., *The Archaeology of Knowledge*, trans. A. Sheridan (London: Tavistock, 1973).

Foucault, M., *Discipline and Punish*, trans. A. Sheridan-Smith (Harmondsworth: Penguin, 1977).

Foucault, M., 'Politics and the Study of Discourse', *Ideology and Consciousness*, no. 3, Spring 1977.

Foucault, M., 'Preface to Transgression', in D. Bouchard (ed. and intro.), *Language, Counter-Memory, Practice: Selected Essays and Interviews by Michel Foucault* (Oxford: Blackwell, 1977).

Foucault, M., 'Nietzsche, Genealogy, History', in D. Bouchard (ed. and intro.), *Language, Counter-Memory, Practice: Selected Essays and Interviews by Michel Foucault* (Oxford: Blackwell, 1977).

Foucault, M., 'Theatrum Philosophicum', in D. Bouchard (ed. and trans.), *Language, Counter-Memory, Practice: Selected Essays and Interviews by Michel Foucault* (Oxford: Blackwell, 1977).

Foucault, M., *History of Sexuality* (Vol. 1), trans. R. Hurley (Harmondsworth: Penguin, 1978).

Foucault, M., 'My Body, This Paper, This Fire', *Oxford Literary Review*, Vol. 4, no. 1, 1979).

Foucault, M., 'Truth and Power', in C. Gordon (ed.), *Power/Knowledge* (Hemel Hempstead: Harvester Wheatsheaf, 1980).

Foucault, M., 'Structuralism and Post-Structuralism: An Interview with Michel Foucault' (conducted by G. Raulet), *Telos*, Vol. 55, 1983.

Foucault, M., 'What is an Author?', in P. Rabinow (ed.), *The Foucault Reader* (Harmondsworth: Penguin, 1984).

Foucault, M., 'Dream, Imagination and Existence', in K. Hoeller (ed.), *Dream Existence: Review of Existential Psychology and Psychiatry* – Special Issue, 1986.

Foucault, M., 'The order of Discourse', in R. Young (ed.) *Untying the Text* (Cambridge: Cambridge University Press, 1987).

Foucault, M., 'Maurice Blanchot: The Thought of the Outside', in *Foucault/Blanchot*, trans. J. Mehlman and B. Massumi (New York: Zone Books, 1987).

Foucault, M., 'The Birth of a World', *Foucault Live* (New York: Semiotext(e), 1989).

Foucault, M., 'About the Beginning of the Hermeneutics of the Self: Two Lectures at Dartmouth', *Political Theory*, Vol. 21, no. 2, 1993, pp. 198–227.

Foucault, M., 'Maurice Florence', trans. by Catherine Porter, in G. Gutting (ed.), *The Cambridge Companion to Foucault* (Cambridge: Cambridge University Press, 1994).

Fraser, N., 'The French Derridians: Politicizing Deconstruction or Deconstructing the Political?', *New German Critique*, Vol. 33, 1984.

Fraser, N., *Unruly Practices* (Cambridge: Polity Press, 1991).

Freud, S., 'Moses and Monotheism', *The Origins of Religion*, Vol. 13 of Penguin Freud Library (Harmondsworth: Penguin, 1990).

Freud, S., 'Civilisation and its Discontents', *Civilisation and its Discontents*, Vol. 12 of Penguin Freud Library (Harmondsworth: Penguin, 1991).

Freud, S., 'The Ego and the Id', in *On Metapsychology*, Vol. 11 of Penguin Freud Library (Harmonsdworth: Penguin, 1991).

Freud, S., 'The Interpretation of Dreams VII: The Psychology of Dream-Processes', in *The Interpretation of Dreams*, Vol. 4 of Penguin Freud Library (Harmondsworth: Penguin, 1991).

Gasché, R., 'Deconstruction as Criticism', *Glyph*, Vol. 6, 1979, pp. 177–215.

Gasché, R., *The Tain of the Mirror: Derrida and the Philosophy of Reflection* (Cambridge: Harvard University Press, 1986).

Goldmann, L., 'The Early Writings of Georg Lukács', *Triquarterly*, Vol. 9, 1967.

Goldmann, L., *Lukács and Heidegger: Towards a New Philosophy* (London: Routledge and Kegan Paul, 1977).

Habermas, J., *The Philosophical Discourse of Modernity*, trans. F. G. Lawrence (Cambridge: Polity, 1989).

Heidegger, M., *Identity and Difference*, trans. J. Stambaugh (New York: Harper and Row, 1974).

Heidegger, M., *Basic Writings*, ed. D. Farrell Krell (New York: HarperCollins 1977).

Heidegger, M., 'The Age of the World Picture', in W. Lovitt (ed.), *The Question Concerning Technology and Other Essays* (New York: Harper Torchbooks, 1977).

Heidegger, M., 'Logos (Heraclitus, Fragment B 50)', in *Early Greek Thinking: The Dawn of Western Philosophy*, trans. D. Farrell Krell and F. A. Capuzzi (New York: Harper and Row, 1984).

Hegel, G. W. F., *Phenomenology of Spirit*, trans. A. V. Miller (Oxford: Oxford University Press, 1977).

Henry, M., *The Geneaology of Psychoanalysis*, trans. D. Brick (Stanford: Stanford University Press, 1993).

Hirst, P., 'Althusser and Philosophy', *Theoretical Practice*, Vol. 2, 1971.

Hirst, P., 'Althusser and the Theory of Ideology', *Economy and Society*, Vol. 5, no. 4, 1976.

Hirst, P., 'Problems and Advances in the Theory of Ideology', in T. Eagleton (ed.), *Ideology* (London: Longman, 1994).

Hobson, M., *Jacques Derrida: Opening Lines* (London: Routledge, 1999).

Honig, B., *Political Theory and the Displacement of Politics* (Ithaca: Cornell University Press, 1993).

Honneth, A., 'History and Interaction', in G. Elliot (ed.), *Althusser: A Critical Reader* (Oxford: Blackwell, 1994).

Howells, C., *Derrida: Deconstruction from Phenomenology to Ethics* (Cambridge: Polity, 1999).

Husserl, E., *The Idea of Phenomenology*, trans. W. P. Alston and G. Nakhnikian (The Hague: Martinus Nijhoff, 1964).

Husserl, E., 'Philosophy as a Rigorous Science', in *Phenomenology and the Crisis of Philosophy*, trans. and intro. by Q. Lauer (New York: Harper Torchbooks, 1965).

Hutchings, K., *Kant, Critique and Politics* (London: Routledge, 1996).

Hyppolite, J., *Studies on Marx and Hegel*, trans. J. O'Neill (New York: Harper Torchbooks, 1973).

Hyppolite, J., *Genesis and Stucture in Hegel's Phenomenology*, Introduction by J. Hekman (Evanston: Northwestern University Press, 1974).

Hyppolite, J., 'Hegel's Phenomenology and Psychoanalysis', trans. A. Richer, in W. E. Steinkraus (ed.), *New Studies in Hegel's Philosophy* (Holt, Reinhart and Winston, 1976).

Jakobsen, R., 'Two Aspects of Language and Two Types of Aphasic Disturbances', in R. Jakobson and M. Halle, *Fundamentals of Language* (The Hague: Mouton Books, 1986).

Jameson, F., 'Imaginary and Symbolic in Lacan', *Yale French Studies*, Vol. 55/56, 1977.

Jay, M., *Marxism and Totality: The Adventures of a Concept from Lukács to Habermas* (Cambridge: Polity Press, 1984).

Jay, M., *Of Downcast Eyes: The Denigration of Vision in Twentieth Century French Thought* (Berkeley: University of California Press, 1993).

Johnson, B. (ed.), *Freedom and Interpretation: The Oxford Amnesty Lectures 1992* (New York: Basic Books, 1993).

Kant, I., *Critique of Pure Reason* (2nd Impression), trans. N. Kemp Smith (London: Macmillan, 1992).

Kerrigan, W. and Smith, J. H., *Interpreting Lacan* (New Haven: Yale University Press, 1983).

Kierkegaard, S., *Philosophical Fragments*, ed. and trans. H. V. Hong and E. H. Hong (Princeton: Princeton University Press, 1985).

Kojève, J., *Introduction to the Reading of Hegel*, trans. J. Nichols (Ithaca: Cornell University Press, 1980).

Kolakowski, L., *Bergson* (Oxford: Oxford University Press, 1985).

Korsch, K., *Marxism and Philosophy* (London: New Left Books, 1970).

Lacan, J., *Speech and Language in Psychoanalysis*, trans. A. Wilden (Baltimore: Johns Hopkins University Press, 1968).

Lacan, J., *Four Fundamental Concepts of Psychoanalysis*, trans. A. Sheridan (Harmondsworth: Penguin, 1979).

Lacan, J., 'Responses to Students of Philosophy Concerning the Object of Psychoanalysis' [1966], *October*, Vol. 40, 1987.

Lacan, J., *The Seminar of Jacques Lacan Book I: Freud's Papers on Technique*, trans. J. Forrester, ed. J. Alain-Miller (Cambridge: Cambridge University Press, 1988).

Lacan, J., *The Seminar of Jacques Lacan Book II: The Ego in Freud's Theory and in the Technique of Psychoanalysis 1954–55*, ed. J. Alain-Miller, trans. S. Tomaselli (Cambridge: Cambridge University Press, 1988).

Lacan, J., *Écrits: A Selection*, trans. A. Sheridan, ed. J. A. Miller (London: Routledge, 1989).

Laclau, E., *New Reflections on the Revolution of Our Time* (London: Verso, 1990).

Laclau, E., 'The Death and Ressurrection of the Theory of Ideology', *The Journal of Political Ideologies*, Vol. 1, no. 3, 1996, pp. 201–20.

Laclau, E. and Mouffe, C., *Hegemony and Socialist Strategy* (London: Verso, 1985).

Lacoue-Labarthe, P., *Typographies: Mimesis, Philosophy, Politics*, ed. C. Fynsk (Cambridge: Harvard University Press, 1989).

Laplanche, L. and Pontalis, J. B., *The Language of Psychoanalysis*, trans. D. Nicholson-Smith (London: The Hogarth Press, 1973).

Lebrun, G., 'Notes on Phenomenology *in* Les Mots et les Choses', in *Michel Foucault: Philosopher*, trans. T. Armstrong (Hemel Hempstead: Harvester Wheatsheaf, 1992).

Lecourt, D., *Marxism and Epistemology: Bachelard, Canguilhem, Foucault* (London: New Left Books, 1973).

Lefort, C., 'The Image of the Body and Totalitarianism', in *The Political Forms of Modern Society* (Cambridge: Polity Press, 1986).

Lefort, C., *Democracy and Political Theory* (Cambridge: Polity Press, 1988).

Lemaire, A., *Jacques Lacan* (London: Routledge and Kegan Paul, 1977).

Lévi-Strauss, C., *The Savage Mind* (Chicago: Chicago University Press, 1969).

Lévi-Strauss, C., 'A Confrontation', *New Left Review*, no. 62, 1970.

Lloyd, G., *Being in Time: Selves and Narrators in philosophy and literature* (London: Routledge, 1993).

Lloyd, G., *Part of Nature: Self-knowledge in Spinoza's Ethics* (Ithaca: Cornell University Press, 1994).

Lloyd, G., *Spinoza and the Ethics* (London: Routledge, 1996).

Lukács, G., *History and Class Consciousness*, trans. R. Livingstone (London: Merlin Press, 1971).

Lukács, G., *The Theory of the Novel*, trans. A. Bostock (London: Merlin Press, 1971).

Lukács, G., *Soul and Form*, trans. A. Bostock (London: Merlin Press, 1974).

Lukács, G., *The Ontology of Social Being: Hegel*, trans. D. Fernbach (London: Merlin Press, 1978).

Lukács, G., *Georg Lukács: Selected Correspondence 1902–1920, dialogues with Weber, Simmel, Buber, Mannheim and Others*, selected and trans. by Judith Marcus and Zoltan Tar (New York: Columbia University Press, 1986).

Lyotard, J. F., *Phenomenology*, trans. B. Beaklek, Foreword by G. L. Ormiston (New York: SUNY Press, 1991).

Macey, L., *Lacan in Contexts* (London: Verso, 1988).

MacCannell, J. Flower, *Figuring Lacan: Criticism and the Cultural Unconscious* (Beckenham: Croom Helm, 1986).

Macksey, R. and Donato, E. (eds), *The Structuralist Controversy: The Languages of Criticism and the Sciences of Man* (Baltimore: Johns Hopkins University Press, 1972).

Major, R., 'Reason from the Unconscious', *Oxford Literary Review*, Vol. 12, 1990.

Márkus, G., 'The Soul and Life: The Young Lukács and the Problem of Culture', *Telos*, Vol. 23, 1977.

Martin, B., *Matrix and Line: Derrida and the Possibilities of a Postmodern Social Theory* (New York: SUNY Press, 1992).

Marx, K., *Early Works*, ed. D. McLennan (Oxford: Blackwell, 1972).

Marx, K., *The Marx–Engels Reader*, 2nd edn, ed. R. C. Tucker (New York: W. W. Norton, 1972).

Marx, K. and Engels, F., *The German Ideology: Part One* (London: Lawrence and Wishart, 1985).

Melville, S., *Philosophy Beside Itself: On Deconstruction and Modernism* (Manchester: Manchester University Press, 1986).

Mergill, A., *Prophets of Extremity* (Berkeley: University of California Press, 1987).

Merleau-Ponty, M., 'Western Marxism', in *Adventures of the Dialectic* (Evanston: Northwestern University Press, 1973).

Merquior, J. G., *Western Marxism* (London: Paladin Press, 1986).

Miller, J. A., 'Jeremy Bentham's Panoptic Device', trans. Richard Miller, *October*, Vol. 41, Summer 1987, pp. 3–29.

Montag, W., 'The Emptiness of a Distance Taken: Freud, Althusser, Lacan', *Rethinking Marxism*, Vol. 4, no. 1, Spring 1991.

Montag, W., 'Spinoza and Althusser Against Hermeneutics: Interpretation or Intervention?', in A. Kaplan and M. Sprinkler (eds), *The Althusserian Legacy* (London: Verso, 1992).

Montag, W., 'The Soul is the Prison of the Body: Althusser and Foucault 1970–75', in J. Lezra (ed.), *Depositions: Althusser, Balibar, Macherey and the Labour of Reading* (New Haven: Yale University Press, 1995).

Montag, W., *Bodies, Masses, Power: Spinoza and his Contemporaries* (London: Verso, 1999).

Nancy, J.-L., 'The Compearance: from the Existence of "Communism" to the Community of 'Existence'", trans. T. B. Strong, *Political Theory*, Vol. 20, no. 3, 1992, pp. 371–98.

Nancy, J.-L. and Lacoue-Labarthe, P., *The Title of the Letter: A Reading of Lacan*, trans. F. Raffoul (New York: SUNY Press, 1992).

Navarro, F., 'An Encounter with Althusser', *Rethinking Marxism*, Vol. 10, no. 3, Fall 1998.

Negri, A., *The Savage Anomaly: The Power of Spinoza's Politics*, trans. M. Hardt (Minneapolis: Minnesota University Press, 1991).

Negri, A., 'The Later Althusser', in A. Callari and D. F. Ruccio (eds), *Postmodern Materialism and the Future of Marxist Theory: Essays in the Althusserian Tradition* (Hanover, NH: Weslyan University Press, 1996).

Nietzsche, F., *Beyond Good and Evil: Prelude to a Philosophy of the Future*, trans. W. Kaufmann (New York: Vintage, 1966).

Nietzsche, F., *The Will to Power*, trans. W. Kaufmann and R. J. Hollingdale, ed. W. Kaufman (New York: Vintage, 1968).

Nietzsche, F., 'On Truth and Lies in an Extra-Moral Sense', *The Portable Nietzsche*, trans. W. Kaufmann (Harmondsworth: Penguin, 1976).

Nietzsche, F., *The Genealogy of Morals*, ed. K. Ansell-Pearson (Cambridge: Cambridge University Press, 1994).

Norris, C., *Derrida* (London: Fontana Press, 1987).

Norris, C., *Spinoza and the Origins of Modern Critical Theory* (Oxford: Blackwell, 1991).

Norris, C., 'What is Enlightenment? Kant according to Foucault', in G. Guttings (ed.), *The Cambridge Companion to Foucault* (Cambridge: Cambridge University Press, 1994).

Parsons, S., 'Foucault and the Problem of Kant', *Praxis International*, Vol. 8, 1988–9, pp. 317–28.

Patten, P., 'Althusser's Epistemology'. *Radical Philosophy*. no. 19, 1978.

Poster, P., *Existentialist Marxism in Post-war France* (Princeton: Princeton University Press, 1975).

Philips, M., 'Foucault on Power: A Problem in Radical Translation?', *Political Theory*, Vol. 11, no. 1, February 1983, pp. 29–53.

Piccone, P., 'Dialectic and Materialism in Lukács', *Telos*, Vol. 11, 1972.

Plato, *The Republic*, trans. D. Lee (Harmondsworth: Penguin, 1987).

Rabinow, P., 'Modern and Countermodern: Ethos and Epoch in Heidegger and Foucault', in G. Gutting (ed.), *The Cambridge Companion to Foucault* (Cambridge: Cambridge University Press, 1994).

Ragland-Sullivan, E., 'Stealing Material', in Alexandre Leupin (ed.), *Lacan and the Human Sciences* (Lincoln: University of Nebraska Press, 1991).

Rajchman, J., *Michel Foucault: The Freedom of Philosophy* (New York: Columbia University Press, 1985).

Rajchman, J., 'Ethics after Foucault', *Social Text*, Winter 1985.

Readings, B., 'The Deconstruction of Politics', in Lindsay Waters and Wlad Godzich (eds), *Reading De Man Reading* (Minneapolis: University of Minnesota Press, 1989).

Ricoeur, P., *Lectures on Ideology and Utopia* (New York: Columbia University Press, 1986).

Ricoeur, P., *The Conflict of Interpretations: Essays in Hermeneutics* (Evanston: Northwestern University Press, 1974).

Ricoeur, P., *Oneself as Another*, trans. K. Blamey (Chicago: Chicago University Press, 1992).

Rockmore, T., *Heidegger and French Philosophy: Humanism, Antihumanism and Being* (London: Routledge, 1995).

Rorty, R., *Contingency, Irony and Solidarity* (Cambridge: Cambridge University Press, 1989).

Rose, G., *Hegel Contra Sociology* (London: Athlone Press, 1978).

Roth, M. S., *Knowing and History: Appropriations of Hegel in Twentieth-Century France* (Ithaca: Cornell University Press, 1988).

Roudinesco, E., *A History of Psychoanalysis in France 1925–1985*, trans. J. Mehlman (London: Free Association Books, 1990).

Roudinesco, E., *Jacques Lacan*, trans. B. Bray (Cambridge: Polity Press, 1997).

Rousseau, J. J., 'A Discourse on the Origin of Inequality', *The Social Contract and Discourses*, trans. G. D. H. Cole (London: Everyman, 1983).

Rousseau, J. J., 'Essay on the Origin of Language', trans. J. H. Moran, in *On the Origin of Language* (Chicago: Chicago University Press, 1966).

Roustang, F., *The Lacanian Delusion*, trans. G. Sims (Oxford: Oxford University Press, 1990).

Said, E., 'The Problem of Textuality: Two Exemplary Positions', *Critical Inquiry*, Vol. 4, no. 4, 1978.

Saussure, F., *Course in General Linguistics*, trans. W. Baskin (London: Fontana, 1974).

Schrift, A., *Nietzsche's French Legacy* (London: Routledge, 1995).

Shanahan, D., *Towards a Genealogy of Individualism* (Amherst: University of Massachusetts, 1992).

Smith, J. and Kerrigan, W. (eds), *Interpreting Lacan* (New Haven: Yale University Press, 1983).

Smith, P., *Discerning the Subject* (Minneapolis: University of Minnesota Press, 1988).

Spinoza, B., *The Ethics*, trans. S. Shirley (Indianapolis: Hackett, 1992).

Staten, S., *Wittgenstein and Derrida* (Lincoln: Nebraska University Press, 1984).

Stedman Jones, G., 'The Marxism of the Early Lukács: an evaluation', *New Left Review*, no. 70, 1971.

Taylor, T., 'Foucault on Freedom and Truth', in David Hoy (ed.), *Foucault: A Critical Reader* (Oxford: Blackwell, 1986).

Taylor, T., *Sources of the Self* (Cambridge: Cambridge University Press, 1989).

Thacker, A., 'Foucault's Aesthetics of Existence', *Radical Philosophy*, no. 63, Spring 1993.

Vajda, M., 'Lukács and Husserl', in Agnes Heller (ed.), *Lukács Revalued* (Oxford: Blackwell, 1983).

Visker, R., *Michel Foucault: Genealogy as Critique* (London: Verso, 1995).

Wilden, A., 'Lacan and the Discourse of the Other', in J. Lacan, *Speech and Language in Psychoanalysis* (Baltimore: Johns Hopkins University Press, 1968).

Wilke, S., 'Adorno and Derrida on Husserl', *Telos*, no. 84, 1990.

Williams, C., 'Feminism, Subjectivity and Psychoanalysis', in K. Lennon and M. Whitford (eds), *Knowing the Difference: Feminist Perspectives on Epistemology* (London: Routledge, 1994).

Williams, C., 'Philosophy and Psychoanalysis: Lacan, Kojève and Hyppolite on the concept of the subject', *Parallax*, Vol. 4, 1997, pp. 41–54.

Williams, C., 'Structure, Language and Subjectivity: Lacan', in *The Edinburgh Encyclopedia of Continental Philosophy*, general ed. Simon Glendinning (Edinburgh: Edinburgh University Press, 1999), pp. 548–57.

Wood, D., 'An Introduction to Derrida', *Radical Philosophy*, Vol. 21, 1979.

Wood, D., '*Différance* and the Problem of Strategy', in David Wood and Robert Bernasconi (eds), *Derrida and Différance* (Coventry: Parousia Press, 1985).

Wood, D., *Philosophy at the Limit* (London: Unwin Hyman, 1990).

Wordsworth, A., 'Derrida and Foucault: Writing the History of Madness', in R. Young (ed.), *Untying the Text* (Cambridge: Cambridge University Press, 1987).

Wright, E. (ed.), *Feminism and Psychoanalysis: A Critical Dictionary* (Oxford: Blackwell, 1992).

Yovel, V., *Spinoza and Other Heretics: The Adventures of Immanence* (Princeton: Princeton University Press, 1989).

Žižek, S., *The Sublime Object of Ideology* (London: Verso, 1989).

Žižek, S., *For They Know Not What They Do: Enjoyment as a Political Factor* (London: Verso, 1991).

Žižek, S., *The Ticklish Subject: The Absent Centre of Political Ontology* (London: Verso, 1999).

INDEX